MEDIÆVAL LEGENDS OF CHRIST

By

A. S. RAPPOPORT, Ph.D.

Author of Myth and Legend of Ancient Israel,
History of Palestine, etc.

NEW interest is being taken in the legends that
have grown round the figure of Christ. At one
time these stories, which reflect the dreams and hopes
of simple people, were regarded as only suitable for
the nursery. Now scholars of the highest attainments
find in them material of the utmost value. In historical
and literary research, in the study of religious development and the work of religious education, a
knowledge of these hallowed fancies of the popular
mind is becoming more and more essential.

Hitherto there has been no collection of these
beautiful and astonishing stories in a form which
would make them accessible to the interested reader.
They were scattered through many literatures,
written in many languages, and locked in the privileged
editions of learned societies. As a master of Oriental
and European languages, Dr. Rappoport has explored
the vast storehouse of ancient and mediæval literature,
and brought within the compass of a household volume
the most treasured examples of legendary lore concerning the earthly life of our Lord.

In addition to stories from the Apocryphal Gospels,
and the Legenda Aurea of Jacobus de Varagine he has
drawn upon the Cursor Mundi, the Historia Scholastica
of Comestor, the Miracle Plays, the publications of the
Early English Text Society and many mediæval
writings, for the material of this work, and in several
cases compares the legends he has found with similar
narratives in Buddhistic, Jewish, and Mohammedan
lore. He has, by his earlier works, won considerable
distinction in this branch of literature, for he brings to
it, not merely scholarship, but the heart of a religious
mystic which sees in these creations of a reverent
phantasy an attractive symbolism, and not infrequently
a moral lesson.

MEDIÆVAL LEGENDS OF CHRIST

MEDIÆVAL LEGENDS

OF

CHRIST

A. S. RAPPOPORT
Ph.D.

1934
Ivor Nicholson and Watson
Limited . . London

FIRST EDITION 1934

PRINTED IN GREAT BRITAIN BY
MORRISON AND GIBB LTD., LONDON AND EDINBURGH

CONTENTS

NUMEROUS DEFINITIONS OF THE TERMS *myth* and *legend*
have been given by scholars. The two terms are
etymologically parallel and in ordinary discourse are
frequently used interchangeably, but they must be
kept separate when strict accuracy is required.

Various terms are applied to stories which do not
strictly conform to reality, and frequently these terms
are used as synonyms. Indiscriminately we speak
of myths, legends, fables, and stories, and thus
confusion arises. Now a myth, a legend, a fable, or
a story, have this in common that they are the
spontaneous products of popular genius and not
artificial creations, but there is a difference, a subtle
difference perhaps, but a difference all the same,
between, say, a myth and a legend. Myth is applied
to everything which has no existence in reality, and
a mythical character is one which only existed or
exists in the imagination of the inventor. Myths
further imply the personification of abstract forces
or ideas ; in other words, they are the explanations
given by the uncivilized mind to natural phenomena,
while a legend usually has an historical or topo-
graphical basis. It attributes to some real personage
imaginary qualities and characteristics, and makes
him the hero of imaginary happenings. Phaeton
driving the solar chariot too near the sun and so
causing the fruits to perish, or the Valkyries hovering

over the battlefield to receive the souls of falling heroes, are myths, but the story of Alexander the Great visiting the gates of Paradise is a legend. Legend thus confining itself to certain localities or to certain persons, invents fantastic stories and accounts, and in contradistinction to a myth or a story, presupposes some historical fact or character which is the subject of the legend or serves as its pretext. " This," writes Delehaye,[1] " is the first essential condition of the legend. The historical fact, however, may have been embellished or entirely disfigured by popular imagination ; if the latter, it is no longer history, but legend." In other words, the *fictitious* element is the principal characteristic trait of a legend.

Various other definitions of the term " legend " have been given. Thus Wundt writes that " when the edifying and improving nature of a tale predominates, it is a legend,"[2] while, according to Harnack (*Legenden als Geschichtsquellen*), a legend is " the judgment passed on History in the form of an untrue historical account."[3] The best definition, however, seems to me to be that which connects the legend with historico-religious occurrences, incidents, and personalities.[4] A legend, therefore, may be defined as a tale which bears a religious character and is connected either with a person or with an object. The word *legend* is derived from the Latin

[1] *Les Légendes Hagiographiques,* p. 20.

[2] See Wundt, *Völkerpsychology,* pp. 29, 476.

[3] See also H. Günter, *Die christliche Legende des Abendlandes,* 1910, p. 200.

[4] See Bernheim, *Lehrbuch der historischen Methode,* 1894, p. 383.

legendum, and was originally limited to the histories of the lives of the Saints.

Many Christian legends are the result of the literal interpretation of a text in the Gospels or in the writings of the Church Fathers, and exactly the same process may be noticed in Jewish legends. The Church, for instance, chanted

> " *O lachryma gloriosa*
> *Christi præclarissima*
> *Gemma coeli pretiosa*
> *Lymphaque purissima.*"

The expression *gemma* was taken literally by one of the mediæval monks, and the result was a legend, beautiful and symbolical in itself, according to which one of the tears which Jesus shed over the death of Lazarus had been gathered up by an angel and changed into a precious stone. This tear, legend further relates, was brought to Marseilles by Mary Magdalen when she landed there with her brother Lazarus and her sister Martha ; and Vendôme declared that the precious relic was in his possession.[1]

Legend and Religion

The pious yearnings of nations, their dreams and aspirations, their hopes and desires, are mirrored in their legends. The spirit of religion, of the Christian and the Jew, of the Moslem and the Buddhist, can perhaps be gauged better from the popular legend and the folk-tale than from the dead letter of the law or ritual. All religious codes demand of the faithful, honesty and truthfulness, faith and trust in God, and

[1] See J. B. Thiers, *Dissertation sur la Sainte larme*, vol. ii. p. 3.

love of our neighbour, but it is in the popular legend and in the folk-tale that we learn how the people themselves applied these commandments to daily life. They show how the religious teachings were interpreted and how the law was translated into life and action. They reveal the conceptions of the people, of naive and simple believers.

While the religious thought of the spiritual leaders and teachers is laid down in the literature which they have created, legend, as the product of the popular mind, expresses popular piety and sentiments. However childish, however naive a legend may appear to us, it is therefore a valuable document as far as the religious psychology of the people, of the humble and unsophisticated, is concerned. More than once a legend, or a mere folk-tale, shows the people's faith. They believe everything is possible with God, and in this conviction, which is expressed in their legends, they find consolation in all their hours of doubt and despair, of suffering and sorrow.

Among the people, the promises which the Prophets and the Saints made, and expressed in poetical flights of imagination, are not just fancies. They are seen as promises which have been fulfilled in human life. For instance, the poetical expression of Isaiah : "When thou passest through the waters, I will be with thee ; and through the rivers, they shall not overflow thee : when thou walkest through the fire, thou shalt not be burned ; neither shall the flame kindle upon thee " (xliii. 2), is embodied by the pious Jew or Christian in a legend which he relates of one of the Patriarchs, a Christian saint, or of Christ himself.

Again, " Thou shalt tread upon the lion and the adder ; the young lion and the dragon shalt thou trample underfoot " (Ps. xci. 13), sings the Psalmist, which the pious mind of the people, firmly believing in the power of God, sees corroborated in many a legend. For God rewards those who deserve His favour and to them He vouchsafes His protection.

Legends of miracles wrought in favour of a saint, be he a Christian or a Jew, also usually teach a lesson in morality. For the favourites of God are not saints because they were miracle-workers or had miracles performed for them, but because they were good and righteous. The Christian legend applied this belief to Christ himself. Christ is the Messiah not because he worked miracles, but because he was the Messiah, he could and did work miracles whenever his mission made it necessary. By the touch of his staff, as many a legend in the following pages will show, he raised the dead and healed the sick, but woe unto those who dared imitate him, imagining that they, too, could produce the same effect with Christ's staff.[1] " Not with the help of my staff," Christ will say in one of the legends I shall relate, " have I called the dead back to life, but by my *faith* in the Father in heaven."

A similar idea is found in Jewish legendary lore. Rabbi Hanina ben Dosa was bitten by a serpent, but its bite had no effect on him. Carrying the serpent on his shoulders into the school of learning, he told his disciples that it was not the serpent but the sin that killed.[2]

[1] See the legend of the smith and his wife (p. 234).
[2] See *Berachot*, 33a ; see also Bergmann, *Die Legenden der Juden*.

Legend, therefore, while it often entertains and amuses, in most cases also instructs and strengthens the piety of the people, consoling the believer and lending him courage to suffer for the sake of religion. It is the love of, and the attachment to, religion which is at the bottom of most legends, Christian, Jewish, Moslem or Buddhist, and in the mediæval legends of Christ it is the mediæval Christian religious spirit that is constantly being mirrored.

The virtues extolled in the Christian legends, as in all legends connected with the saints, unlike those of pagan mythology—Greek, Roman, Slavonic, and Teuton—are of a positive and negative character. Charity, self-sacrifice, and repentance are highly praised, but lessons of humility, forgiveness, and suffering are also given. In some of the legends connected with Christ, the Saviour appears as a severe judge and a fighter, but he is not a fighter in the sense in which Teuton mythology depicts Thor. Christ's severity is mitigated not only by justice but also by forgiveness, while his fight is directed against sin and not against the sinner. He forgives St. Peter who had denied him, and the Apostle's tears of repentance are changed into flowers, or, according to another version, into pearls. He forgives Judas who had betrayed him and calls him back. More than once, as is related in several legends in the present volume,[1] Christ does not merely forgive the deceivers and the men of little faith who try to imitate his miracles, but he also saves them from certain death.

[1] See chapter on " The Wanderings of Christ on Earth."

Legend and History

Legend, in more than one way, is the very antithesis of history. While the latter is aiming at truth, the former usually introduces elements of poetry, of fiction, and of imagination into the narrative. It either begins where history has left off and is silent, and continues the record in its own way, or it simply contradicts the historical facts. In other words, it completes history, supplements it, tries to fill out the gaps, and to shed a light on questions wrapped in obscurity. The Canonical Gospels, for instance, refer to the Adoration of the Magi, to the flight of the Holy Family to Egypt, to the life of Christ when he had reached the age of thirty, but the Gospels give no details, and these details the legends connected with Christ try to supplement.

It must, however, be remembered that legend, as I have defined it, is a product of the popular mind, and that the naive and simple souls are fond of exaggeration, of all that is wonderful, miraculous, strange, and supernatural, of all that is calculated to strike the imagination. That same yearning to grasp the mysterious and unknown, to touch the hidden springs of existence, to know what is behind or beyond natural phenomena, which has led the philosophers to metaphysical speculations and the scientists to scientific discoveries, results, in the uncultured, in superstitions, myths, and legends. It has been said that " the metaphysician is a poet who has lost his vocation, because he is searching beyond facts." In like manner it can be said that the mythographer or the inventor of legends is searching for something above historical facts. Voltaire says somewhere that "metaphysics constitute the romance of the mind and are more entertaining than geometry"; instead of undergoing the perpetual trouble of calculating and measuring, we can dream pleasantly. In like manner, one might say that legend is "the romance of Theology and History." Instead of reasoning and collecting facts, the religious mind in legend can dream pleasantly and be instructed as well as entertained.

Harnack (*Reden und Aufsätze*, 1904) once defined legend as the "creeper of history," and considered it to be the "worst enemy of history." This definition, however, does not seem to me to be quite correct. The strict historian may show an absolute contempt for the legends clustering round great historical characters, heroes, and saints, but for the student of the psychology of the people and of religion they are valuable, for they contain the people's religious philosophy of history.[1]

The Motif of Legend

Just because legends are mostly the product of popular speculation, the answers of the people to questions dictated by religious sentiments, legendary lore all over the world is full of contradictions and repetitions. I have said that the characteristic trait which distinguishes the legend from the historical fact is its preference for the wonderful and exaggerated, but another characteristic may be added,

[1] See Bergmann, *Die Legenden der Juden*, p. 234.

namely, that of *constant repetition.* " Repetitions always bear the hall-mark of the legend." [1] Exactly the same story and wonder-tale may be told of different persons who have lived in different ages and in different climes. The people who are the inventors of legends and myths and in their flights of fancy, like children, create an imaginary reality in which they believe, are conservative in their tendencies. Moreover, their imagination and powers of invention are limited. The number of themes employed is therefore not only limited but is constantly being repeated in the legends of various nations widely differing from one another both in language and religion.

In his learned articles on the lives and miracles of the mediæval saints,[2] Peter Toldo has enumerated a list of motives which constantly occur in the legends connected with the Christian saints. These same motives are also found in the legends woven round the Patriarchs and Prophets of the Old Testament, and in the legendary lives of Krishna and Buddha, and even of the heroes and gods of pagan antiquity. The main themes occurring in legendary lore are briefly the following :

1. Birth and childhood : the signs announcing the birth of the Patriarch, the Prophet, or the Saint ; the miraculous way in which the newly born are fed by divine messengers or angels.

2. The divine wisdom and intelligence vouch-

---

[1] See Bernheim, *Lehrbuch der historischen Methode,* p. 353.

[2] See *Zeitschrift für Vergleichende Litteraturgeschichte,* vol. xiv. (1901).

safed unto the person with whom the legend is connected ; his ability to speak immediately after his birth and even before.

3. The obedience of the elements, of creation, of beasts, birds, and trees, to his commands.

4. The invisibility of the heroes of the various legends in moments of distress.

5. Their omnipresence : space and time offer no obstacles to them.

6. The imprints of the footsteps of the legendary characters.

7. The hurling down and smashing of idols at their approach.

8. The sudden endowment of animals with the power of speech to address the hero or the saint.

9. The weeping of statues or sweating of blood.

10. The obeisance of trees, which bow down before them or offer them shelter.

11. The power of the legendary character to command the sun and the moon, and to hang an object on a sun-ray.

12. The miraculous power innate in an object belonging to the hero of the legend, etc.

MIGRATION OF LEGENDS

The mediæval Christian legends, the legends of Christ and the Saints, are the product of the religious mediæval mind. The *terra* of mediæval men was the land of religious passion where their romance lay, whither their thinking pointed and their yearning drew. It surged through mediæval thought, and not only moved priests and religious philosophers, monks and scholars to measures of glorifying and pulsating emotions, but also penetrated the life of the people attached to the Christian religion.

The fact, however, that parallels to many of the legends woven round the Saviour are found in the legendary lives of the Christian saints, of the Patriarchs and the Prophets, and also in those of Buddha and the heroes of pagan antiquity, proves that popular speculation and popular imagination are running in the same groove all over the world, in the East and in the West. What men have been dreaming and imagining in bygone ages they may also be dreaming to-day, and the flights of fancy and religious imagination of people differing in culture and language often bear a striking resemblance.

It would, however, be wrong to imagine that one nation does not borrow its myths and legends from another. I have shown elsewhere [1] that Jewish legends, although a product of the Jewish national spirit, have been subject to many foreign influences. Egypt, Persia, Babylonia, and India have left their traces upon these legends. The remark applies no less to the mediæval legends woven round Christ. Indian, Jewish, and Moslem thought, and later on Slavonic, Teutonic, and Celtic conceptions, beliefs, and ideas penetrated into Christian mediæval legendary lore and gained citizen right. And as in the case of Jewish legends, the Christians, too, either changed or adapted many a pagan legend to suit either a Christian saint or Christ himself.

[1] See *Myth and Legend of Ancient Israel*, vol. i. p. xx.

2

Religious ideas wander all over the world, and more so do myths and legends. They are carried hither and thither like light leaves by the breeze, from the East to the West and from the West to the East.

INDIAN INFLUENCES

That Buddhist tradition and Indian literature in general exercised an influence upon Christian legendary lore, and particularly upon the Apocryphal Gospels, is more than probable. There is little doubt that legends connected with Vishnu and Gautama Buddha were brought to Palestine and to Europe and adapted to the life of Christ. Even before the times of Alexander the Great a considerable traffic existed between East and West. King Solomon, as we read in the Old Testament, had commercial relations with Ophir, which, in the opinion of some scholars, stands for India.[1] Even if Ophir designates South Arabia,[2] the possibility of traffic and trade between Palestine and India is not excluded. Solomon's ships, plying the Mediterranean Sea, traded to the islands of Kittim, Kaphtor (Cyprus and Crete), and Dedan. They carried wheat and balm and oil, and brought back cloth, purple, and scarlet, silver and tin, lead and brass. " And Hiram sent in the navy his servants, shipmen that had knowledge of the sea, with the servants of Solomon. And they came to Ophir and fetched from thence gold "

[1] See Weber, *Indische Skizzen*, 1857, p. 74 ff.
[2] See Eduard Meyer, *Geschichte des Altertums*, i. (1884) ; and Rhys Davids, *Buddhist India*, 1903, p. 38.

(1 Kings ix. 27, 28). " And the navy also of Hiram, that brought gold from Ophir, brought in from Ophir great plenty of almug trees and precious stones " (1 Kings x. 11). From Ezion-Geber, on the shores of the Red Sea, the vessels sailed for Tarshish, a Phœnician colony, and hence on much longer voyages to India. " Once in three years came the navy of Tarshish, bringing gold and silver, ivory and apes and peacocks " (*ibid.* x. 22).

The inhabitants of India, like the Phœnicians, had many " shipmen that had knowledge of the sea " and had trade relations with Western Asia. Both the *Jatakas* and the *Rig-Veda* contain passages which clearly prove that the Indians were used to long sea voyages.[1] By land also India had commerce with Babylon, and for over 150 years the North-West was under the survey of the Achæmenidæ. From Herodotus we learn that in the armies of Xerxes Indians fought against Greece, and thus entered into contact with that country (iii. 91 ; vii. 65).

Now along these trade-routes, either by sea or by land, not merely material merchandise but also intellectual products must have been carried. Spiritual values are inseparable from the traffic of material goods, and wherever there is an exchange of merchandise there is also an exchange of ideas.

Before the age of Alexander the Great—who had conceived the idea of binding together the East and the West by means of the Greek civilization—India and Western Asia had been exchanging ideas. There can be but little doubt, therefore, that Semitic

[1] See *ZDMG*, xlvii. p. 606 ff.

legends entered Indian literature, while Indian fables and traditions were carried to the West. Similarities between Indian thought and conceptions and Greek philosophy are numerous, and some scholars even assert the influence of India upon the doctrines of Pythagoras.[1]

The relations, both politically and intellectually, between India and the West became even closer after Alexander the Great, and friendly relations existed between the courts of the Seleucidæ and the Indian rulers. In 256 B.C. Antiochus Theos concluded an alliance with King Asoka,[2] and in 216 Antiochus III. the Great made a treaty with the Indian king, Saub-Nagasena. Traces of these relations are found both in the East and in the West.

The relations were further strengthened in the first two centuries of our era under the Roman Emperors, and philosophical and mythological ideas would thus be carried from India by way of Alexandria and Antioch to Western Asia and hence to Europe.[3] At this time Buddhistic doctrines penetrated into the West, and along with them the doctrines of the Essenes and Greek gnosticism, which it is claimed had their origin in India.[4] Many Indian legends and fables doubtless also migrated to

---

[1] Eysinga van den Bergh, Indische *Einflüsse auf evangelische Erzählungen*, Göttingen, 1894, p. 93 ; see also L. V. Schroeder, *Pythagoras und die Inder*, 1884 ; Gompertz, *Griechische Denker*, i. p. 103.

[2] See A. Smith, *Asoka*, 1901 ; Rhys Davids, *Buddhist India*, 1903, pp. 272–307.

[3] See S. Beal, *Abstract of Four Lectures on Buddhist Literature in China*, 1882, p. 159 ff.

[4] See *Journal of the Royal Asiatic Society*, 1902, pp. 377–415 ; J. Kennedy, *Buddhist Gnosticism*.

the West to appear later in a Jewish or Christian dress. There is indeed every probability that Jewish and Buddhistic ideas and beliefs have influenced more than one mediæval Christian legend, for the currents of intellectual life, of philosophical thought and popular fancy mixed and mingled in Rome, Alexandria, and Antioch. And if doctrines and laws have always been reciprocally borrowed by one religion from another, much more may this process be noticed in the case of romance and legend.

Naturally, in the course of their long wanderings and migrations, these legends changed their aspect and were altered and adapted by the various nations to suit their own peculiar and characteristic ways. The Haggadists of the Talmud and the Midrashim will tell the same legend of Adam or Abraham, of Moses or Solomon, while the author of an Apocryphal Gospel or a mediæval friar will connect it or a similar popular folk-tale with a Christian saint or even with Christ himself. " The same stories," wrote Cowell,[1] " may in the course of their long wanderings come to be recognized under widely different aspects, as when they are used by Boccaccio and Poggio merely as merry tales, or by one Welsh bard to embellish King Arthur's legendary glories, or by some mediæval friar to add point to his discourse."

The Early Converts to Christianity

In fashioning the Christian legends, other influences besides Indian, Persian, and Jewish were at work. When Christianity triumphed over paganism,

---

[1] See *The Jatakas, or Stories of Buddha's Former Births*, i. p. vii.

it was embraced by people of various nations, who brought to their faith a spirit and an imagination peculiar to their climate and characteristic of their trend of thought. The majority of these converts spoke either Hebrew, Arabic, Greek or Latin, and the Apocrypha, which are one of the sources of the legends connected with Christ, were written in one of these languages. Moreover, during the first three centuries of Christianity many heresies arose, and it was only natural that their supporters should add passages to the Apocrypha showing the nature of their teachings. Now, nearly all the Apocrypha which have come down to us are the work of Oriental Christians, some of them Arabs and others subjects of the Greek or Roman Empire. The first interwove in their Apocryphal narratives brilliant fables or legends, the product of facile Eastern imagination and of a love and an admiration for everything that is wonderful and marvellous. The latter were more inclined to reality, and showed their predilection for Roman or Byzantine life and habit.

Thus the Arabic authors or compilers of the legends presented Christ during his early childhood, even from the very first moment of his birth, as a sort of powerful magician, a king of nature which he commanded, changing and altering its laws. The Greeks, on the other hand, presented the God-man of Christianity in the image of the men-gods and heroes of Greek antiquity. Numerous legends are, therefore, woven round the personality of the Founder of Christianity, for which parallels are found in both Arabic legendary lore and in Greek mythology.

On the other hand, when the sunbeams of Christianity scattered the mythological mist of paganism, the Church tried, to a certain extent, to adapt herself to the habits and even the beliefs and superstitions of the pagans. The descent of the Gods to earth, mixing with and wandering among the mortals, is a characteristic trait of all mythologies, and often, therefore, the legends of Christ and his Apostles are really old legends of wandering pagan gods in a Christian dress. Thus, in some of the legends related in the following pages, which deal with the wanderings of Jesus and St. Peter, a half-digested heathen idea can be detected. The legend, for instance, of " The Smith and his Dame " shows how the miraculous attributes of Christ were adapted to current mediæval superstition.

It was quite natural for early Christianity, when it tried to penetrate into and convert to a new religion the pagan world, to adopt a language which was not entirely new. The Church could not systematically repudiate *all* the forms of religion ; all the beliefs and superstitions to which the people whom the Church was anxious to convert had been clinging for centuries. The new religion, if it was to be successful in pulling down the walls and abolishing the boundaries, the isolation and exclusiveness, which had hitherto existed between Judaism and paganism, was bound to be conciliatory. Whenever external signs of the cult did not implicitly manifest a recognition of polytheism but served to express the religious instinct of the masses, they were tolerated by the Church. The more Christianity spread among the uncultured and even ignorant masses and was no longer the religion of a few elect, the more it was overwhelmed by the crowd, the more the Church was bound to reckon with the popular instinct and to make allowance for the polytheistic sentiments and beliefs still fermenting in the minds and hearts of the new converts.

The door had to be left half-open and admitted the air wafted from pagan antiquity, although it may not have been either fresh or pure. In the case of the saints and the legends clustering around their lives, the door was more widely opened, and the pagan current entered freely. Legend frequently confounded the heroes of pagan antiquity with the saints of the Church, and gradually pressed even the Redeemer into a legend told of a pagan god or hero.[1]

Thus pagan Rome had become Christian, but the early Christian Church could not so easily eradicate the worship of the pagan gods and the celebration of pagan festivals. The Church, therefore, and the priests recognized the necessity of introducing many customs into Christian worship, and of allowing pagan beliefs to remain under the veneer of Christianity. Hence a symbolism which can easily be recognized as pagan is associated not only with many Christian saints but even with the Madonna and the Saviour himself.

Not only Christian scholars, but also ecclesiastics, have admitted that numerous motives in Christian mediæval legends have been borrowed from pagan classic antiquity. They are like the light leaves

---

[1] See Delehaye, *Les Légendes Hagiographiques*, p. 181.

carried hither and thither by the breeze. The themes, for instance, of which legends always make use, namely, a letter or a statue falling from heaven, or holy images or statues weeping or sweating, are not inventions of mediæval Christianity, but were already known to pagan mythographers, and are to be met with in the legends of classic antiquity.[1]

All these legends applied to the Saviour, and glorifying him appealed to, and flattered, the taste and love for the wonderful and marvellous so prevalent during the Middle Ages. With avidity the pious mediæval men and women listened to the accounts contained in the legends, gracious or pathetic, showing the lions and tigers worshipping the Holy Infant, or trees bending down their branches and offering their ripe fruit unto the Virgin.

Considering the origin of the authors who compiled the Apocrypha, and the nations and races among whom all later mediæval legends have arisen, especially Teutons and Slavs, it will be easily understood that Christ is not always represented in the true light. One often misses the Christ of the Gospels, who, on the starlit mountain of Galilee, sought to regenerate the heart of man, and who, when he was suffering on the Cross, uttered the words : " Father, forgive them, for they know not what they do."

What value we give to a legend depends largely upon the source from whence it emanated, and the character of the nation in which it arose, whether Hindus, Persians, Jews, Greeks, Romans, Slavs, or

[1] See E. von Dobshütz, *Christusbilder Texte und Untersuchungen*, N.F., vol. iii. (1899) ; Delehaye, *l.c.* p. 38.

Teutons. Many a legend shows Christ in his true nature, kind and charitable, the benefactor of humanity, while in others, to our great surprise, he is represented as revengeful. In some we are reminded of the Buddha or of the prophet Elijah, while in others he appears as a Teuton god, an Odin or a Thor, hurling his curses just as the latter brandished his hammer.[1]

LEGEND AND ART

Christian mediæval poets and painters have always delighted in the flower-strewn meadows of tradition and legend, and just as many mediæval poems owe their inspiration to the legends current among the Christians of the earliest days, so also many of the great pictures of the mediæval artists can be traced to the same influence. The majority of the legends woven round the earthly life of Christ were known to the mediæval artists. Almost a complete legendary history of Christ and of the Virgin Mary can be constructed from the pictures of these early artists. There are beautiful paintings of the life of Mary in the temple, and of her marriage to Joseph, as, for instance, the " Sposalizio of the Brera " by Raphael, and the picture of Ghirlandajo. The Visitation has been treated by Raphael, by Andrea Sabbatini of Salermo, and by many others. Most of the legends of the Nativity seem to have been known to the mediæval artists, for they did not confine their art to the portrayal of the simple and brief accounts given in the Gospels. I refer in the following pages

[1] See Le Roux de Lincy, *Le Livre des Légendes*, Paris, 1836.

to the legend of the Sibyl Tiburtina, whom the
Emperor Cæsar consulted. This tradition, as Mrs.
Jameson has pointed out,[1] suggested the *Pollio* of
Virgil, which, in its turn, suggested Pope's *Messiah*,
and furnished a subject to more than one mediæval
artist. " It was painted by Cavallini, about 1340,
on the vault of the choir of the Ara-Coeli, and by
Pietro da Cortona in a picture at Hampton Court." [2]

The legends of the ox and the ass kneeling before
Christ, worshipping and warming the Holy Infant
on the cold winter night, most probably were suggested by the passage in Isaiah : " The ox knoweth
his owner, and the ass his master's crib " (Isa. i. 3).
The legend was doubtless accepted by the early
Church because it showed how the humblest animals
recognized the Divinity of Christ whom men had
misunderstood. It has also found a place in the
liturgy of the Catholic Church.[3] In these brief notes
I will refer only to Correggio's " Nativity." The
legend of the two midwives, Zeloni and Salome,
which St. Jerome counted among the " deliramenta
apocryphorum," became, nevertheless, popular among
the mediæval artists. We find the scene depicted in
the cathedral of Lyons. I have myself admired the
same subject on the stained-glass windows in the
cathedrals at Chartres and at Le Mans.

It was, however, the legend of the Adoration of
the Magi which gave full scope to the creative genius
of the mediæval artists. Imagination travelled to the

---

[1] *Legends of the Madonna as represented in the Fine Arts*, p. 223.

[2] *Ibid.* p. 214.

[3] See E. Male, *L'art Religieux du XIII. Siècle en France*, 1898, p. 275,
note 1.

distant Orient, and Ludolphe le Chartreux in his
Vie de Jésus Christ (chap. xi.) mentions a tradition
according to which the Magi were the descendants of
Balaam, whose secrets of magic they had inherited.
The tradition may be connected with the passage in
the Book of Numbers : " There shall come a star
out of Jacob, and a sceptre shall rise out of Israel "
(Num. xxiv.). The majority of the legends woven
round the Magi were known to Jacobus de Voragine,
the author of the *Golden Legend* (chaps. x. and xiv.),
and must have been familiar to the Florentine and
Venetian painters, Angelico, Parmigiano, and Ghirlandajo.[1]

Of the legends connected with the Flight to
Egypt, the one which describes the fall of the idols
appears to have appealed strongly to the artistic
mediæval imagination. A reproduction of it is
among those which describe the Childhood of Christ
on a stained-glass window at Le Mans.

The legend of the palm or the date tree which
bowed down its branches and offered shade and
refreshment to the Holy Virgin was very popular,
and art has preserved it on canvas and in glass. A
picture by Antonello Mellone is mentioned by Mrs.
Jameson (*l.c.* p. 253), and the scene is depicted on
the stained-glass windows at the cathedrals of Lyons
and Tours (Male, *l.c.* p. 285).

There are numerous pictures of the legends connected with the Passion. It was natural that the
men of the Middle Ages should turn to the scenes of
the Passion, and round Golgotha weave a web of

[1] See Mrs. Jameson, *l.c.* pp. 235–236 ; and Male, *l.c.* pp. 280–281.

fancy. What scope for the artistic imagination, for piety coupled with genius, in the idea of the death of the Saviour ! The Cross was readily associated with the wood of a tree in the Garden of Eden, first the tree of knowledge, and then the tree of life. The legends of the angels at the Cross gathering the blood from the wounds of Jesus, of the Centurion Longinus, of the Saint Graal at the feet of Christ, of St. Veronica lending her handkerchief to Christ to wipe his brow, were so symbolical of religious sentiment that they could not be omitted from the canvases of the mediæval masters.

Art, just as much as legend, was the handmaiden of religion. It brought the Christian faith near to the heart of the people. For the men of the Middle Ages, even those who were pious, were mostly unlearned, and could not be satisfied with an abstract faith, with the ethical teaching of Christ and a recital of passages from the Gospels ; they wanted something which could make a more direct appeal to their feelings. The Church, therefore, encouraged the picture-lessons given by the mediæval artists in their paintings and sculptures. The followers of Christ could thus strengthen their faith by the contemplation of a picture or a series of sculptures which graphically portrayed a legend.

The Sources

The sources from which I have drawn the material for the present volume are, in addition to the Apocryphal Gospels, *The Historia Scholastica* of Comestor, the *Miroire Historique* of Vincent de Beauvais, the

Golden Legend of Jacobus de Voragine, and the *Vie de Jésus-Christ* by Ludolphe de Chartreux (which he wrote in 1350). I have also consulted numerous collections of European folk-lore—Slavonic, Celtic, Teutonic, etc.

Among the English sources which I have utilized I will mention in chronological order : Kynewulf's *Crist* ; the collection of *Old English Legends* (*Altenglishe Legenden*, edited by Horstmann, 1875 and 1878) ; the *Cursor Mundi*, a Northumbrian MS., consisting of about 30,000 lines, edited by the Rev. Richard Morris, and published for the Early English Text Society, which poem I have already had occasion to consult for my *Myths and Legends of Ancient Israel*.

I have also consulted John Lydgate's *The Life of our Lady*, composed at the instigation of Henry V. It was printed by William Caxton, England's first printer, and enjoyed a great popularity. Some of the legends related in the present volume have been drawn from Christmas carols.

I have further consulted the Townley and Coventry Mysteries and the Chester Plays. Thus, in the play *Salutation and Nativity* in one of the Chester Plays, reference is made to the legends of the midwives, the prophecy of the Sibyl, and the fall of the idols in the hour of the Nativity.[1] And last, but not least, the numerous collections of folk-tales of several European nations, and written in different languages, have been laid under contribution. These are the quarries from which the stones for my humble structure were drawn.

[1] See R. Reinsch, *Die Pseudo-Evangelien von Jesu und Marias Kindheit*, Halle, 1879, pp. 127–138.

" Gaude, Virgo, mater Christi,
Quæ per aurem concepisti,
Gabriele nuntio."

MARY, SO LEGEND RELATES, sprung of the royal stock
and family of David. She was born in the city of
Nazareth and brought up at Jerusalem in the temple
of the Lord. Joachim and Anna were respectively
the names of her father and mother. Her father
hailed from Nazareth in Galilee, while her mother
came from Bethlehem. Mary's parents led a pious,
simple, and upright life before the Lord, and a
blameless one before men. All their substance and
possessions they divided into three equal parts ; one
portion they gave to the temple and the servants of
the temple, another they distributed among the poor,
while the third part they reserved for themselves and
their family. They had made a vow to the following
effect : Should the Lord bless them with offspring,
they would yield the child to the service of the Lord.
And thus Mary was brought up in the temple. She
was in the habit of working, spinning, sewing, and
embroidering the silk and velvet curtains for the
temple.

THE ANNUNCIATION AND THE VISITATION

When Mary was fourteen years of age, Zacharias
the priest inquired of the Lord concerning her.

Thereupon an angel of the Lord came to him and said to him : " Go forth and call together all the widowers of the people, and let each of them bring his rod in his hand, and he to whom the Lord shall show a sign, let him be the husband of Mary." Zacharias the priest did as the angel had commanded him, and he made a proclamation accordingly. Joseph, who was a carpenter by trade, threw down his axe, took his staff in his hand, and went with the rest of the widowers. When he appeared before the priest and presented his rod, lo ! a wonder happened, for a snow-white, dazzling dove issued forth from the rod, settled on his head, and then flew towards heaven. Thereupon Zacharias the high-priest said to him : " Thou art the man chosen to take the Virgin Mary and espouse her." Joseph, however, was afraid, and invoking his advanced age drew back, but he was prevailed upon to take Mary to his house and to be betrothed to her.

Another version of the rod of Joseph runs as follows : All the suitors who aspired to the honour of marrying Mary, and the number included the son of the high-priest, deposited their rods or wands in the temple overnight. When on the following morning they came to fetch their rods, behold ! the rod of Joseph, like the rod of Aaron, had budded forth into leaves and flowers. Thereupon, in their disappointment and despair, all the other suitors broke their rods. One of them, a young man of a noble family named Agabus, fled to Mount Carmel where he became an anchorite.

Another legend relates that, as a rule, Joseph

carried an ordinary staff, but when the angel announced to him that he was destined to be the husband
of Mary, he became radiant with joy, and his staff
flowered in his hand.   In Tuscany the oleander is
known as Joseph's Staff.

The Rod of Joseph

The legend of a staff which blossoms and brings
forth leaves is a *motif* quite frequent both in Christian
and in pagan legendary lore.   Thus St. Christopher,
who carried Christ and hence received his name,
planted his staff in the ground ; it took root, became
a tree, and bore foliage and fruit.   The staff of St.
Francis grew into an oak tree which remained for a
long time.   The staff of St. Polycarp was changed
into a cherry tree, and was visible at Smyrna.
The author of the *Legenda Aurea* relates that St.
Sebinian planted his staff in the ground and it took
root, brought forth foliage, branches, and flowers in
the presence of a great concourse of people, and
one thousand one hundred and eight immediately
embraced Christianity.[1]

A similar story of a staff which blossomed is told
of David and Solomon.   When David was well
advanced in years, both he and his people asked
themselves who should reign after him, until an angel
brought the king a golden letter from heaven, wherein
a number of questions were written.   " Call thy sons
together," said the angel, " and ask them the questions written down in this letter.   Whosoever shall
answer all the questions rightly shall sit on thy

[1] See Maury, *Croyances et legéndes du moyen âge*, p. 385.

throne." And David obeyed the command of the Lord, called his sons together, and read to them the questions written down in the letter. But none of David's sons could answer the questions.

Thereupon Solomon, who was the youngest of David's sons, said unto his royal father : "Oh my father, read me the questions, perchance I might be able to answer them."

And David read the questions one by one :

" What is the most beautiful thing in the world ? "

And Solomon answered : " The most beautiful thing in the world is when God forgives men and they forgive one another."

" What is the sweetest thing in the world ? " David asked again.

And Solomon answered : " The sweetest thing in the world is love, for love is the spirit of the Lord in His Creation."

And many other questions written down in the golden letter sent down by God from heaven did David ask, and to all of which Solomon gave the right answer.

Then David said that Solomon should rule over the children of Israel. But although Solomon had answered all the questions rightly, the people murmured against being ruled by so young a prince, and they asked for another test. Thereupon David ordered that the chiefs of the tribes and Solomon should each take a rod and write their names upon them. " Whichever rod," said David, " bore fruit, its owner should be declared the King's successor." And when the chiefs of the tribes and Solomon had

written their names on the rods these were left under
seal and watch was kept over them.   In the morning
the rods were brought forth, and, behold ! it was
Solomon's rod which had borne fruit.   Thus the
Lord made it known that Solomon had been chosen
to sit on the throne of David.[1]

The Visit of Gabriel

" The flower of Jesse," wrote St. Bernard, " was
born of a flower, in the season of flowers."   These
words are, of course, an allusion to Nazareth, which
means a flower (*flos nascit voluit de flore, in flore, et
floris tempore*).   It happened two months after the
Holy Virgin had been betrothed to Joseph.

It was in early spring-time, at eventide, soon after
sunset.   The maid of Galilee was walking over fields
and meadows to draw water from the fountain, when
suddenly she heard a voice which said, " Hail, Mary,
that art full of grace."   She was troubled ; she looked
to the right and to the left, and seeing no one, returned to her house and sat down to her work.   It
was the house which Mary had inherited from her
parents, Joachim and Anna, who were people of
substance.

Thereupon the winged spirit from on high, the
angel Gabriel, spread his lucid wings and took flight
to Nazareth.   He was accompanied by a train of
lower angels, who were eager to pay reverence to
the Queen of Heaven.   They, however, remained
at the gate, and Gabriel alone entered.

[1] See Migne, vol. ii. col. 849 ; Salzberger, *Die Salomon Sage*,
pp. 65-68.

With grave and serious mien, winged, beautiful, and radiant with eternal youth, Gabriel went in, bearing a lily in his hand, and in his angelic musical voice he said, " Ave Maria gratia plena——"

At that moment Mary was reading the Book of the Prophet Isaiah, and when the wondrous vision burst upon her she had just reached the verse : " Behold, a virgin shall conceive and bear a son." In great humility she thought within her heart : How blessed the woman of whom these words are written ! Would I might be but her handmaid to serve her, and be allowed to kiss her feet ! It was then that the prophecy was realized in herself.

According to another version it happened at dawn.

It was an hour of silence, freshness, and peace, which Mary so much liked. It was the hour when nature in the East awakes from its slumbers, mirthful and perfumed, when the grass on the fields has drunk the dew of the night and the birds are beginning to sing their first hymns to the Creator of the Universe. It was the hour when the heart of man, in the midst of silence and peace, communes with the Father of all, when Mary felt her soul filled by a heavenly sweetness, and in her ecstasy she exclaimed : " Lord of the Universe, God of Abraham, of Israel and of Jacob, be it thy wish to deem me worthy of contemplating her one day, the virgin who is destined to bear Christ under her heart."

Thereupon she took the purple she was spinning for the curtain in the temple of the Lord, and being seated, turned her wheel. And lo ! an angel of the

Lord stood before her, saying, " Fear not, Mary, for thou shalt conceive at His word." But when Mary heard this she disputed in herself, saying, "How shall I conceive from the Lord, the living God, and bear as every woman beareth ? "

Then the angel of the Lord said, " Not so, Mary ; for the power of the Lord will overshadow thee ; wherefore that holy thing which is born of thee shall be called the son of the Most High ; and his name shall be called Jesus, for he shall save his people from their sins." And Mary said :

" Behold, the servant of the Lord is before him ; be it unto me according to thy word."

A Russian legend runs as follows : Mary told the Archangel Gabriel that she would give credit to his words if a fish, one side of which she had already eaten, were to come to life again. And lo ! at that very moment the fish came to life, and was put back in the water.[1] This tale reminds one of similar stories in Western and Eastern legendary lore, where it is related that the shape of the sole is due to the fact that after one half of it had been eaten the other half had been thrown into the sea again (*l.c.* p. 330).

The *motif* of a half-eaten fish which came to life again is frequent, both in Jewish and Mohammedan legendary lore. It is told of Moses and Joshua, that when they had eaten one half of a fried fish the other half was brought to life again by the Lord. The same story is referred to by Kazwini in his *Cosmography* — where the Arabic author describes the wonderful creatures found in the Mediterranean Sea.

[1] See Ralston, *Russian Folk-tales*, p. 330.

And the Spaniard Abu Hamid said : "In the vicinity of Ceuta I have seen a fish which is an off-spring of that fried fish one half of which Moses and Joshua had eaten and the other half of which the Lord brought to life. And the resuscitated half of the fish found its way back into the sea. This fish until this very day has offspring in this place. It is a fish measuring more than one yard in length and an inch in width. Both its sides consist of fish-bones, and its bowels are surrounded by a delicate skin. It has only one eye and its head is only the half of a head. Whoever looks at the fish from this side imagines it to be dirty, thinking that it had already been eaten and was dead, while its other half is really clean." (Kaz-wini, *Cosmography*, Ethe's translation, p. 258.)

THE VISITATION

Thereupon Mary arose and went up into the hill country, journeying with haste to the house of her cousin Elisabeth, whom she saluted. Mary loved and greatly honoured her kinswoman, a woman well stricken in years, and when she heard that Elisabeth had been exalted to a miraculous motherhood in spite of her advanced age, she made haste to visit her. She did not, however, go to her kinswoman for advice, but to reveal what had happened to herself. And when the two mothers, the two exalted women, the mother of Christ and the mother of John, met, Elisabeth knew what had happened, for even before Mary had opened her lips she exclaimed : "Whence is this to me that the mother of my Lord should come to me ?"

Mary dwelt for three months with her cousin, and often she would walk in the garden and meditate on the strange and wonderful destiny which was in store for her. Legend relates that one day the Holy Virgin touched a flower in the garden which had hitherto had no scent, and lo ! it became fragrant and has remained so ever since.

At length Mary left the house of Zacharias and returned to Nazareth to her own dwelling, where Joseph met her. When he beheld his wife he noticed that she was about to become a mother and his mind was troubled. But he was a charitable man and in the habit of treating an offending person with leniency and forbearance. He emulated, even before the Lord's birth, the forgiveness, pity, and mercy of his foster-son. But while Joseph was pondering in his heart, Gabriel, the angel of the Lord, appeared unto him in a dream and told him not to fear. When Joseph awoke he obeyed the divine voice, and entreated forgiveness of Mary whom he had wronged in thought. Kneeling before her, he pleaded for pardon, and the Virgin mother extended one hand, raised him, while with the other she pointed to heaven.

FLOWERS IN THE FOOTSTEPS OF THE MADONNA

Numerous legends are connected with flowers which are believed by the faithful to have grown under the footsteps of the Madonna, just as flowers are said to have grown under the footsteps of Adam or of Buddha. In the Scandinavian countries of Denmark and Norway, flowers formerly named after the heathen goddess Freya, the Venus of the North, are now called after Mary, Queen of Heaven. Different ferns are known as the Herb of Mary or *Mariengrass*. Botany, once full of the heathen Venus, the Queen of Beauty, is to-day full of the Madonna. The floral attributes of Isis, Venus, and Freya, are now bestowed on her whose whole life had been passed in the pastoral surroundings of Galilee and its flower-strewn meadows. The rose of Jericho, a legend which will be related in a subsequent chapter, is said to have blossomed forth in the desert at a spot which the Virgin had touched with her foot. This flower, it is believed, comes up and blossoms on Christmas night.

Chapter III

The Nativity

" Now when Jesus was born in Bethlehem of Judæa in the days of Herod the king, behold, wise men from the East came to Jerusalem, saying, Where is he that is born king of the Jews ? for we saw his star in the East and are come to worship him."—MATT. ii. 1, 2.

AN INTERESTING INCIDENT which happened at the time of the birth of Christ and found a place in Christian legendary lore is the prophecy of the Sibyl. One day the Emperor Augustus Cæsar went to the Sibyl Tiburtina to inquire whether he should allow himself to be worshipped as the Senate had decreed with divine honours. The Sybil asked for a few days of meditation. When the Emperor returned to inquire her verdict, she took him apart and showed him an altar in the sky. Above the altar he saw a beautiful virgin in the glory of a brilliant light, holding in her arms an Infant, and he heard a voice saying : " This is the altar of the Son of the living God." Thereupon Augustus Cæsar caused an altar to be erected on the Capitoline Hill with the following inscription : " Ora primogeniti Dei." [1]

Soon after this Sibylline prophecy a decree went forth that the world should be taxed. And Joseph saddled his ass, set his wife on it, and went up from Nazareth to Bethlehem. Long and steep and weary

[1] See Virgil's *Pollio* and Pope's *Messiah*.

was the way, and Joseph, following the ass led by his son, was troubled in his mind. I will enroll my children, he thought, but what shall I do with Mary ? I cannot enroll her as my wife nor can I enroll her as my daughter, but the Lord will make it plain how He willeth it. Once, when Joseph looked up, he saw an expression of sadness in her eyes, and he thought unto himself, perhaps her burden troubleth her. But when he looked up again, the Holy Virgin was laughing, and he said unto her :

" Mary, what aileth thee, because I see thy face at one time sad and at another laughing ? "

And Mary said to Joseph, " I see two peoples before me, one weeping and the other rejoicing."

Then said Joseph unto her :

" Thou speakest superfluous words, and hadst better sit on thy beast and not trouble."

At that moment a beautiful youth, clothed in white array, appeared before Joseph and thus he spoke :

" Why didst thou call superfluous the word Mary hath spoken ? Indeed, she saw two peoples, one weeping and the other rejoicing, and they were the Jews and the Gentiles, who will be made nigh to the Lord as He promised unto our fathers Abraham, Isaac, and Jacob ; the time is come when in the seed of Abraham a blessing will be bestowed on all nations." And thus speaking, the beautiful youth, who was an angel in disguise, departed.

When they came in the midst of the road Mary said to Joseph :

" Take me down from the ass, for my burden

urgeth me to be delivered." And Joseph took her
down from the ass and said unto her : "Whither
shall I take thee, for I see no inn nor resting-place."
And he lifted his eyes, and beheld a cave near the
grave of Rachel, the wife of the Patriarch Jacob, and
the mother of Joseph and Benjamin. So he took
Mary down from the animal and led her to the cave,
which was below a cavern. There was never any
light in it, but always darkness, because the cave
could never receive the light of day. As soon as the
Madonna entered the cave it became light with all
brightness, as if it had been the sixth hour of the day.
And as long as she remained in that cave the divine
light which illumined it never failed either by day or
by night. There she brought forth a male child,
whom angels instantly surrounded and adored.

The rough rocky cave, as the stable afterwards,
became forthwith a temple full of light and religion
where the Holy Infant was worshipped. Angels with
olive branches were floating around the roof, singing
Gloria in Excelsis, for the Prince of Peace who was
destined to bring universal peace on earth and good-
will towards men was born there.

In the meantime, Joseph had gone out to seek
midwives in the country of Bethlehem, and looking
up into the sky he saw strange and wonderful things.
He noticed that the air was violently agitated, but
the pole of heaven was stationary, and the birds of
heaven were trembling. Looking at the earth he
saw a vessel with working-men sitting around it.
He watched them put their hands in the vessel ; but
those who should have lifted their hands did not lift

them, and those who should have presented the food
to their mouths did not present it, and all their faces
were turned heavenwards. Around him Joseph saw
sheep scattered, but the sheep were standing still.
The shepherd lifted up his hand to strike them, but
his hand remained up. Then Joseph looked at the
river, and he saw that the mouths of the kids were
down over the water, but they were not drinking, for
everything was intercepted and stopped in its course.
Joseph marvelled greatly.

He lifted his eyes and behold ! a Hebrew woman
was coming down from the hill country, and he
called unto her and said : " Blessed art thou, I am
seeking a Hebrew midwife ; come with me to yonder
cave." And the woman asked : " Art thou of
Israel ? " And he answered "Yes." " And who,"
asked the woman, " is it that bringeth forth in
yonder cave ? " And Joseph answered : " It is a
woman who is espoused to me."

" Is she not thy wife ? " asked the woman, to
which Joseph replied : " She is Mary who was
brought up in the temple of the Lord, and she was
allotted to me as wife, but she is not my wife, but
hath conceived by the Holy Spirit."

And the midwife said : " Tell me the truth."
Whereupon Joseph answered : " Come and see."
And the woman went with him, and when they stood
in front of the cave there was a bright cloud over-
shadowing it. And the midwife was overawed and
exclaimed : " To-day my soul is magnified, because
mine eyes have seen strange and wonderful things,
for salvation is born unto Israel." But suddenly the

cloud withdrew and the cave was filled with a light which was more beautiful than the glittering of lamps and candles, and brighter even than the light of the sun, so that the eyes could not bear it.

The woman refused to enter the cave, but Joseph went in and said unto Mary : " I have brought thee Zeloni and Salome, two Hebrew women who are midwives, but they are standing without, not daring to enter the cave for the too great splendour." Mary smiled at this. But Joseph said : " Do not smile, but be cautious that they may visit thee, lest perchance thou shouldst require medicine." Thereupon Mary bade the women enter. Zeloni alone entered the cave and gradually the great light withdrew until the babe was seen, and it came and took the breast of its mother Mary.

Then the midwife cried out and said : " To-day is a great day to me, for I have seen this novel sight. Never hath it been heard, or suspected, that the breasts of any woman should be full of milk, and the child born show its mother to be a virgin. There is no defilement of blood on the child nor is there any pain in the mother. A virgin has conceived, and a virgin she hath continued."

After this the midwife went out of the cave and called Salome. And the latter said : " As the Lord my God liveth, except I put out my hand and touch thee I will not believe Zeloni's words that a virgin hath brought forth. Can this be true ? " Mary smiled and said : " It is true, for as there is no child like mine, so there is no woman like unto his mother."

That Jesus was born in a cave is not only related

in the Apocryphal Gospels but also by Justinus
Martyr and Eusebius.[1] According to legend it was
on the third day after the birth of the Holy Infant
that Mary carried him into a stable and laid him in a
manger, where the ox and the ass worshipped him.

The birth of the Saviour has made a deep impression upon popular imagination, and many
legends found in the folk-lore of the Christian nations
are woven round this event. Nature and the whole
world was hushed, and everything stood still. It
was a moment of solemn silence until angels appeared
saying : " A Saviour is born unto you this day."
On that day, too, three suns were seen in the East
which were immediately joined into one to signify
that divinity, soul, and flesh were all combined in
Christ, and were made one sun, one man, Jesus.

On the night of the Nativity there appeared in
the East a star in the centre of which was a child
with a cross on his forehead, who spake unto the
Magi saying that they were to go into Judæa to
worship him that was born King of the Jews. On
that night, too, all the elements bore witness unto the
Holy Infant, for the darkness of the night was changed
into the light of day. At Rome, too, strange things
happened. A fountain of oil gushed out and flowed
into the Tiber, and a temple fell to pieces. The
Romans, enjoying peace for the first time since six
centuries, had erected a magnificent temple to Peace
and placed in it the statue of Romulus, the founder

---

[1] See Justinus Martyr, *Apologia*, i. 34 ; *Dialogus cum Tryphone
Jedæo*, c. 78 ; Eusebius, *De Vita Constantini*, iii. 43, and *Protoevangelium
Jacobi*, c. 18.

of Rome, the Eternal City.   They consulted Apollo
to ascertain how long peace would prevail on earth,
and the oracle replied that peace would continue
until a virgin gives birth to a child.   " Then peace
will be eternal," said the Romans, and on the Temple
of Peace they inscribed the words :   " Templum
pacis æternum " (Peace for ever).

In the fields round the stable where the Holy
Infant lay, close by the tower of Eder, where the
Patriarch Jacob once pastured his herds, some
shepherds were looking after their flocks.   Towards
midnight an angel appeared unto them bringing
them the glad tidings that in the city of David,
Christ was born, wrapt in swaddling-clothes and
lying in a manger :

" Let us be off and go to Bethlehem to see whether
this is true," said the shepherds, and hastily proceeded to the city, where they found the Holy Infant.
The news soon spread all over the country place.
On that night the vineyards of Engaddi, which
produce balsam, suddenly appeared in full bloom,
and a delicious perfume was wafted far and wide.

A valiant Arab tribe dwelling in the mountains
heard the news from the shepherds and came to
Bethlehem to render homage to the newly born King.
They returned to their lonely camp carrying in their
simple hearts the remembrance of the Holy Family.
Often in the evenings, when the caravans in the
desert stopped at the foot of a solitary palm-tree by
this camp, one of the tribe would repeat the story of
the miraculous Nativity as the Egyptian travellers
or the wealthy Assyrian merchants exchanged the

merchandise of their native land for the perfumes of Arabia. When the tale was told, the Arab would prostrate himself before an image representing the Holy Virgin holding the Holy Infant in her lap.

Similar legends are found in the life of Buddha and in Jewish folk-lore.

At the moment when Buddhisatta was reborn in the womb of his mother all the ten thousand worlds suddenly trembled and shook. A great light gleamed in the ten thousand worlds, and the blind who had been yearning for the light suddenly regained their eyesight ; the deaf began to hear, the mute started to speak, and the hunchbacked suddenly became straight. Fetters and chains fell off, and the imprisoned found themselves free. The fires in hell were extinguished, and hunger and thirst disappeared. Animals lost the feeling of fear, while in the whole universe disease disappeared. All creatures, men and animals, spoke kindly ; pleasantly neighed the horses and trumpeted the elephants ; all musical instruments began to play by themselves without being touched by the hand of man, and ornaments worn by women began to tinkle. A cool, pleasant, and salutary wind blew over the world, and water gushed forth from the earth. Flowers began to blossom, and heavenly instruments resounded in the air.[1]

Legend also relates that even before his birth, Krishna emitted a dazzling light. No one could bear to gaze upon Devaki on account of the light that

[1] See Dutoit, *Das Leben des Buddha*, Leipzig, 1906, pp. 7–8.

invested her ; and those that contemplated her radiance felt their minds disturbed.[1]

When Abraham was born, the radiance of his countenance shed a brilliant light in the cave where his mother Emtelai was hiding from Nimrod.[2]

Jewish legendary lore further relates that miracles happened at the birth of Moses and at the Revelation at Mount Sinai. When Moses, the future redeemer of Israel, who was to lead the sons of Israel from the brickfields of Egypt to the promised land of Canaan, was born, the whole house was filled with a radiance like the dazzling splendour of the sun and moon.[3]

In Greek mythology we read that a shepherd who had found the boy Æsculapius, perceived a brilliant and dazzling light emanating from him.[4] When Servius Tullius was a small boy the household saw a brilliant light over him while he was asleep.[5] A light is said to have shone over the head of Proclus, the Neo-Platonic philosopher, when he was lecturing.[6]

Similar wonders and miracles accompanied the Revelation on Mount Sinai. Mount Sinai rose from the earth and became taller than all the mountains of the world. The heavens opened, and the summit of the holy mount towered through the opening.[7] Nature was hushed, the whole universe stood still, and no creature uttered a sound. The birds did not

---

[1] See Wilson, *Vishnu-Purana*, 1840, ii. p. 500, quoted by Eysinga, *l.c.* p. 76.

[2] See Rappoport, *Myth and Legend*, vol i. p. 229 and vol. ii. p. 217.

[3] See *Pirke de Rabbi Eliezer*, ed. Friedlander, ch. 48 ; Rappoport, *Myth and Legend of Ancient Israel*, vol. ii. p. 217.

[4] See Gunter, *l.c.* p. 51.

[5] *Ibid.* p. 62.   [6] *Ibid.* p. 67.   [7] See *Pirke de Rabbi Eliezer*, ch. 41.

4

sing, nor did the oxen low ; the sea ceased its roaring, the heavenly spheres their motion, and the Seraphim themselves no longer uttered their cry of " Holy ! " A breathless silence prevailed, and there was a stillness never witnessed before and never to occur again. In the midst of this solemn and supernatural silence, the voice of the Lord resounded, saying : " I am the Lord, your God." The divine voice travelled from one end of the world to the other, and was heard by all inhabitants of the earth, by old and young, by the aged and the suckling, by the youth and the maiden. And the divine voice divided itself into seventy tongues and travelled from one end of the world to the other, so that all could understand it. Each individual understood it in his own way, according to his own intelligence, and scarcely had the words been uttered, when they became tongues of flame and visible to the whole world.[1]

The Animal World

Great joy prevailed among the animals and birds on Christmas night. All creatures communicated one to the other the glad tidings, announcing in their respective tongues and in different sounds the birth of the Saviour. At midnight the cock announced the glad event, and crew : " Christ is born."

" Where ? " asked the dog.

" At Bethlehem," answered the gnat.

And the hen clucked : " Go there, go there at once."

The raven is said to have been the first bird to

[1] See Rappoport, *l.c.* pp. 306, 307.

know of the birth of Christ. It was just roving about on the meadow when the angels appeared to the shepherds and told them the glad news. Ever since the raven lays a single egg in the winter, namely, at midnight on Christmas. Unable to hatch the egg at once, the raven covers it up with resin, hides it in the branches of the fir tree, and whoever discovers this egg is destined to acquire great wealth. Winter, however, never leaves the land before the raven has fetched its egg and begun to hatch it. It is then that spring makes its appearance.[1]

There is a belief that on Christmas Eve the cattle have the gift of language and confide one to the other many secrets, but to eavesdrop on them is a sin, and many legends are connected with this belief. The idea that the cock sings all night on Christmas seems to have been known to Shakespeare.

" Some say, that ever 'gainst that season comes
Wherein our Saviour's birth is celebrated,
The bird of dawning singeth all night long.
And then, they say, no spirit can walk abroad ;
The nights are wholesome ; then no planets strike,
No fairy takes, nor witch hath power to charm.
So hallow'd and so gracious is the time."

(*Hamlet.*)

THE ASS AND THE HORSE

A Slavonic legend relating the birth of Christ runs as follows :

When Jesus Christ was born in a shepherd's hut the Holy Mother, rolling him up in swaddling-clothes, put him on the straw in the manger. Thereupon she

[1] See Knoop, *Volkstümliches aus der Tierwelt*, 1905, p. 38.

laid herself down on the straw near the manger to watch over the Infant. At sunset the shepherds returned with their cattle from the pasture, and the ox, the cow, and the horse as usual went into the stable and approached the manger. The Holy Mother, anxious for the comfort of the Holy Infant, rose to her feet and gathering straw from the manger heaped it in a corner of the stable for the animals to eat. When the ox and the cow had eaten up the straw they lay down and began to ruminate, but the horse returned to the manger where a little straw remained and on which Jesus lay. It began to eat this straw. The Holy Mother tried to keep the animal away, first with her hands and then by flustering her dress, but as if to spite her the horse fell to and would not move away. Thereupon the Holy Mother took up the Holy Child in her arms and thus she spoke :

" Ox and cow, you and your offspring shall be blessed, but thou, oh horse, thou and thy kindred shall never be filled to satiety, and men shall lay heavy burdens on thee." [1]

Another version of this legend is given by Afanassieff : [2] When Herod was pursuing the Holy Child, the Holy Mother placed it in a manger and covered it up with hay. All through the night the voracious horse devoured the fodder, which concealed the Holy Infant, while the bull not only ceased to eat but gathered the scattered hay with its horns, and threw it over the child to cover it up. The

---

[1] See Krauss, *Sagen und Märchen der Sudslaven*, vol. ii. p. 121 ff.

[2] *Russian Popular Legends*, London, 1859.

Lord thereupon cursed the horse for its greediness, and blessed the bull. Consequently the horse is always feeding but never has its fill.

THE COW AND THE MULE

In other legends it is not the horse but the mule which is cursed and condemned to remain for ever barren on account of its conduct on Christmas night.

The Holy Virgin, to hide the child and to keep it warm, had placed it between a cow and a mule. The latter, however, constantly drew the hay aside, while the cow, gathering the hay, covered the newly born child and kept it warm with its breath. Thereupon the Holy Virgin said unto the cow :

" Thou shalt have the honour of being pregnant for nine months, even like a woman ; in all seasons of the year, be it summer or winter, thy snout shall be moist and indicate health, and thy breath shall be warm in reward for thy kindness on this night. The mule, however, Mary condemned to barrenness.[1]

It is believed by some that at one o'clock on Christmas morning the cattle turn their heads eastward, and even get down upon their knees and worship him who was born in a stable.

THE DAISY AND THE ROSE

Not only the animals but the plants also are said to have rejoiced on the night of the Nativity. A pious tradition declares that the plants and flowers rejoice on every Christmas night. Fruit trees and

---

[1] See Sébillot, *Folk-lore*, iii. 73 ; *Revue des Traditions Populaires*, v. 244.

flowers burst forth into blossom in some southern countries, such as the Rose of Jericho, the balsam, the apple, and the cherry.

A legend connected with the daisy and accounting for the tinge of red in it is current in France.

When the wise men of the East and the shepherds came to offer their gifts to the Holy Infant, there was also a poor small shepherd boy who had no gift to offer. He was sore at heart, as he could not appear empty-handed, and so he plucked a white daisy in the field and held it up close to the lips of the Holy Child. Jesus kissed the flower, and where His lips had touched it there is a red rosy tinge on the edge of the leaves.[1]

Another legend explaining the origin of the Christmas rose is connected with the little shepherdess, Magdalen.

The Holy Child was lying in the stable stretched on some hay between an ox and an ass. Mary was watching near the manger, while Joseph, with folded hands, was adoring the child. The ox was lowing : " Moo, moo, what a great day," while the ass was braying : " How beautiful is the child. Ih, ah." Night came, outside there was storm, snow, and frost, while inside the stable was full of brilliance. The three Kings of Saba entered, arrayed in velvet and silk, their dresses studded with precious stones. Balthazar brought gold, Melchior myrrh, and Caspar incense. From another direction came the shepherds. Pelion brought whistles, Ysambert a calendar of wood from which the days and the months could be

[1] Sébillot, *Folk-lore*, iii. 446.

learned, while Aloris brought a rattle to soothe the child when it was crying.

Behind the shepherds, timid, curious, and enraptured, a small, blue-eyed girl, the little shepherdess Magdalen, stood on tiptoe. Oh, how she loved the child Jesus, and how happy she would have been to hug it and offer some precious gift. But, alas, she was so poor and had nothing to offer. Her little hands were empty, and in her inconsolable distress at her poverty she burst into tears.

But when the angel Gabriel saw her distress, he descended from heaven and gently asked her :

" What is it thou dost desire ? "

" Oh, I do not know," she answered.

" And why art thou crying ? "

" Because I should have dearly wished to offer some gift to the child Jesus, but I have none."

" And what gift wouldst thou wish to offer him ? "

" Alas, the shepherds and the kings have already given Him everything."

" Have they not forgotten anything ? Reflect and think about it."

" Yes, if I only could offer Him roses ! The dear child has not received a single flower, but it is freezing and spring is still far away."

Thereupon the angel Gabriel took Magdalen by the hand and led her outside where a brilliant light shone around them. The angel touched the ground with his staff, and suddenly the earth was covered with pretty and dainty flowers, tender and exquisite wild roses. Magdalen, the little shepherdess, could now embrace Jesus, for Christmas had its roses.[1]

A French legend runs as follows : Whilst Jesus was lying in the manger a spray of the rose-coloured Sainfoin was found among the dried grass and herbs which served for the Infant's bed. Immediately the Sainfoin began to expand its delicate blossoms, and to the wonder of Mary it formed a wreath around the head of the Holy Child.

I have pointed out in the Introductory chapter that when the pagan world became Christian the Church could not help recognizing the importance of transferring certain legends to the characters of the New Testament. So legends told of Freya were applied naturally by popular imagination to the Holy Virgin, while those clustering around Buddha were adapted to Christ.

In the legends connected with the Madonna and the Nativity pagan floral symbolism was woven into beautiful fancies which adorn the legendary life of the Holy Virgin. When Diana, Venus, and Juno disappeared from the centre of popular fancy the Virgin Mary took their place. She became the incarnation of grace, the queen of heaven and of earth. The plants which were worshipped by pagan antiquity were in course of time connected with incidents in the life of the Madonna, and the origin of the choicest fruit and flowers were ascribed to her. Floral offerings were now laid on the shrine of the Madonna. She has become the Rose of Sharon, the Lily of the Valley, and the whole bloom and

[1] See *La Tradition*, vol ii. p. 335, and vi. 345.

colouring of the fields have been ascribed to her, while some of the choicest flowers, unknown in her native Galilee, have been named after her.

THE CHERRY TREE

Before the birth of Jesus the Virgin Mary, desiring to refresh herself with some luscious cherries hanging in clusters upon the branch of a tree, asked Joseph to gather some for her. But Joseph mockingly replied : " Let the father of thy child bring them to you." Instantly the branch of the cherry tree inclined itself to the Madonna's hand, so that she could herself reach the ripe cherries and refresh herself. It is for this reason that the cherry has been dedicated to the Madonna.

The legend is told somewhat differently in the Provence. Mary and Joseph on their way from Bethlehem to Nazareth came upon a gardener who was climbing an apple tree, and Mary asked him for an apple. The gardener politely told her to help herself and pluck one. When Joseph, however, tried to pluck an apple, the branches went up and the fruit was beyond his reach.

THE ADORATION OF THE MAGI

The Canonical Gospels nowhere inform us that the wise men from the East were either kings or that their number was three. But legend and popular imagination found ample scope in this incident connected with the Far East for details of pomp and splendour. The visit of the Magi struck the mediæval mind more forcibly than the simplicity of the visit of the shepherds. Consequently, the Magi were converted into kings, eastern potentates, who brought royal gifts. They came to Bethlehem with mules, camels, and horses loaded with great treasure, and with a multitude of people to do homage to the Saviour. Their names were specified, and their appearance and stature minutely described, making the legend an attractive subject to the mediæval artists (Van Eyck, Dürer, Rubens).

There is a golden reliquary in the cathedral at Cologne, where, in an odour of sanctity, the relics of the Magi, the three eastern potentates, the wise men, are preserved. The Magi, these " truth-seekers " as they have rightly been called, greatly attracted popular fancy.

In an old German legend by Johann von Hildesheim,[1] it is related that the three kings who followed the star started on their journey at the same moment, but that none of them knew anything about the other two. Caspar came from Tharsis, Balthazar from Saba, and Melchior from Arabia. They met on the way to Bethlehem. The three Magi had been informed of the birth of Christ by different miraculous events. Thus in the night of the Nativity an ostrich in the possession of King Caspar laid two eggs, out of which a lamb and a lion respectively came forth. In Balthazar's garden a flower suddenly blossomed, and out of it a bird arose and took flight; while unto Melchior a child was born on that night, which announced the birth of Christ and its own death in thirty-three days.

[1] Edited by Gustav Schwab, 1823.

On their return to their native lands, the three kings of the East exterminated paganism and were subsequently converted to Christianity by the Apostle Thomas when he went to Persia. They died as Christian bishops while partaking of the Lord's Supper. Their bodies were conveyed from Persia to Constantinople and buried in the Church of St. Sophia, though subsequently their remains were transferred to Milan. In 1163, when Frederick Barbarossa sacked Milan, the Archbishop Reinald carried away the coffins containing the mortal remains of these three kings of the East to Cologne, where they are to-day guarded with veneration.

There is a story connected with the Magi in the *Gesta Romanorum* (No. 47) which runs as follows :

A Danish king once undertook a pilgrimage to Cologne to the tombs of the three Magi, and carried with him three precious crowns for the three kings. On his return home he had a curious dream. Three saints appeared to him, each of them offering him a gift in return for those he had made, namely, three boxes, one containing the gold of wisdom, the other the myrrh of penitence, and the third the incense of humility. On the king's awakening, his visitors had disappeared, but the boxes were there. The pious king lived for another thirty-three years in happiness.[1]

The names of the Magi are said to have been Melchior, Caspar, and Balthazar, but other traditions ascribe unto them different names : Apellus, Amerus, et Damascus, or Ator, Sator, Peratoras.[2]

[1] See *Gesta Romanorum*, ed. Graesse, No. 47.
[2] See Peter Comestor, *Historia Scholastica*, Hist. Ev. ch. viii.

According to a mediæval author, Jacques d'Ausoles, in his *Traité de l'Epiphanie*, the three kings from the East, like the three travellers who visited Abraham in the plain of Mamre, were three immortals in disguise, namely, Enoch, Elijah, and Melchi-Zedek, two of whom had never tasted death.

Other mediæval authors, however, maintain that the three wise men from the East were kings in reality and ruled over the kingdoms of Tharsis, Nubia, and Sheba or Saba, respectively. Their respective ages were : twenty, forty, and sixty years, and they thus represented the three stages of human life—adolescence, manhood, and old age.

In connection with the legendary description and the physical details of the Magi I must mention another legend which runs as follows :

In the distant and far East, hard by the ocean, dwelt a people who preserved a book bearing the name of Seth and in which the appearance of the guiding star and the offering of gifts were written down. This book was handed down as a precious heirloom from the fathers to their sons. Twelve men were chosen whose function it was to watch for the appearance of the star and to follow it. When one of the twelve died another immediately took his place. These watchers were called in the language of the people, Magi. Every year, after the wheat harvest, they ascended a mountain called Victorialis, a pleasant spot on account of its grottoes, trees, and springs, and here they watched for the star. At last, one day the promised star appeared, and in it was the face of a child and above it the sign of the cross.

The star itself shone to the watchers, and bade them go to Judæa. The journey lasted two years, but during all the time the travellers lacked neither food nor drink.[1]

This legend, by the way, was evidently known to the mediæval artists. An altar-piece by Hemling presents the three kings as standing on the top of a mountain and watching from afar the child surrounded by a radiant light.[2]

The star which guided the Magi is said to have disappeared in a well at Bethlehem, in front of which now stands the Greek Church of St. Elijah. Legend affirms that the star still abides in the well, but that only virgins are able to see it.

In the Ethiopic Book of Adam and Eve the following passage referring to the worship of the Magi occurs :

"And when he (Christ) was born at Bethlehem in the land of Judah, a star in the East made it known, and was seen by the Magi. That star shone in heaven, amid all the other stars ; it flashed and was like the face of a woman, a young virgin, sitting among the stars, and holding in her arms a little child of a beautiful countenance. The loveliness of his face filled the heaven and earth with beauty and light, and around his head was a radiance like a crown. It was a custom of the Chaldeans to observe the stars and to take counsel from them. So when they saw the star and the figure we have just men-

---

[1] See R. Hofmann, *Das Leben Jesu nach den Apokryphen*, pp. 131–132.

[2] See also Sepp, *Symbolik zum Leben Christi*, v. Regensburg, 1846, p. 13 ; see also Hofmann, *l.c.* pp. 125–134.

tioned, they were greatly troubled, and said among themselves, ' Surely the King of the Helouæans is putting himself in battle array against us ! '

" But they inquired among soothsayers and philosophers, until they ascertained the fact, and discovered that it was the King of the Children of Israel who had been born. So they set out to seek him, taking with them the presents they had prepared ; that is, gold, frankincense, and myrrh, which had been with Adam in the Cave of Treasures —gold, as unto a king ; frankincense, as unto God ; and myrrh, as for his death." [1]

THE CIRCUMCISION

When the time for the circumcision came, which is the eighth day, the child was circumcised according to the Law. Therefore Joseph and Mary betook themselves to Bethlehem where the Child was circumcised, and they called him Jesus. An old Hebrew woman took the umbilical cord and laid it up in a vase of oil and spikenard, and hid it. But she had a son who was a perfumer by profession to whom she committed the vase. " Take care," she said to her son, " not to sell this vase of ointment even if people were to offer thee 300 dinars." It was this vase which Mary Magdalen afterwards bought and poured its contents upon the head and the feet of Jesus, which she afterwards wiped with her hair.

On the fortieth day from the birth of Jesus, Mary brought him into the temple and offered sacrifices

---

[1] *The Book of Adam and Eve,* by the Rev. S. C. Malan, London, 1882, pp. 204–205 ; see also Nino, *Usi e Costumi,* vol. iv. pp. 18–23.

for him, as is commanded in the Law.[1] There was, however, a pious and just man in the temple of the name of Simeon, who had reached the age of 113 years. He knew that he would not die before he had seen the Christ with his own eyes. When he saw the child shining as a pillar of light in the arms of Mary, he said :

" Now I can go in peace, for mine eyes have seen the mercy which God hath prepared for the salvation of all peoples ; a light to all nations and a glory to the people of Israel."

The prophetess Hannah, the daughter of Phenuel, was also there, and she gave thanks to God, for in this child, she said, is the salvation of the world.

It is interesting to notice that this legend found credence in the Church, for it seems that the umbilical cord and the stone on which Jesus was circumcised were for a long time preserved as holy relics in the churches of St. Mariæ populi and of St. Jacobi Scossa respectively. Winkler, in *Anecdota Eccles*, i. p. 787, mentions a number of other legends to which the mediæval Church has given credit.

[1] Exod. xiii. 2 ; see also Luke ii. 23 ; Hofmann, *l.c.* p. 120.

" Now when they were departed, behold, an angel
of the Lord appeareth to Joseph in a dream,
saying : Arise and take the young child and his
mother, and flee into Egypt."—MATT. ii. 13.

ON THE DAY before Herod issued his decree to
massacre all the infants of Bethlehem an angel of the
Lord appeared to Joseph in his sleep and thus spoke
to him : " Arise and take with thee Mary and the
Child, and travel through the desert to Egypt."
Joseph did as the angel had bidden him, and set out
on his way before the cock crew. The Holy Family
came to a cave and stopped there for a little rest.
Mary dismounted and sat down, holding the Child
Jesus in her lap. Three men-servants and one maid-
servant accompanied Joseph and Mary on their
journey, for Salome had joined the Holy Family.

MEETING WILD BEASTS

Now it happened that dragons suddenly emerged
from the depth of the cave, and the frightened men-
servants cried aloud, in an agony of fear. Thereupon Jesus arose from his mother's lap and stood on
his feet, in front of the dragons, but the beasts
prostrated themselves, worshipped him, and then
went their way. The Child, however, walked before
the beasts and commanded them not to harm any
one.

Mary and Joseph were both in great agony, afraid lest the dragons should harm the Holy Child. Thereupon Jesus thus spoke unto his parents : " Do not look on me as a mere child, for I am indeed a perfect man, and all the beasts in the forest will become tame in my presence."

In like manner the lions and the panthers worshipped him, and escorted the Holy Family through the desert. Walking in front of them, they showed the fugitives the way, and from time to time they bowed their heads and worshipped Jesus. Mary was greatly frightened when she beheld the lions and the other wild beasts for the first time, but Jesus looked into her face and joyfully said : " Have no fear, mother, for these beasts have come hither not to harm thee but to do my bidding." And thus speaking he banished all fear from his mother's heart.

The lions walked along by the side of the travellers, together with the oxen, asses, and other beasts of burden which carried their belongings. They hurt no one, but were tame among the sheep and the rams which had been brought from Judæa. The Holy Family met packs of wolves, but none of the beasts harmed the fugitives.

This legend, related in the so-called Apocryphal " Gospel of the Infancy," is evidently inspired by Ps. xci. 13, where it is said : " Thou shalt tread upon the lion and the adder : The young lions and the serpent shalt thou trample under feet."

The obedience and submission of wild beasts which worshipped and prostrated themselves before saints and heroes is a *motif* quite frequent in the

5

legendary lore of many nations. It is told of many Christian saints, as well as of Jesus. Just as the celestial beings, angels, and demons are submissive to the saints and the holy and pious men on earth, so also are the beasts. Deeply rooted in the heart of humanity is the belief that animals are susceptible to the supernatural. It is to this belief that all the legends about the worship of animals give expression. In the Talmud there are many legends of pious and holy men who were cast into a cage of lions without being harmed. By order of the Roman Emperor, Rabbi Tanchuma was thrown into a lion's cage but came out safe, for the beast refused to touch him.[1]

Our first parent, Adam, is also said to have been worshipped by all the beasts of creation. A profound impression was produced by Adam upon the beasts of the earth and the birds of the air. Seeing him adorned with the divine image, they all came to prostrate themselves before him. But Adam said to the beasts of the earth and to the birds of the air: "Why have ye come to worship me, who am only a creature of clay and whom the Creator has fashioned in His image? Come ye all and let us clothe ourselves in glory, and let us praise the Lord and acknowledge Him as king over us all." Thus spoke Adam, and he chose God as King of all the world and as Ruler of the Universe. And all the beasts, fowls, and fishes listened to the word of Adam and did likewise.[2]

In a Christian source, *The Cave of Treasures*, written in the sixth century by a disciple of St.

[1] *Aboda Zara*, 18b.   [2] Rappoport, *l.c.* vol. i.

Ephrem, we read that all the wild and tame beasts and all the fowls of the air gathered before Adam, our first parent, bowed their heads, worshipped, and served him.[1]

Legend also relates that lions gambolled round Moses and Aaron like dogs round their masters. It happened when the brothers appeared for the first time before the Pharaoh of Egypt. Two fierce lions were stationed before the royal palace, and any one approaching the gates without permission was immediately torn to pieces. A visitor could penetrate into the palace only when the magicians led the beasts away. When the keepers heard that Moses and Aaron were coming, they let the beasts loose, so that they might devour them. But as soon as the sons of Amram approached the gates of the royal palace, the fierce lions joyously bounded towards them, bowed their heads in salutation and followed them wherever they went.

Similar legends are told of King Solomon, both in Jewish and Christian sources. All the beasts of the earth, all the birds of the air, and all that dwelt in the sea paid homage to the wise king of Israel.

Many parallels are found in the legendary lore of other nations—of the Egyptians, the Greeks, and the Romans. Deep down in the heart of man lies the love of the unexpected and the wonderful. The lives and deeds of heroes and saints, of men with a divine mission, appeal to the mind, and dreams are woven into the real events of their lives. A halo

---

[1] *The Cave of Treasures*, ed. C. Bezold, 1888, pp. 3, 4; see also Grünbaum, *Neue Beiträge zur Semitischen Sagenkunde*, 1893, pp. 57, 58.

surrounds the saints of Christianity as it does the characters of the Old Testament and the heroes of pagan antiquity. One nation, however, eagerly learns from another, and foreign elements are quickly assimilated. Many a feature taken from elsewhere is added to those already in the possession of a people. Hence the parallels between the legends of nations separated both by faith and language and the similarity of the legends told of Christ or of Moses and those culled from the literatures of the nations of pagan antiquity. Lucian mentions an Egyptian sage before whom the wild beasts bowed. The fierce dogs in the temple of Dictyma, on the island of Crete, bounded towards Apollonius and met him like an old acquaintance when he entered the building in the middle of the night.[1]

There was one animal, however, which never bowed to Jesus and ignored his divine mission. It was the horse. It obstinately refused to render any service to the Saviour. " I have no time," said the horse ; " I am taking my food and have not yet had my fill." And the Saviour cursed the horse and condemned the stupid animal to eat to the end of the world, but never to be filled.[2]

LADEN FRUIT TREES

On the third day after the Holy Family had set out, it came to pass that Mary became exhausted in the desert through the excessive heat of the sun. When, therefore, she saw a tree, she thus spoke unto

---

[1] See Lucius, *Anfänge des Heiligenkults*, p. 511.
[2] See Sébillot, *Folklore*, iii. 74.

Joseph : " Let us rest a while under the shadow of this tree." So Joseph hasted, and led her to the palm, lifting her off her beast. Now when Mary sat down and looked up to the top of the palm tree she saw that its branches were laden with fruit. " I desire, if it is possible," she said unto Joseph, " to eat of the fruit of this palm tree." And Joseph said unto her : " I marvel that thou speakest thus, since thou seest how high the branches of this palm tree are. What I am extremely anxious about is *water*. It has now been exhausted in our skin-bottles, and we have none to fill them and quench our thirst."

Thereupon the child Jesus, who lay with joyful countenance in his mother's, the Virgin Mary's, bosom, said to the palm tree : " O palm tree, move thy branches, lower them and refresh my mother with thy fruit." And behold ! instantly the palm tree at his word bowed its head to the very sole of Mary's feet. And they all plucked the fruit which the palm tree bore, and ate and were refreshed. Afterwards, when all its fruit had been plucked and eaten, the palm tree still remained bent, waiting to rise up at the word of him by whose command it had bowed down.

Thereupon Jesus said to the palm tree : " O palm tree, arise and be of good cheer, and be thou the companion of my trees in my Father's Paradise. Open thou, however, with thy roots the spring that is hidden in the ground and let water flow forth from that spring to quench our thirst."

At that moment the palm tree stood erect, and from amid its roots came forth streams of water, crystal clear, cool, and very sweet. When they beheld the streams of water they rejoiced exceedingly, and quenched their thirst and that of their beasts of burden ; they were all satisfied and praised God.

At the hour of their departure on the following day, Jesus said unto the palm tree : " O palm tree, I command thee that one of thy branches be carried by my angels and planted in my Father's Paradise. And this blessing I bestow upon thee that to all those who will be victorious in a good fight it shall be said : ' Thou hast borne away the palm.' " And as he thus spoke, behold, an angel of God appeared above the top of the tree, and taking one of the branches of the tree, soared up to Heaven, carrying the branch in his hand.

When they saw this they were greatly frightened, but the child Jesus thus spoke to them : " Why hath fear entered your hearts ? Know ye not that this palm tree, which I have commanded to be carried to Paradise, shall one day be to the saints in the abode of bliss what it has been unto you in the desert ? "

The entire legend of Mary and the palm tree, as related above, is found in a collection of old English legends dealing with the Infancy of Jesus, and in the *Cursor Mundi* of the fourteenth century.[1] It is also told by Martinus Polonus in his *Chronicle*, by Sozomenos in his *Ecclesiastical History*,[2] by Vincent de Beauvais, and by several mediæval writers.[3] In

[1] See *Early English Text Society*, vols. i.–v.
[2] See Gubernatis, *l.c.* p. 278.
[3] Maury, *l.c.* p. 229.

some versions it is a peach tree. Sozomenos also quotes a Spanish tradition according to which a demon had taken up his abode in the tree there to receive the adoration of the people. When, at the approach of Jesus, the demon was hurled into an abyss, the tree bent down in order to express its gratitude.[1]

The legend of Mary and the palm tree was known to Mohammed. It is found in the *Koran*, Sûra xix., where, however, it is connected not with the Flight to Egypt but with the Nativity. The Virgin, says the *Koran*, gave birth to the Child at the foot of a palm tree, the tree best known to the Arabs. At the moment of his birth Christ directed the tree to let fall upon Mary freshly gathered dates, and he also told his mother that a streamlet was flowing at her feet. " Eat, therefore, and brighten thine eye (rejoice)."

A parallel of the legend of Mary and the palm tree is found in Buddhist literature. When Queen Maya, the mother of Gautama the Buddha, was with child and knew that her confinement was close, she obtained her husband's permission to return to her family and relations, to be delivered there, in accordance with the custom of the country. She then set out on her journey to the country of Dewah. One day the queen and her maidens entered a beautiful forest where they saw water-lilies shooting forth from the main branches of each tree, for all the trees seemed to share in the universal joy. Queen Maya greatly admired the abundant flowers which

[1] See Migne, *Patrologia*, vol. clxxii. col. 837.

she saw on the trees. Gently she rose from the couch upon which she was seated, and with her right hand tried to reach and break a small branch, which she wanted to carry away. And instantly the tree, like the end of a stick well softened with steam, bent its head, and all the branches lowered their extremities, offering themselves, as it were, to the hand of the queen. The branch came within the reach of Maya's hand, and she unhesitatingly seized and broke the extremity of one of the young boughs. And at that moment, just as she stood grasping the branch of the tree, her child was born.[1]

In another Indian source we read that Buddha, who in a former birth was a prince called Vessantaro, was once banished by his discontented people from his kingdom, along with his wife and children. They were wandering through the forest to the distant mountains, where they hoped to find an asylum, tormented by the scorching heat of the sun. The children grew hungry, and seeing fruit-bearing trees they wept for the fruits to satisfy their pangs of hunger. And behold, the great, lofty, giant trees seeing the children weep, bowed themselves down towards the children, who were thus able to ease their hunger.[2]

THE ARROGANT ASPEN

The only tree which refused to worship Jesus was the aspen, and for its arrogance the Saviour pronounced a curse upon it : " As thou didst not

[1] See Bigaudet, *The Life of Gaudama*, 1880, i. p. 35.
[2] See Eysinga, *l.c.* p. 79.

bow to me in salutation, thou shalt tremble for ever."
The leaves of the aspen have ever since been seen
trembling.

> " Once as our Saviour walked with men below,
>   His path of mercy through a desert lay,
> And mark ! how all the drooping branches show
>   What homage best a silent tree may pay.
>
> Only the aspen stood erect and free,
>   Scorning to join the voiceless worship pure.
> But see ! He cast one look upon the tree ;
>   Struck to the heart, she trembles evermore."

There is a Polish legend of the aspen and the
hazel which runs as follows : On their flight to
Egypt the Holy Family, fleeing from the wrath of
Herod, sought safety under an aspen, but the tree
refused to give protection to the fugitives, afraid lest
it might be cut down by King Herod. The Holy
Family then hasted to hide under a hazel, which
gladly offered them protection, screening them with
its scanty branches. As a punishment for its lack of
hospitality the aspen was cursed by the child Jesus
to tremble for ever, even when no wind was blowing,
while it was promised to the hazel that whoever
sought shelter under it during a storm would be protected, as no lightning will ever strike it.[1]

There seems to be no statement in the Canonical
Gospels for the legends related above, but the *motif*
of trees bowing in salutation to saints, obeying their
commands and offering them their branches and

---

[1] Dähnhardt, *Natursagen*, vol. ii. p. 39 ; see also X. Marmier,
Lettres sur l'Islande, p. 106.

fruit, is quite frequent in legendary lore. In the
Talmud we read that once the hired labourers of
Rabbi José had had no food for a whole day. Thereupon the son of the pious Rabbi said unto the
fig tree : " O fig tree, bring forth thy fruit, so that
the labourers of my father may relieve their hunger."
And instantly the fig tree brought forth fruit.[1]

The trees, so legend further relates, not only
bowed to Jesus in salutation and provided the Holy
Family with food, but gave them protection during
their flight to Egypt. Not far from Old Cairo stands
a fig tree, which opened its trunk and thus hid the
Holy Family from a band of robbers.

THE OLIVE

An Italian tradition connects this legend with the
olive tree. So many troops of Pharisees were searching for the Holy Family that at every moment Mary
and Joseph perceived their pursuers. One troop
being close on their heels, nothing was left to the
fugitives but to run as fast as they could. There was
neither house nor hut, not even a cavern which could
offer them shelter, while they could hear the voices
of their enemies shouting : " Stop ! "

Thereupon Mary beheld an olive tree and implored it to save them.

" Have pity," she prayed, " and hide us : save
us in our dire necessity."

When lo ! the olive tree opened like a hut, and
Joseph and Mary and the Holy Child entered, whereupon the olive tree closed up. And the Holy Family

[1] *Taanit,* 24a.

was not in darkness, but had light inside the tree, as there was no lack of oil. The Pharisees who a moment ago had seen the Madonna with their own eyes did not understand how she could have disappeared so suddenly and miraculously. In vain did they explore the olive grove, searching all through the night, but when morning came they angrily gave up their quest and returned home.

Thereupon the olive tree opened again and Mary, Joseph, and the Holy Infant came out. And Mary said to the olive tree : " May thy fruit be sacred ! " And therefore people speak of the sacred oil and apply it to wounds, tumours, and scalds ; and therefore we also say : " Olive oil, thou that once didst give light to the Lord Jesus, take away from the baptized all pain." [1]

Legends of trees offering shelter to prophets and saints are very numerous. In a Persian story we are told that through the kindness of God a tree once opened its trunk to hide Shah Djemshid.[2] A Jewish legend relates that a cedar tree once opened and gave shelter to the prophet Isaiah who was being pursued by the king.[3] Tabari relates a similar miracle of the prophet Zacharias who was hiding from the Jews. Another legend explains the reason why the tamarind is red, and attributes the colour to the blood of the prophet. The prophet Zacharias, who was being pursued by his enemies, had sought shelter in the hollow of a tamarind. The pursuers

---

[1] De Nino, *Usi e Costumi Abbruzzesi,* vol. iv, *Sacre leggende,* 1887, pp. 42–43.

[2] See Rudolf Hofmann, *Das Leben Jesu,* p. 138.

[3] See Kautzsch, *Die Pseudæpigraphen des Alten Testaments,* p. 127.

having discovered the prophet's hiding-place, summoned him to leave the hollow of the tree. The prophet, however, ignored the summons, and his enemies decided to saw the tree through, but in so doing they hurt the fugitive, and his red blood flowed abundantly over the tamarind. Hence the red colour of the tree.[1]

The Holly and the Juniper

An Italian legend states that during the flight to Egypt Joseph, being an old man and unable to run, continually lagged behind. Once the Holy Family saw the Pharisees riding along. And Mary, in her agony, exclaimed : "Run, Joseph, run !" The Holy Family was just in the midst of a thicket of juniper bushes, and Mary begged one of the bushes to hide the Holy Child. The bush immediately opened, received the Child, and closed up again ; and when the Pharisees came near they only saw a woman and an old man.

After a while another troop of Pharisees came riding along. As they were standing on a rock they saw that there was no tree in the vicinity except a holly, but the holly spread out its branches, and Mary and Joseph went beneath them and were hidden from view. The Pharisees, not finding the fugitives, continued their way. Thereupon Mary blessed the holly and said : "Thou shalt remain evergreen." [2]

This legend may seem to account for the custom of using branches and berries of the holly or holy tree

[1] See *Revue des Traditions Populaires*, xvi. 265.
[2] See de Nino, *l.c.* p. 44–45.

for the decoration of churches and houses at Christmas. It should, however, be remembered that
among the Romans it was already customary to send
boughs of holly to friends with new-year's gifts, as
emblematical of good wishes.

As the juniper bush also opened its branches and
offered shelter to the Holy Child, it is customary in
Italy to decorate the houses with juniper branches.[1]

Numerous other legends are connected with
plants and trees which, in order that the Virgin might
conceal herself and the Holy Infant from the assassins
sent out by King Herod, either stretched out their
branches or enlarged their leaves.

Not all plants, however, were ready to offer
shelter to the fugitives. Some of them, by the noise
they made, drew the attention of the soldiers of
Herod to the spot where the travellers had halted.
These plants accordingly received the maledictions
of the Madonna, and one of them was the Lupine.

The Flax and the Lupine

On their flight to Egypt the Madonna, carrying
the Holy Child, passed over a lupine field, and the
plants, dry and prickly, hurt the feet of Mary. To
escape from the pain she ran forward and entered a
field where broad beans were just being planted.
The Holy Virgin in joy blessed the field, and the
broad beans immediately grew up. In the meantime the pursuers, who had reached the border of the
field, inquired of some peasants whether they had

[1] See A. de Gubernatis, *Mythologie des Plantes*, vol. ii. p. 153 ; see also
La Tradition, vol. xx. p. 72.

seen a woman carrying a child accompanied by an elderly man.

" Yes," replied the peasants.

" When ? " asked the pursuers.

" Just when we were planting these broad beans."

When the pursuers noticed that the broad beans were in full growth they retraced their steps and returned home.

Thereupon Mary and Joseph came to a field of flax, and once more they beheld their pursuers, who were quite near. " Flax, O flax," prayed Mary, " hide my child " ; and the flax hid the Holy Infant. It began to wave to and fro so that the glimmering wave-lines dazzled the pursuers, who saw nothing. When the danger passed, Mary said :

" Blessed be thou, O flax ! " and ever since there has been so much flax in the world that the women have grown tired in spinning it.[1]

Another legend of plants offering shelter to the Holy Family runs as follows :

Joseph, warned in a dream that Herod had determined to put the Holy Child to death, was commanded by the angel of the Lord to flee to Egypt. In order to prevent the pursuers sent out by Herod from finding out the whereabouts of the fugitives from the traces left by the footsteps of their mount, Joseph decided to shoe his ass the wrong way. And thus the Holy Family went on their journey. At dawn the fugitives entered a lupine field, hoping to find there a hiding-place. But, alas, the dry husks made a noise, and the fugitives were obliged to re-

[1] De Nino, *l.c.* pp. 36–37.

trace their steps. Thereupon they entered a rye field, but here too they could find no shelter, for the ears bent their heads and did not rise up again, so that the Holy Family remained unprotected. At last the fugitives came to a curcitta field, where they found a safe shelter. And the Lord blessed the curcitta field, and henceforth men satisfy their hunger completely by eating the bread of curcitta.[1]

THE BASIL AND THE MINT

In Roussillon the following legend of plants which offered shelter to the Holy Family during their flight to Egypt is related :

Herod the Great, King of Judæa, had determined to massacre all the infants in order to get rid of Jesus who was destined to bring light to the world. Greatly frightened, Mary pressed the Infant to her heart and fled over the fields seeking shelter from the pursuers whom Herod had sent out. She perceived a peasant in a cornfield sowing his seed.

" Peasant, dear peasant," begged Mary, " run home and fetch thy family to help thee mow the field and bind the sheaves."

The peasant looked incredulously at the Virgin and shrugged his shoulders.

" Thou art mocking me," he said ; " dost thou not see that I am only throwing out the seed ? "

" Go," repeated Mary, " and obey."

She had spoken these words with such conviction that the good peasant, moved to obedience, ran home to fetch his family. When he returned, a miracle

[1] Pitré, *Usi e Costumi Credenze e preguidizi*, vol. iii, pp. 294-295.

had happened, for the corn was ripe. Quickly he began to mow the field and to bind the sheaves. And Mary with her child hiding under the sheaves commanded the good peasant to be silent and not betray her. But the sheaves not being long enough, the corner of her garment could be seen. Thereupon the branches of a basil standing near by bent down, entwined themselves, and formed a bush which completely hid from view Mary and her child.

Suddenly the sound of horses was heard. Herod himself, accompanied by his sinister warriors, appeared.

" Hast thou seen a woman carrying a child in her arms ? " asked the king of the peasant.

" Yes, O king," replied the peasant, " I have seen such a woman, but it was when I was sowing the corn."

" If such be the case," said Herod furiously, " then she must be far away, for I perceive that thy harvest is finished."

At this moment Herod might have heard a murmur issuing from a neighbouring bush. It was a mint standing near by which was saying : " Under the sheaves, under the sheaves " ; while a jay was repeating his words : " Under the sheaves, under the sheaves."

Luckily, however, Herod failed to catch the sounds and went his way.

Mary was saved. The happy mother now blessed the basil, and said : " May the Lord bless thee, and mayest thou flourish and bear fruit." And ever since the basil has been a favourite plant of young maidens, who make nosegays of it and stick them in their bodices.[1]

THE MINT AND THE SAGE

A Provençal legend runs as follows :

Joseph and Mary asked a man who was working in the field to save them from Herod, and the man told them to hide under mint. The mint, however, depressed its leaves so as not to afford the fugitives any concealment. For this treachery the mint was cursed, and though it flowers, it does not seed. The good man then told them to hide under sage, and the sage at once stretched itself and covered them.[2]

WAYSIDE FLOWERS

The flowers, too, joined in their silent worship of Jesus. Thus the rose of Jericho is said to have sprung up during the flight to Egypt, marking the footsteps of the Holy Family. Ever since it has been called " Mary's rose," or the rose of the Madonna. In Italy, women attribute to this flower the virtue of facilitating childbirth. In Germany this rose of Jericho is known as " Maria's Hand," the " Hand of Mary." [3]

THE DOG-ROSE

In modern folk-lore the origin of the dog-rose is attributed to the miraculous effect of the linen of the Holy Infant. One day, during the flight to Egypt,

---

[1] H. Chauvet, *Folk-lore Catalan*, p. 95.

[2] See Arbaud, *Chants populaires*, ii. 245 ; Briz, *l.c.* iv. 69.

[3] See Angelo de Gubernatis, *Mythologie des plantes*, vol. i. p. 324.

6

Mary having washed the Child's linen, looked round for a place whereon to dry it. Perceiving a withered bramble bush which only bore thorns, she hung the linen on it to let it dry. After a time Mary noticed that the linen was gently rising and falling, and when she removed it from the bush she saw to her amazement that the withered bush was covered with roses, varying in hue from red to white. In the places where the wet linen had touched the bush, red roses had blossomed forth, whereas the touch of the dry linen had produced white roses.[1]

Similar legends exist in the Holy Land, in France, Belgium, and Germany.[2] The German legend, which thus explains the origin of the dog-rose, adds that it was on a Friday that Mary had washed the linen. The Madonna was in the habit of washing the linen on a Friday, the day of preparation for the holy Sabbath, and therefore the sun must always shine on a Friday, were it only for a few moments. The white dog-rose is particularly honoured, and witches are afraid to pluck it, for they run the risk of being detected.[3]

FRIENDLY AND UNFRIENDLY ANIMALS

Legendary lore connects the cross on the back of the ass with its conduct in the night of the Nativity.

In other legends, however, this distinction is attributed to the willingness of the ass to carry on its back the Holy Family on their flight to Egypt.

---

[1] See Dähnhardt, *l.c.* vol. ii. p. 27.
[2] See Sébillot, *Folk-lore de France*, vol. iii. p. 368.
[3] See Perger, *Deutsche Pflanzensagen*, p. 239.

When the Holy Virgin and Joseph implored the horse to carry them on its back, and thus save them from the assassins sent out by King Herod, the horse who was just then eating its fodder turned away its head and continued to eat. A plaintive sound escaped the lips of the Child, and immediately such a ravenous hunger came over the horse that henceforth he can never eat his fill. Full of oats and hay, he nevertheless greedily continues to pluck leaves from trees and grass growing between the stones on the pavement. Thereupon Mary and Joseph approached the ass, which abandoned his meagre fare, and joyfully granted their request. Henceforth the ass has remained very frugal ; thistles satisfy him as well as pure oats, and the despised blades of grass he finds quite tasty. But because this modest animal carried the Holy Infant, the sign of the cross is visible on his back.[1]

THE HEN AND THE SOW

One day, on their flight to Egypt, the Madonna was looking for a hiding-place in order to protect the Holy Child pursued by Herod's murderers. Perceiving a heap of straw, she hid the Child beneath it, but a hen came along and with its feet began to scatter the straw so that the Child could be seen by all passers-by. Thereupon Mary seized the Child and hid it in a refuse heap. A sow standing near by helped her with its snout. And Mary said :

" May the hen require more time to lay one egg

[1] Sébillot, *Folk-lore de France*, iii. 74. See also ch. viii. " The Passion."

than the sow to give birth to seven young." " And ever since," say the Italian peasants, "the hens have great trouble to lay an egg, while the swine can cast several suckling pigs in a very short time and without any difficulty." [1]

THE BEETLE

Another version of the legend of the sower is current in Ireland :

After the massacre of the Innocents in Bethlehem the Holy Family on their flight to Egypt met several sowers and begged them for help, which was readily granted. As a reward for the sowers' kindness the corn they had sown suddenly ripened. And when Herod's hirelings reached the spot they asked the sowers who were proceeding to mow the corn whether they had seen the fugitives. Anxious not to tell a lie, the mowers replied that they had not seen any fugitives since they had sown the corn. Herod's hirelings were on the point of proceeding on their way when a wicked insect, the beetle Staphylinus, which was hiding under a stone and had seen and heard everything, crept out and told all it had overheard. Hitherto the beetle had been of a beautiful carmine-red colour, but by the will of the Lord it was changed into diabolical black. It is now despised by the whole world, and whoever kills it with the thumb of his right hand is looked upon as a benefactor of humanity, and the seven mortal sins are forgiven unto him. [2]

---

[1] *Rivista delle trad. pop.*, ii. 42.
[2] *Transactions of Phil. Soc.*, 1859, 94.

The Spider

The legend of the spider which is said to have
protected the Holy Infant when he lay in the manger
is told in connection with the flight to Egypt, but in
a somewhat different version :

When the Madonna, carrying the Holy Child, was
fleeing from Herod she hid in a cave. Thereupon a
spider came along and weaving its web round the
entrance, covered it as if with a curtain. Soon afterwards a dove appeared and laid an egg in the cobweb.
And when Herod's pursuers reached the cave they
were on the point of penetrating into it to look for
the fugitives. But one of them, pointing to the cobweb and the egg, said :

" We are only wasting our time, for no one has
entered this cave, and heaven knows how long the
cobweb has been covering the entrance to it."
Saying this, the pursuers proceeded on their way.

Thereupon the Madonna blessed the spider, and
permitted the insect to spin its web in the abodes of
man. The Madonna also blessed the dove, and
endowed it with the capacity of laying eggs every
month.[1]

Similar legends are related of King David in
Jewish folk-lore, and of Mohammed in Moslem lore.[2]

The Ibises

One day the Holy Family went on board a ship
which was sailing for Egypt. When the vessel was

[1] Shishmanoff, *Légendes religieuses Bulgares*, No. 49.
[2] See M. Grünbaum, *Neue Beiträge zur Semitischen Sagenkunde*, p. 195.

leaving port thousands of little birds were flying about, and some of them even came into the cabin to the fugitives, warning them that a storm would soon break out. The holy Joseph, understanding the warning of the birds, asked for a boat to take them back to the shore. While the boat was crossing the water the birds were singing above the heads of the passengers. They were happy to have thus saved the Holy Family, for soon afterwards the storm broke loose, the vessel sank, and was lost. The birds were small ibises, and as a reward for their action the Lord blessed them and ordained that their nests should never fall into the hands of cruel children.[1]

[1] See *Revue des Traditions Populaires*, xiv. 697 ; Sébillot, *Folk-lore*, iii. 170.

Chapter V

The Resting-Places during the Flight to Egypt

" My people shall abide in a peaceful habitation, and in sure dwellings, and in quiet resting-places."—ISA. xxxii. 18.

DURING THEIR FLIGHT into Egypt the Holy Family often rested by day or night, and many legends are connected with the difficulties they encountered and people they met at these times.

THE SHORTENING OF THE WAY

Travelling first through the hilly country of Judæa and taking the road to Joppa or Jaffa, Joseph and Mary afterwards pursued the way along the coast. It was a long and perilous journey, which for ordinary mortals, and under ordinary circumstances, would have taken five or six weeks, but space and time were miraculously shortened for the travellers.

They passed beautiful plains enamelled with flowers, shaded by fruit trees and watered by murmuring streams. But more than once they had to cross rivers and lakes and traverse thick forests or vast stretches of desert land, to wander through wildernesses or venture into hidden paths and solitary defiles, where their lives were often in danger. And one day Joseph said unto the Holy Infant : " The heat is great and we are exhausted ; shall we not proceed along the coast and travel through the towns and villages so that we may rest there from time to time ? " And Jesus said unto Joseph : " Fear not, for I will shorten the way, and in one day we will cover the distance of a thirty days' journey." And lo ! scarcely had he spoken these words when they perceived the hills and villages of Egypt.

Similar legends are related of the Hebrew Patriarchs, and also of the Apostles. A miracle, we read in Jewish legendary lore, was worked for Jacob on his journey from Beer-Sheba, when he fled from his brother Esau. From Beer-Sheba to Mount Moriah, a two days' journey, the Patriarch covered in three hours.[1] St. Thomas is said to have travelled to India in three months, or, according to another version, in seven days—a journey which required three years.[2] Eliezer, the servant of Abraham, travelled from Hebron to Haran in three hours. Under ordinary circumstances the journey would have taken him seventeen days.

IN AN IDOLATROUS TOWN

Great was the joy of the Holy Family when they reached a town called Sotinen. Now there was an idol in this place to whom all the idols and divinities of Egypt were in the habit of offering presents and paying homage. The priest ministering to this idol frequently announced to the inhabitants of the country the words spoken by Satan through the mouth of the idol. This priest had a son three years

[1] Targum, *Genesis* xxviii. 10, 11. [2] See Lipsius, *l.c.* 1249.

old, who was possessed by a number of demons and evil spirits who were always talking. Whenever the evil spirits seized the boy, he would tear off his clothes, run about naked, and throw stones at the passers-by. In the vicinity of the temple consecrated to this idol was a hospital to which the Holy Family proceeded. Suddenly a great fear came over the inhabitants. Thereupon all the elders and priests assembled and thus addressed the idol :

" What is the meaning of this fear, confusion, and disturbance which have come over us ? "

And the idol replied :

" The unknown God has arrived in your midst. He is truly God, and there is none worthy of divine worship as he is, for he is the true Son of God. It is on account of his arrival in the town that the whole district is so disturbed and frightened, for even we idols fear the greatness of his power."

It happened that when Mary, holding the Holy Infant in her arms, entered the temple, all the idols were suddenly hurled down to the ground by an invisible hand, and smashed to pieces. They lay on their faces as if they were nought. Now when the governor, named Afrodisius, heard what had occurred, he betook himself to the temple, accompanied by a numerous suite of soldiers. The priests, seeing the governor accompanied by his army on his way to the temple, said : " He is surely going to wreak vengeance on those who have caused the Egyptian idols to fall down and be smashed."

But such was not the intention of Afrodisius, for when he perceived the heathen idols lying prostrate on their faces or smashed to pieces, he approached Mary and worshipped the Holy Infant whom she was holding in her lap. And when the governor had finished his adorations he thus addressed his friends, his army, and all the inhabitants of the town, who had assembled to witness the punishment of the strangers :

" Know ye that this is the true God, for were he not God, then our own gods would never have fallen on their faces before him, lain prostrate, or been smashed to pieces. By their silence our gods themselves have proclaimed him to be the Lord. We, however, if we do not worship him and prostrate ourselves before him, even as our own gods have done, run the great risk of being sent to perdition, even as King Pharaoh was when he hardened his heart and refused to obey the commands of God." The governor, so tradition adds, subsequently came to Gaul and preached the Gospel in Gallia Narbonensis. He became the first bishop of Béziers.

This legend, which was adopted by the Church, as it served to justify a canonical text, was known to the religious artists of the thirteenth century, and has often been represented on the stained-glass windows of cathedrals.[1] A similar legend is related of Abraham. When the Patriarch proclaimed the only God, the ruler of the Universe, before Nimrod, all the idols in the throne-room were immediately thrown to the ground by an invisible hand.[2]

[1] See *supra*, p. 28.

[2] See Jellineck, *Beth-Hamidrash*, vol. i. ; see also Lipsius, *l.c.* ii. 27, where it is told that all the idols at Athens fell down at the appearance of Jesus in His glory.

Thereupon it happened that the possessed son of the priest had again a fit of his usual disease, and in his wanderings he came to the hospital where the Holy Family still abided. Now Mary had just washed the linen of the Holy Infant and hung it on a line, and the possessed son of the priest pulled down a piece of linen and put it on his head. And lo ! immediately the demons and evil spirits who possessed him and had taken up their abode in his body hurriedly departed, escaping through his mouth and flying away in the shape of ravens and serpents. The boy, who had thus been cured by the command of the Lord, began at once to praise him and to render thanks unto him. And when the priest saw his son cured from his disease and delivered from the demons and evil spirits, he said unto the boy : " My son, what has happened unto thee and in what manner hast thou been cured ? "

And the boy replied : " When the evil spirits and demons began to torment and torture me, I went into the hospital and met an honourable woman who had just washed the linen of her child and hung it on a line. I tore down a piece of linen and placed it on my head, and lo ! all the demons who had chosen their abode in my body left me and fled away in dismay and confusion."

And when the father heard his story he was greatly rejoiced, and thus he spoke : " My son, the evil spirits and demons cannot bear the presence of the Divinity, and are afraid of it. The very name of God sends them away in confusion. He must surely be the son of God who has created heaven and earth, for as soon as he came here all our idols have been hurled down, smashed to pieces, and crumbled to dust as if they had been destroyed by a mysterious and superior power."

Thus spoke the priest, but Mary and Joseph did not feel quite safe in this place, for a great fear had entered their hearts. "When we were in the land of Israel," they said, "Herod tried to put the Infant to death, and he has massacred all the innocent children in Bethlehem and in the neighbourhood. The shrieks and lamentations of heart-rent mothers have gone up to heaven. And now, when the Egyptians will hear how their idols have been hurled to the ground and smashed to pieces, they will surely condemn us to the flames." Thus saying, they hurriedly left the town.

AT THE CROSSWAYS

Then they came to a city where they met a woman whom Satan had oppressed one night when she went out to fetch water. She could neither endure clothing on her body nor stay in the house, and whenever they bound her with straps or chains she broke them, and, escaping from the house, fled into desolate and deserted places. Sometimes she would sit at the crossways and throw stones at the passers-by, so that her relatives and friends were sorely grieved. When the Holy Virgin saw the poor woman she pitied her greatly and made Satan leave her immediately. Addressing himself to Mary, he thus spoke unto her : "Woe has befallen me, O Mary, through thee and thy Son."

And thus the demoniac woman was healed from her disease. When she became self-conscious and saw that she was naked, she blushed, and felt greatly ashamed. She returned home, put on clothing, and told her father and her relatives how it was with her. Thereupon the family of the poor woman, one of the noblest in the city, hospitably received Mary and Joseph and entertained them honourably.

In a City Street

Well supplied with provisions for the journey, the fugitives from the wrath of Herod departed on the following morning, and in the evening reached another city. A marriage was just being celebrated there, but, alas ! through the arts of Satan and the work of the enchanters the bride had been struck dumb and was bereft of speech. And when Mary, carrying the Infant in her arms, entered the city, the dumb bride saw her. She at once stretched out her hands towards Jesus, and drawing him to herself, took him into her arms. Embracing him closely and tenderly, she kissed him several times, pressed him to her breast, and rocked him to and fro. And lo ! her tongue was loosed and her ears were opened, and she could hear and speak. And because the Lord had restored her to health, she gave praise and rendered thanks to God. And that night the inhabitants of the city were greatly rejoiced, for they thought that God and his angels had come down to them.

Legends of demons who take possession of men and women are numerous in the folk-lore of Eastern and Western nations. In the Old Testament, although the melancholy of King Saul is attributed to an evil spirit which the Lord had sent,[1] no mention is made of demoniac or possessed persons. But in the New Testament, in the Apocryphal Gospels, and in the works of the Church Fathers, which mirror the popular conceptions of the Jews at that time, there are numerous references to the casting out of devils. Josephus relates that demoniac persons were given certain plants to smell, and the devil was thus expelled. In the Talmud there are many legends of possessed persons healed by the Rabbis. Thus the famous Rabbi Yochanan ben Zakkai expelled devils who had entered the bodies of men or women.

There is a legend of a demon called Ben Temalion (or Ben Talmion) who had entered the body of the daughter of the Emperor of Rome, and who was expelled by Rabbi Simeon ben Yohai. It has been suggested that the legend of Ben Talmion is really a Christian legend about the apostle Bartholomew which had found entrance into the Talmud. This may be true, but there is no real reason for the assertion that the legends about demons expelled by saints are peculiar only to Christian literature during the first centuries of our era.[2]

In Jewish legendary lore and in Christian mediæval folk-lore, legends of saints who healed possessed men are numerous and have found en-

[1] See 1 Sam. xvi. 14–23 : "And an evil spirit from the Lord troubled him."

[2] See Geiger's *Zeitschrift*, vol. ii. pp. 273–278 ; *Revue des Études Juives*, vol. viii. pp. 200–202 ; vol. x. pp. 68–93 ; Migne, *Dictionnaire des Apocryphes*, ii. col. 153–157 ; Fabricius, *Codex Novi Test.*, p. 674 ; Benfey, *Pantshatantra*, i. p. 520.

trance into the general folk-lore of European nations. In Jewish folk-lore the spirit who entered a person became known as a *Dibbuck*, and was exorcised by means of magic formulas and amulets.

That demons are particularly afraid of the vicinity of the Divinity, as in the case of Mary and Jesus in the legends related above, is a *motif* frequently met with in Jewish legends, especially in those related of King Solomon. Thus Ashmodai, king of the demons, is cowed and conquered as soon as he finds himself bound by a chain upon which the ineffable name of God had been engraved. To break an ordinary chain would have been child's-play for him.

The majority of the legends about demons possessing mortals are traceable to the East, and some of them are of Indian origin. They were imported into Europe by the Crusaders, the Moors of Spain, and the Jews. An amusing story of a demon is told in the *Cuka Saptati*, and runs as follows :

Once upon a time there lived a Brahman who was wise but very poor. His wife, unfortunately, was such a shrew that a demon who lived in a tree near the house of the Brahman escaped to the desert on account of the woman's abominable character. Soon the Brahman himself, unable any longer to stand the temper of his wife, was compelled to leave home. He met the demon who—knowing what his life had been—took pity on the poor Brahman and offered him his services.

" Go to the town of Mrigavati," said the demon, " where I will enter the body of the daughter of the

King. Thou wilt heal her and expel me and a good reward will be thine."

The Brahman obeyed the instructions of the demon and went to Mrigavati. Here he expelled the demon from the king's daughter, and was generously rewarded. Thereupon the demon entered the body of another princess, but when the Brahman was again called, the spirit refused to obey the Brahman's command to leave his new abode. Seeing that his adjurations were of no avail, the Brahman suddenly whispered into the ear of the princess : " Here cometh my wife Karagara."

Scarcely had the demon heard these words, when he took fright, left the body of the princess, and fled away.[1]

An almost similar story is told by Dunlop [2] of the demon Belfegor.

IN A SORROWING HOME

The fugitives stayed in the city for three days and lived in plenty, and again being supplied with provisions, they departed and came to another town, where they passed the night. Now there was in that city an excellent woman possessed by Satan. In the shape of a serpent he leaped upon her one night when she went to the river to wash, and twined himself about her body. And as often as night drew on he vexed her greatly. When this woman saw Mary and the child in her lap she was moved with a great desire for him, and she said :

---

[1] See *Cuka Saptati*, trans. by R. Schmidt, 1894, pp. 66, 67.
[2] *History of Prose Fiction*, vol. i. pp. 186–188.

" Oh, Mary, give me the Child that I may hold him in my arms and kiss him." And Mary granted her request, but as soon as the Infant was moved towards the demoniac woman, Satan left her and fled away, and never again did he trouble her. All who were there praised the great God, while the woman herself, who had thus been miraculously healed, showed great kindness and liberality to Mary and the child.

On the following morning the happy woman took perfumed water and washed the Holy Infant. Afterwards she poured the water on a girl who was sitting there and suffering from leprosy. And behold ! so great was the power of the water wherein the Holy Infant had been washed that the girl was immediately cleansed from leprosy. And the people who witnessed the miracle said : " There is no doubt that these three travellers are Gods and not men."

As for the girl who had been cured from leprosy, she would no longer leave the Holy Family. When Mary and Joseph were ready to depart, she begged permission to accompany them. Her request was granted, and she followed them on their wanderings.

In a subsequent chapter I will refer to another legend where Abgar, king of Edessa, regained his health after looking upon an image of Christ.[1] Similar legends are also found in Jewish lore. The sick who approached Abraham were immediately healed.[2] On his breast the Patriarch wore a precious stone, and the patient who gazed at it was

---

[1] Lipsius, *l.c.* ii. 171.
[2] Yoma, 28b, *Rashi* ; Josephus, *Antiquities*, i. 8. 2.

at once cured from his disease.[1] The daughter of Pharaoh was suffering from leprosy, but her disease disappeared and she was restored to health as soon as she had touched the basket wherein Moses lay.[2] A Mohammedan legend relates that the seven daughters of the king of Egypt were cured of their diseases as soon as they had gazed upon the face of Moses (Weil, *Biblische Legenden der Muselmänner*). The oven, wherein the friends of Daniel had been thrown, was afterwards filled with water, and all those who bathed in it were cured.[3]

AT A PRINCE'S CASTLE

At length the fugitives came into a city in which was the castle of a very famous prince who had a house for the reception of guests. When they reached the house the girl, who now accompanied them, betook herself to the wife of the prince, whom she found sad and weeping bitterly.

" Tell me, O princess," asked the girl, " why art thou so sad and weeping ? "

" Wonder not at my weeping," replied the princess, " for a great sorrow oppresses me, and I have never yet dared to tell it to any one."

The girl, however, insisted, and begged the sorrowing princess to tell her the secret of her grief.

" If thou wilt reveal thy secret unto me," she said, " I shall find a remedy for it."

" Thou art a stranger unto me," replied the princess, " but I will tell thee my secret. Know then that for a long time after my marriage to the

[1] *Genesis Rabba,* 16.　　[2] *Exodus Rabba,* 1.　　[3] *Seder Hadorot,* i. 131.

prince I had no child, and when at last I gave birth to a son he was a leper. The prince, my husband, then turned away from me and ordered me either to kill the child or to give him to a nurse to bring him up in some lonely place whence no tidings should ever come. That is the cause of my grief, and therefore am I perplexed and sad at heart."

When the girl heard the sad tale she was glad, and thus she spoke : " Did I not tell thee that I shall have a remedy for thee ? Know thou that I, too, was a leper, but Jesus, the Son of Mary, healed me."

" And where is this God who has worked such a miracle ? " asked the princess.

" Behold Joseph and Mary," said the girl, " but the child which is with them is Jesus, and it is he who has healed me of my disease and suffering."

" But by what means wast thou healed of thy leprosy ? " asked the princess, " wilt thou not tell me ? "

" I will tell thee," replied the girl. " I received from his mother the water in which his body had been washed and this water I poured on me, and so I was cleansed from my leprosy."

Thereupon the princess arose and invited them to use her hospitality and she prepared a great feast for Joseph with a company of men. And on the following morning she took the perfumed water wherein the Infant Jesus had been washed, and washed her own son with it, and he was immediately cleansed from his leprosy. The princess then gave thanks and praise to God and said : " Blessed is the mother who has thee, O Jesus." And she offered rich gifts to Mary and sent her away with much honour.

In a Thief's Stronghold

Thereupon the Holy Family departed and came into a desert country which was not safe for travellers, for it was infested by robbers and thieves who haunted the district. Joseph and Mary therefore thought it best to pass the place by night and under the shelter of darkness. But as they went, behold they came upon a gang of thieves and robbers who were asleep, except two, whose names were Titus and Dammachus. Now Dammachus would have plundered the travellers and maltreated them, but Titus, the merciful thief, interfered.

" I pray thee," he said to his companion, " suffer these travellers to depart freely so that our companions who are now asleep observe them not. Do not harm them, and I will give thee forty drachmas and this my girdle as a pledge."

And saying this, he took off the girdle with which he was girdled and handed it over to his companion, so that he should not open his mouth and speak. His offer was at last accepted by Dammachus. Then Titus led the travellers to his stronghold on the rock where he gave them lodging for the night, and when morning came he accompanied the travellers some distance and showed them the right way.

Now when Mary saw what the merciful thief had

done to save them from his companions who were asleep, she said unto him : " The Lord God shall sustain thee with his right hand and grant thee remission of thy sins."

And the child Jesus answered, and thus he spoke : " Mother dear, thirty years hence I will be crucified at Jerusalem, and with me will be nailed on the Cross these two thieves, Titus on my right, and Dammachus on my left, and after that day Titus shall go before me into Paradise." [1]

" May God avert this from thee, my son," said Mary.

Thereupon they went hence and came to a city of idols, which was changed into a heap of sands at their approach.

The legend of the merciful thief, which is of Arab origin, and describes the influence of the Infant Jesus on thieves and robbers who were moved to repentance and generous acts, finds parallel in modern folk-lore. One legend runs as follows :

The Frightened Robbers

They continued their journey and reached a cave, which was the dwelling-place of thieves and robbers, and as they drew near they saw some peaceful travellers attacked and taken captive. While Joseph, Mary, and the Infant Jesus were wondering what to do, the robbers suddenly heard a great noise, as if a king and his army were marching through the town. Greatly frightened, the robbers abandoned their captives and their booty and took to flight.

[1] See Hofmann, *l.c.* pp. 176-179.

The freed prisoners now collected their belongings and prepared to continue their journey as the Holy Family approached them.

"But where is the king and his army," they asked Joseph and Mary, "whose arrival has frightened away our captors?"

"The King," said Joseph, "is following."[1]

THE CANNIBAL AND HIS SON

When the Holy Family was travelling in Egypt on their flight from Herod's soldiers, it happened that they met a woman who was the wife of a robber. To their request for a night's lodging in her home, the woman replied :

"Go ye hence, for my husband is a robber, and he will not only rob you but kill you, for he is fond of human flesh."

But the Virgin mother entreated the woman so eagerly to give them shelter that at last she yielded. She led the fugitives into her chamber, where she had just bathed her little boy, who was suffering from leprosy. When Mary beheld the leprous child a wave of divine pity swept over her, and addressing the mother, she thus spoke unto her : "If thou wilt bring me clean water wherein to bathe my child I will render thee a service."

The wife of the robber brought clean water, and Mary, having bathed the Infant Jesus, said unto the woman : "Now place thy child in this water, bathe it, and dry its body with my hair, and it will be cured from leprosy."

[1] Hofmann, *l.c.* pp. 156–159.

The woman obeyed, although she had but little faith in the cure. But lo ! when the child was dry its body became as white and smooth as a peeled radish. And when the mother beheld the wonderful and miraculous cure which had been worked on her leprous child, her gratitude knew no bounds.

"Henceforth," said Mary, "the water wherein the little one will be bathed shall cure many diseases, and whoever shall be suffering from an ugly disease shall be healed if he touches the body of a pure virgin and dries himself with her hair."

Soon afterwards the robber returned home, and even before he had reached the door of his house, he shouted : "Ah, I can smell human flesh, and the flesh of a virgin is particularly pleasing to my palate." Thereupon he rushed into the chamber, but his wife hastened to meet him, holding in her arms their son who had been so miraculously restored to health. When the father beheld his child, he grew calm and humble, and welcomed the travellers in his house. On the following morning he accompanied the Holy Family a long distance, and showed them the right way.

When the little leper who had been so miraculously cured grew up, he also became a robber, and was later on nailed on the Cross by the side of Jesus, whom he recognized. Being convinced of the innocence of Jesus, and remembering how he had once been cured of leprosy by Mary, he repented of his wicked life and of his many sins, whereupon Jesus promised him Paradise.[1]

[1] See Dähnhardt, *Natursagen,* vol. ii. p. 28.

A Gipsy Tent

The wife of the cannibal robber was not the only charitable person whom the weary wanderers encountered on their journey. An old Provençal legend relates that one day on their arrival in Egypt they met a gipsy (Zingarella) who offered them hospitality. When she saw the fugitives, tired and weary, and without a place where to lay their heads, she bade them alight and offered them a resting-place.

" Come to my humble home," she said, " and I will give you a night's lodging, and straw and fodder for your ass." When the gipsy had brought the travellers to her hut she begged leave to tell them their fortunes. She first recounted to the Virgin Mary her past history, and then examined the palm of the child, crossed it, and, in gipsy manner, foretold his future. She praised the child's divine beauty, " but, alas ! " she added, " I see suffering in store for him." And to the great grief of Mary, the gipsy foretold the wonderful and terrible life of Christ and all that he was destined to endure upon earth.

The Journey's End

After a long journey the Holy Family finally rested in the village of Matarea, beyond the city of Hermopolis or Heliopolis. It is here that a fountain miraculously sprung up for the refreshment of Mary, and is still called by the Arabs " The Fountain of Mary."

" The Egyptian sycomore," writes De Gubernatis,[1] " is honoured on account of the protection it offered to the Madonna and the child when they reached Egypt. About a few miles from Cairo lies Matarea, and there is a house where the Madonna lived for several years. There is also a source wherein, according to legend, she washed the linen of the child—and in the neighbourhood they show a garden where once the balsam shrub could be seen." The legend runs as follows :

When they reached the district near Matarea they rested under a palm tree round which there was much grass, enough for the ox and the ass to browse over. Now Mary, being exhausted and thirsty on account of the great heat, took the child into her lap, and he stuck his finger into the ground. And lo ! a fountain at once gushed forth.[2]

Thereupon Mary washed the child's linen in the fountain. And when the sweat emanating from the linen mixed and mingled with the water, such a blessing was vouchsafed unto the source that the whole district henceforth produced the best renowned balsam in the world.

In another source we read that the inhabitants of the district had planted many balsam shrubs which, however, had never borne any fruit. One day, therefore, the people conceived the idea of watering the plants with the water from the source wherein Mary had once washed the linen of the Holy Infant. They conducted the water from the source over the

---

[1] *Mythologie des Plantes*, vol. ii. p. 356.

[2] The spring is said to continue until the present day ; see Borchardus, *Descriptio terræ sanctæ*, ii. 4.

entire plantation, and thus it came about that the
district watered by that source produced the best
balsam in the world.[1] The balsam was greatly
renowned not only for its excellency but also for the
many other wonderful qualities it possessed.

This legend is also referred to by Kazwini. In
the neighbourhood of Elma Tarijja, a village in
Egypt, is situated the place where the balsam shrub
grows. The plant is watered by a well which possessed
a peculiar virtue. It is said that the Messiah once
washed himself in this well. The water is sweet
and contains a fine oily substance. There is no other
place in the world where the balsam shrub grows,
and even here the oil cometh forth only when the
plant is watered with the water from this particular
well.[2]

Other legends attribute the origin of all hot
springs to the fact that the Madonna had once bathed
the Holy Child in them. Mary, on her flight to
Egypt, having no bath-tub, bathed the child wherever
she could. She blessed all the springs she had used,
and hence there are hot springs in the world.[3]

In the vicinity of the town of Emmaus, runs one
version of this legend, near the so-called tower of
the forty martyrs, there are several hot springs.
Popular belief attributes their origin to the fact that
in one of the springs the child Jesus had once bathed
his feet. The springs were stopped by the Emperor
Julianus Apostata.[4]

[1] See Xaverius, *Hist. Ch.*, p. 202 ; Jansenius, ch. xi.
[2] Kazwini, *Cosmographie*, p. 412.
[3] See Shishmanoff, *Légendes Bulgares*, No. 48.
[4] See Sepp, *l.c.* vol. v. p. 21.

Chapter VI

The Early Childhood of Christs

*" The child grew, and waxed strong, filled with
wisdom : and the grace of God was upon
him."*—LUKE ii. 40.

THE SYNOPTIC GOSPELS tell us little, if anything, of
the childhood of Jesus till he was twelve years old.
They record no facts and give a very bare outline
of the boy Christ. He grew up as other children
grow up, although he was " stainless, sinless, and
advanced in wisdom." He grew up " as the flowers
of roses in the spring of the year, and as lilies by the
water."

Legend, however, not satisfied with the scanty
statement in the Gospels, has woven a web of gold
and azure round his childhood and invented wonderful tales and pretty anecdotes respecting his boy-
hood. It shows Jesus as a child in whom childish
innocence is subtly blended with something deeper
and more divine. He plays with other children of
his age, but he is a child with a grave look, endowed
with supernatural powers. All the early legends and
later folk-tales originated in the desire of the people
to reinforce the existing stock of Christian beliefs.
Like the Jewish *Agadoth* and *Midrashim*, they were
invented and collected for the purpose of both instruction and amusement. Some of them are sublime

and pleasant ; others are crude and grotesque ; it all depends in what *milieu* they originated. A good many of the earlier ones introduce new doctrines, like Gnosticism, but the majority of these legends and folk-tales appear to have been created to extol the virtues of justice, charity, pity, mercy, and forgiveness.

Several of these legends of the early childhood of Jesus were apparently known to the mediæval artists. I will only mention one which adorns many of the thirteenth-century canvases. It is found in the *Arabic Gospel of the Infancy.* According to this narrative, the children playing with the boy Christ crowned him with flowers and waited on him as on a king. Moreover, they made the passers-by come and adore him. The legend runs as follows :

Now in the month of Adar, Jesus assembled the boys as if he were their king ; they spread their garments on the ground and he sat upon them. Then they put on his head a crown wreathed of flowers, and, like attendants waiting on a king, they stood in order on his right hand and on his left. And whoever passed that way, the boys took him by force, saying : " Come hither and adore the king, and then proceed on your way." [1]

The Boy who was nearly Blind

When the Holy Family returned to Bethlehem they saw there a number of infants suffering from sore afflictions of the eyes. One woman whose sick son was already nigh unto death, brought the boy

[1] *The Arabic Gospel of the Infancy,* ch. xli.

to the Virgin Mary while the latter was washing Jesus Christ. Then said the woman : " Lady Mary, regard this my son, who is suffering grievous pain."

When Lady Mary heard her she said : " Take a little of this water with which I have washed my son, and sprinkle it over the boy."

The woman took a little of the water, as Lady Mary told her, and poured it on her own son. And lo ! immediately the boy's pain ceased, and when he had slept a little he awoke quite sound and well. And the mother of the sick boy brought him to Mary, but the Virgin said unto the happy mother : " Give thanks to God, for it is He who hath healed thy son."

Now there was another woman, a neighbour of her whose son had thus been healed thanks to the virtue of the water wherein Christ had been washed, whose son, afflicted with the same disease, was nearly blind. " Why dost thou lament night and day ? " said the first woman. " Why not carry thy son to Lady Mary, who healed my son when he was nigh unto death ? "

And when the woman heard this she, too, went to Mary and received some of the water wherein the Holy Infant had been bathed. She washed her sick son with it and he, too, was healed. Then Mary told her to give thanks to God, and commanded her not to tell the matter to any one.[1]

The Boys who had a Fever

In the same city there were two other women, the wives of one man, each of whom had a son ill with fever. One of these women was called Mary,

[1] *The Arabic Gospel of the Infancy*, chs. xxvii.–xxviii.

and the name of her son was Cleopas. One day this woman arose and, taking with her a beautiful cloak, went to Mary, the mother of the Holy Infant.

"Lady Mary," she said, "take this beautiful cloak as my offering, and give me for it one of the swaddling-bands of thy son." Mary granted her request, and the woman who had shown such faith in the Holy Infant went away and made a shirt of the swaddling-band for her own son. When the child was dressed in the new shirt his disease ceased and he was healed.

In the meantime, the son of the other wife, her rival, died, and the grieved mother was jealous of Cleopas and hated his mother. Now these two were in the habit of managing the affairs of the household on alternate weeks, and on one occasion the turn of Mary, the mother of Cleopas, came on. She heated the oven to bake bread for the household, and going away to fetch the dough she had kneaded, she left her son Cleopas near the oven. Her rival, the woman whose son had died, seeing the boy alone, seized him and thrust him into the oven, where a huge fire was burning. When Mary returned she was horrified and amazed to see her boy in the midst of the oven lying there and laughing as if it had been a garden of roses.[1]

The happy mother took her boy out of the oven, carried him to the Virgin Mary, and told the latter all that occurred. "Keep silence," said the Madonna, " and do not divulge this miracle vouchsafed unto thy son." The wicked woman, however, who so

[1] Cf. the legend of Abraham, Jellineck, *l.c.* vol. i. pp. 29–34.

hated Cleopas and his mother, tried to destroy the boy on another occasion.

One day she went to the well to draw water, and seeing Cleopas sitting near the well and playing, she seized him and thrust him into the well. But once more, thanks to the miraculous virtue of the shirt he wore, he was saved. When men came to fetch water from the well, they saw the boy sitting on the surface of the water, and they brought him out. Once more the happy mother, whose son had been saved for the third time, took the child to Lady Mary and told her all that had happened. "It is impossible," cried the mother, "that she should not one day succeed in her efforts and destroy my boy."

"No," said the Virgin Mother, "God will not only protect thy son, but also avenge thee upon thine enemy. Is it not written : 'They dug a well deep, but they fall into the pit which they had prepared ?'"[1]

And indeed, as Mary had prophesied, so it soon happened. One day the wicked woman who had attempted to destroy an innocent child again went to draw water at the well, but her feet became entangled in the rope and she fell into the well and was drowned.[2]

The Boy who was Dead

There was also another woman in the city whose two sons fell sick, one of whom died, while the other still lived. So the grieved mother took up the boy

---

[1] Ps. vii. 15, vii. 7 ; Prov. xxvi. 27 ; Eccles. x. 8.
[2] *The Arabic Gospel of the Infancy*, ch. xxix.

who was still alive and, weeping bitterly, brought him to Mary.

"Lady Mary," she wailed, "help and succour me. See, I had two sons, one of whom I have now buried, and the other is on the point of death. I am begging and praying to God to help me and leave me my second son." And the woman began to pray to God, and said : "O Lord, thou art kind and merciful and good ; thou gavest me two sons, but one of them thou hast since taken away ; leave me at least this one."

Seeing the grief of the poor mother and the violence of her weeping, Mary, the mother of Christ, pitied her and said : "Put thy child in my son's bed, and cover him with my son's clothes." And the woman obeyed, and put her son, who was already dead and had closed his eyes, in the bed in which Christ was lying. As soon as the smell of the garments of Jesus Christ reached the boy, he opened his eyes, and called with a loud voice, asking for bread.

And the happy mother praised God, and said unto Mary : "Now I know that the power of God dwelleth in thee, for they who partake of the same nature as other men healeth them after they have touched his garment." [1]

A GIRL AND THE DRAGON

Now there was a girl in a city not far from Bethlehem who was afflicted by Satan. He appeared to her from time to time in the shape of a huge dragon preparing to swallow her. So that

[1] *The Arabic Gospel of the Infancy*, ch. xxx.

whenever it approached her, she screamed aloud and said : " Alas, alas, that no one should deliver me from this wicked dragon." Her father and mother and all the members of her family stood around her in great confusion, but they could only weep and lament with her while she wept and begged them to save her from the monster. They were, alas ! helpless to do anything.

One day the daughter of a prince, who had herself been healed of leprosy, heard of the distress of the suffering girl, and sent for her mother. " If thou wilt keep my secret," said the princess, " I will help thee to make thy daughter quite well again." And when the weeping mother had promised to keep the secret, the princess continued : " Know thou that I was a leper and I was healed by Lady Mary, the mother of Christ. I therefore advise thee to take thy unhappy daughter to Bethlehem and seek out Lady Mary, and I am sure that thou wilt return hither with thy daughter rejoicing in good health."

And when the woman heard this she went home, took her daughter with her, and proceeded to Bethlehem, where she visited the mother of Christ. To her Mary gave a little of the water in which she had washed the child Jesus, and also a strip of the clothes of Christ. " Take this strip of cloth," said Mary to the girl, " and show it to thy enemy as often as thou seest him." The two women now departed and returned to their home.

As the time drew near when Satan in the guise of a dragon was wont to assail the girl, her mother said unto her : " Fear not, my child, but show him

8

the strip of cloth which Lady Mary gave thee."
When therefore Satan appeared, the girl, shuddering
for fear of him, took the strip of cloth and put it on
her head so that it covered her eyes, and lo ! flames
and flashes of fire blazed forth. Immediately the
dragon, who was Satan in disguise, saw the strip of
cloth and the flames and flashes of fire darting at
his head, he was greatly frightened, and cried out in
a loud voice : "What have I to do with thee, O
Jesus, son of Mary ! Whither shall I flee from thee !"
And turning his back with great dread, he departed
from the girl and never after appeared to her.[1]

The Boyhood of Judas

Many legends are connected with the disciple
who betrayed Christ even in his childhood. Judas
is represented as wicked and cruel. But Christ, who
forgave Judas his last crime, is shown in these
legends as forgiving him also the cruelties he prac-
tised when they played together as children. Nay
more, for by virtue of the magic or divine power
which emanated from the child Jesus, Judas is said
to have been healed of a terrible disease just at the
very moment when he bit the Saviour.

The following legend is told in the *Arabic Gospel
of the Infancy* (chapter xxxv.) :

In the same place there was also a woman whose
son was often vexed by Satan. The boy, Judas by
name, whenever Satan seized him bit all those who
approached him. And if he could find no one near
him he would bite his own hands in his frenzy. Now

[1] *The Arabic Gospel of the Infancy*, chs. xxxiii. xxxiv.

when the mother of Judas heard how many people had been healed thanks to the divine powers emanating from the person of the child Jesus, she arose and took her son Judas to Mary. In the meantime James and Joses had taken the child Jesus, and gone to play with other children. When Judas came nigh to the playing children, Satan had just assaulted him and his demoniac fit was on him. He sat down by the side of Jesus and in his fit of frenzy tried to bite him, but could not.

Then Judas struck the right side of Jesus and made him cry. But this contact with the child Jesus was sufficient to frighten away Satan, who forthwith went out of the boy in the shape of a mad dog. This boy, adds the author of the Apocryphal Gospel, was Judas Iscariot, who afterwards betrayed the Lord Jesus, and that side of Jesus on which Judas had smote him was afterwards pierced with a spear by the Roman soldier Longinus.

To a certain extent this legend, which shows Judas as a demoniac in his youth and possessed by Satan, may have been inspired by a passage in Luke xxii. 3, and John xiii. 27, where it is said that Satan had driven Judas to commit his crime.

" Then entered Satan into Judas, surnamed Iscariot, being of the number of the twelve."

" And after the sop Satan entered into him. Then said Jesus unto him, That thou doest, do quickly."

THE GARLAND OF FLOWERS

When Jesus was three years old his mother, the Virgin Mary, wished to give him a flower-wreath as a birthday present. But at Christmas-time in her native Galilee no natural flowers could be found which might have served to make a garland for her son. As for artificial flowers, they did not exist in the small village of Nazareth. The loving mother therefore decided to make a few artificial flowers for the intended garland.

Silently and carefully Mary started her work, embroidering and plaiting all sorts of flowers, big and small, as her artistic sense taught her. One flower, above all, excelled all the others in beauty and magnificence. Mary had taken for this flower a piece of yellow golden silk which had once belonged to her ancestor David, and which she encircled with thick white silken threads. While stitching on one of these threads she pricked her finger with her needle, and drops of blood fell on the dazzlingly white silk, so that in a few places the thread had a red gleam.

When the Holy Infant beheld this flower he grew melancholy, and chose it as his favourite flower. As long as the winter lasted the Holy Infant carefully treasured the flower, but when spring came he planted it in the valley of Nazareth. In holy joy he took the golden goblet which the wise men of the East had presented to him, and hastening to a spring near by, drew some water. After watering the flower and breathing on it with his divine breath, it became alive and grew up in quiet and modest magnificence, spreading over all parts of the globe, and filling the meadows and fields.

Henceforth the flower grows and flourishes from

the first day of spring to the last day of the cold and stormy autumn. Young and old take pleasure in it, and call it the flower of the Madonna, or the daisy.[1]

A Game of Ball

A curious legend which finds parallels in Jewish and Indian folk-lore refers to the pre-existence of Christ, and on this ground explains the creation of the sun, the moon, and the stars. The Holy Child is believed to have existed long before the creation of the universe.

One day when the Holy Infant was following about the Creator of the Universe, the latter said, " Go away and play, as it behoves a child." Thereupon Christ went out to play. He fashioned balls out of clay and put them on bricks to dry. And when the balls were dry he threw them into the air as high as he could.

The Creator of the Universe looked on and was amused, but he blessed the balls, and lo ! one of the balls suddenly stood still in mid-air and became the sun. Another ball again stood still in mid-air and became the moon, while the smaller balls which the Holy Infant had thrown into the air became stars. And when Jesus saw that all the balls which he had thrown into space had remained in mid-air and he had none to play with, he caught a handful of dust and threw it into the air trying to hit the stars and make them fall down. But the Creator of the Universe blessed also the handful of dust which the

[1] See Söhns, *Unsere Pflanzen*, p. 35 ; Warnke, *Die Pflanzen in Sage und Geschichte*, p. 153.

Holy Infant had thrown up, and it was changed into tiny stars. This is the Milky Way.[1]

Another legend describing the creation of sun and moon runs as follows :

One day the Holy Infant reposing in the lap of Mary refused to go to sleep. So Mary took two apples and handed them to the child to play with. Jesus, in childish play, threw one apple into the air, and it became the sun ; he then threw up the second apple, and it became the moon.[2]

BIRDS FASHIONED FROM CLAY

It came to pass after the return of the Holy Family from Egypt, when Jesus was in Galilee and had entered on the fourth year of his age, that he played with other children on the banks of the Jordan. He sat down and made in the mud seven pools, to each of which he made little channels. Thereupon he collected the running waters into the pools and immediately it became pure. He then took some soft clay and fashioned out of it twelve sparrows. But a certain Jew, seeing what Jesus had done, went immediately and told Joseph about it.

"Behold !" he said, "thy child is at the water-course, and he hath taken clay and fashioned twelve birds, and hath profaned the Sabbath." And Joseph came to the place, and when he saw what the child had done, he cried unto him, saying : "Why art thou doing these things on the Sabbath?" Jesus, however, clapped his hands and cried unto the

---

[1] See Strauss, *Die Bulgaren*, p. 32 ; Shishmanoff, *Légendes*, No. 1.
[2] See De Gubernatis, *Mythologie des Plantes*, ii. 305.

sparrows : " Go away ; fly through all the world, and live." Immediately the sparrows made of clay flew up and departed.

When those who were there saw such signs, they were filled with great amazement. Some praised and admired the Holy Child, some blamed him. Others went away and told the Pharisees that Jesus, the son of Joseph, had done great signs and miracles in the sight of the people.

The *Arabic Gospel of the Infancy*, where the spirit of the miracles performed by Jesus during his early childhood is generally of a benevolent character, gives a different version of this legend :

Jesus was playing with other boys of the same age. They were playing with clay, out of which they had made figures of asses, oxen, birds, and other animals, and each of the boys, glorying in his skill, praised his own work. Then Jesus said : " The figures which I have made I will command to walk." Thereupon he commanded the figures of clay to walk, and straightway they began to jump about. And the figures of birds and sparrows flew when he bade them fly, and stood still when he bade them stand still, and ate and drank when he offered them food and drink.

This legend of the birds of clay which, at the command of Jesus, came to life and flew away, is obviously based on a passage in the Gospel of John : " For as the Father raiseth up the dead and *quickeneth* them, even so the Son quickeneth whom he will." [1] It seeks to show that even as a child and long before

[1] John v. 21.

his baptism Jesus possessed the creative power of God the Father, who had fashioned the beasts of the earth and the birds in the air. The legend also bears traces of Gnostic influences. As a child Jesus was above the Sabbath. The number of twelve may be an allusion to the twelve apostles.[1]

In the East the legend obtained wide currency and was generally believed at the time. This, in spite of the fact that no miracles performed by Jesus in his childhood are recorded in the Canonical Gospels. None, we read in the Gospel of John (ii. 11), were performed by him until after his baptism at the age of thirty. The legend of the birds must have been known to Mohammed, who incorporated it in the Koran !

" And when Thou dost create from clay as it were the figure of a bird by my permission, then Thou dost breathe into it, then it becometh a bird by my permission. . . . And when thou dost bring forth the dead by my permission. . . ." [2]

The legend has since been repeated by many Moslem authors, one of whom is quoted by M. d'Ohsson.[3] Speaking of Jesus, he writes :

" God gave him the power to work the greatest miracles. He cured the leprous, made the blind see, raised the dead, walked upon the surface of the waters, and even breathed the spirit of life into a bird which he had fashioned of clay." [4]

It is also referred to by a Moslem author writing

---

[1] Hennecke, *Handbuch der Neutestamentlichen Apokryphen*, p. 135.

[2] *Koran*, Sura v. 119 (110).

[3] *Tableau General de l'Empire Ottoman*, vol. i. p. 188.

[4] See also C. F. Gerock, *Die Christologie des Koran*, pp. 137–138.

in a corrupt Spanish dialect for the benefit of the Arabs who had remained in Spain. " He (Isa) possessed the power to work all sorts of miracles. He fashioned birds out of clay and made them fly by the breath of his mouth." [1]

Similar legends are related both of the Christian Saints and the Rabbis of the Talmud who possessed the power to create life. [2]

It seems to have been very popular during the Middle Ages, for it is related in Middle High German poetry, in the *Cursor Mundi*, in a Provençal Gospel of the Infancy, and in Old English literature. [3] Mediæval poetry and general folk-lore have adopted and adapted this legend according to time and *milieu*. Thus an Icelandic legend runs as follows :

THE GOLDEN PLOVERS

Once on a Sabbath day Christ was amusing himself in the company of Jewish children. They were fashioning birds out of clay. And while they were thus engaged, an old zealous Sadducee happened to come their way. He rebuked and chided the children for profaning the Sabbath and, to the great grief of the youngsters, he seized the birds of clay and broke them all. Now when Jesus saw this, he waved his hands over all the birds he himself had fashioned, and lo ! they forthwith became alive,

---

[1] See *Mahometism fully explained, written in Arabick by Mahomet Rabadan*, translated by Morgan, London, 1723–25, pp. 213–214 ; see also De Sacy, *Chrestomatie Arabe*, vol. i. p. 165 ; Gerock, *l.c.* p. 139.

[2] See Lucius, *Anfänge des Heiligen Kults*, 1904, p. 389 ; *Sanhedrin*, 67 b.

[3] See R. Morriss, *Early English Text Society*.

and, to the great astonishment of the bystanders, soared up into the heavens. The birds are the golden plovers which constantly sing the glory of the Lord who had saved them from the merciless hand of the Sadducee. The note of the plovers, *deerin*, sounds like the Icelandic word *dyr-dhin*, which means glory.[1]

A Spanish folk-tale gives a different version :

The Origin of the Swallows

Once on a Sabbath day the Holy Child was playing with other children in the fields. To amuse themselves they gathered white clay, fashioned birds with outspread wings, and placed them in the sun to dry. Now a zealous Pharisee chanced to come along, and when he saw what they were doing, he chided the children for breaking the Sabbath. He was on the point of stamping his foot upon the birds and of breaking them in pieces, but Jesus clapped his hands, and lo ! the birds of clay became alive and soared up to heaven. They became swallows. Thereupon the birds built their nests of the clay out of which they had been fashioned under the roof of the house in which Jesus lived with his parents. And ever since the swallows are in the habit of building their nests under the roofs of the abodes of poor and humble people, and thus bring luck to the inmates.[2]

---

[1] See Arnason, *Icelandic Legends* ; K. Maurer, in *Zeitschrift des Vereins für Volkskunde*, i. 42.

[2] Caballero, *Cuentos*, Madrid, 1877, p. 227 ; see also Dähnhardt, *Natursagen*, vol. ii. p. 75.

The Origin of the Owl

Another form of the legend of the birds made of clay is found in Polish folk-lore, and a Polish folk-tale runs as follows :

When Jesus was still a child his Jewish playmates were curious to know him better, for they had heard that he was destined to rule the world. Once they mocked him and said : " If thou art capable of creating birds, make one for us too." Jesus took no heed of this taunt, and said not a word, but when the boys repeated their challenge he replied that he indeed possessed the power to create a bird.

Thereupon the boys sat down on the ground and fashioned a bird out of clay, with a head resembling that of a cat. When Jesus saw the clumsy bird fashioned by his playmates, he made a nightingale and sent it among the roses. When the boys again insisted on his fashioning another bird, he made a titmouse, and commanded it to sing in the bush. Thereupon the boys asked Jesus to improve the bird they had fashioned with a head resembling that of a cat, so he commanded the bird to fly up to the branch of a tree, and there to screech in the voice of a cat. And thus the bird fashioned by the Jewish boys became an owl.[1]

The Origin of the Bat

Popular tradition elsewhere connects this legend with the creation of the bat instead of that of the nightingale and the owl. The people refused at first

[1] Dähnhardt, *l.c.* p. 76.

to believe in Jesus. " If thou canst perform a miracle," they said, " we shall believe in thee."

" And what miracle do you expect me to perform ? " asked Jesus.

" Make a bird which looks like leather, has no feathers, bears offspring like the quadrupeds, and nurses its young like the mammals."

Thereupon Jesus moistened the tip of his thumb with spittle and closed his fist on it. After a while he opened his hand, and lo ! oh, wonder ! in the hand of Jesus there sat a bat nursing its young. And the people believed in Jesus.[1]

The legend dealing with the creation of the birds fashioned of clay is also related in the following version :

While Jesus was dwelling in Upper Galilee, Queen Helena, who was ruling over the whole of Israel, sent out horsemen to apprehend him. But the men of Upper Galilee would not permit them to take Jesus, and induced him to give those who sought him proofs of his wonderful and supernatural powers. The Galileans forthwith fashioned birds out of clay ; Jesus spoke the Ineffable Name, and the birds became alive and flew away.[2]

Many legends, like the above, which are connected with the early childhood of Jesus, are of Gnostic or of Indian origin. They found their way into popular tradition, and are repeated in various versions in the folk-lore of many nations. The Gnostics were anxious to prove that Jesus had never belonged to the earthly world, and that as a child he

---

[1] *La Tradition*, vol. x. p. 72.

[2] Dähnhardt, *l.c.*, quoted from S. Krauss, *Das Leben Jesu*.

was above human development and conditions. He therefore had no respect for the traditional religion of the Jews, and ignored its precepts. Often, therefore, these legends are in contradiction to the real character of Christ. Popular fantasy imagined Jesus as a Wonder-Child playing among other children, and depicted him as such. It was a simple matter, therefore, to take the Oriental legends which clustered round the childhood of Buddha and freely transfer and adapt them to Christ.[1]

THE HOLY CHILD AND THE SUNBEAMS

A rather amusing legend is found in the Provençal *Gospel of the Infancy.* One day Jesus was playing with other Jewish children. They entered a house and saw the sunrays penetrating through the open window. Thereupon Jesus sat astride upon a sunbeam and thus soared up to the sun. The children, greatly amused, were eager to imitate the feat of their playmate. They, too, caught hold of a sunray and tried to ascend to the sun, but, alas, they fell down and broke their arms and legs or even their necks. Great was the grief of the parents when they saw their children either mutilated or dead. Wailing and lamenting, they hurried to Joseph and vehemently accused Jesus of being the cause of the disaster. Joseph hastened to the spot and called Jesus back. The Holy Child glided down along a sunray on to the earth, healed the wounded, and brought the dead back to life.[2]

The *motif* of this legend is found in a tale which

[1] See Hennecke, *l.c.* p. 64.   [2] See Bartsch, *Denkmäler*, pp. 279–281.

was very current in the Middle Ages. It is that of
the thief who once tried to break into a house from
the roof, holding fast to a moonbeam, and naturally
broke his neck. The story is found in the *Gesta
Romanorum* (ed. Graesse, Nr. 136).

THE MOONRAY

The fable of the housebreaker who wanted to
descend upon a moonray, as published by Le Grand
and reproduced in the *Gesta Romanorum*, runs as
follows :

A robber had once formed the design of breaking
into the house of a rich inhabitant of the town, in
which he was in the habit of committing many
depredations. One night he climbed up to the roof,
and there waited until the whole family and the
servants had gone to sleep so that he might have an
opportunity to slip into the house. The master,
however, who had gone to bed but was still awake,
perceived the adventurer by the light of the moon.
He was a sharp, cunning fellow, and resolved to play
a trick upon the thief.

Speaking low to his wife, he said unto her :
" Ask me by what method I have succeeded in
acquiring my property. I will make some difficulty
in answering you, but you press me on the subject,
insist upon knowing, and do not give me any rest
until I have disclosed to you my secret ; but, above
all, remember to speak out as loud as you can."

The obedient wife, without inquiring into her
husband's motives, asked the question, as he had
required her to do.

" It is a secret," said the husband in a mysterious manner, "one that I mean to conceal for ever in my own breast. It is really no affair of yours how I had amassed my wealth ; is it not enough for you to be allowed to enjoy in quiet the affluence which I give you ? "

The wife, however, pressed her husband so often on the subject that seeming at length to yield to her importunities, he confessed to her that he had been a thief and had made a large fortune by this profession.

" What, sir," asked his wife, " have you been a thief all your life and never been suspected of any dishonesty ? "

" Yes," replied the husband, " the reason is that I had one of the most ingenious tutors in the business of burgling, such a tutor as will not find his match anywhere. He was in the habit of robbing only in the night, and was sure of robbing without any risk or danger to himself. You see, he possessed the secret of using certain cabbalistical words which rendered him immune. Thus, if he wanted to break into a house he only had to pronounce the mysterious word seven times before the moon, and instantly a ray shot from that luminary and carried him up to the roof of the house, for he always entered by the roof. And when he was ready to descend, he once more spoke the magic word, and, clasping the ray, gently came down again. I inherited the secret from him, and I had no occasion to make use of it for any length of time."

" This is quite wonderful," said the wife, " and if I had a friend or a relation in embarrassed circumstances, I should be extremely anxious to let them know the secret."

Thereupon the wife entreated her husband to admit her into the secret and tell her the magic word. For a long time the husband objected, begged her to desist and let him sleep. The woman, however, was obstinate, and after much solicitation the husband informed her that his secret consisted in repeating seven times the word *seil*.[1] Then wishing his wife a good-night he began to snore as if he had fallen into a profound sleep.

Now the thief had not lost a word of all this conversation, and could not resist the temptation to try the virtue of the charm. He repeated the magic word seven times, and throwing out his arms and imagining that he was clasping the ray of the moon, he sprang from the roof. He fell, of course, straight to the earth and broke his thigh. At the noise of his descent, the master of the house, pretending to awake from his sleep, cried out aloud :

" Who is there ? "

" It is a man," said the poor thief, " to whom the charm has not been so serviceable as to you." He was seized and the next day delivered to the judges, who condemned him to the gallows.[2]

---

[1] In the *Gesta Romanorum* the word is *Fallax* = Deceiver.

[2] See Le Grand, *Fabliaux*, vol. iii. p. 253. The story is also found in the *Disciplina Clericalis* of Petrus Alphonsus (ed. Schmidt, p. 156), and in an old French Fabliau (Barbizan, *Fabl.*, vol. ii. p. 148), and in a mediæval Latin story (Th. Wright, *Latin Stories from MSS. of the Thirteenth and Fourteenth Centuries*, No. 23). In the last-named version the passage runs as follows : " Perceptis denique talibus fur inde gavisus, dicto septies carmine sumpto manu radia lunæ, laxatis manibus et pedibus per fenestram in domum cecidit, et fracto cure et brachio congemuit " (Wright, *l.c.* p. 25). The source of this fable is in my opinion the *Kelilah ve-Dimnah*.

The Pitcher hung on a Sunbeam

Another legend of Jesus and of a sun-ray is found in a mediæval English text. One day Jesus was sent by his mother to draw water from a well in Nazareth. Evidently to amuse himself, he hung his pitcher on a sun-ray. His playmates tried to imitate him, but their pitchers naturally fell down and were broken. Seeing their distress, Jesus immediately made the broken pitchers whole.[1]

This legend is not found in any of the Apocryphal Gospels, but is given in Schade's *Narrationes* (Section xliii).

An imitation of this legend is found in the Old English Poem of *Tom Thumble, His Life and Death* :

> " Of whom to be reveng'd he tooke
>   (In mirth and pleasant game)
> Black pots and glasses, which he hung
>   Upon a bright sonne-beame.
>
> The other boyes to dow the life,
>   In pieces broke them quite ;
> For which they were most soundly whipt,
>   Whereat he laught outright." [2]

The Aster

The aster is a plant with flowers somewhat like stars, and the origin of this plant is told in a legend connected with the early childhood of Jesus.

When Jesus was growing up in the village of

---

[1] See Horstman, *Altenglische Legenden*, 1875, v. 639.

[2] See W. Carew Hazlitt, *Remains of the Early Popular Poetry of England*, 1866, vol. ii. p. 180.

9

Nazareth among other children of his age, the Lord sent an angel to play with the Holy Infant and to tell him about the Heavenly Father. Sometimes the Lord sent little John to play with Jesus and to point him out as the Messiah. John thus frequently visited the house of Jesus' parents and played with the Saviour. In their familiar childish ways, Jesus told John all that he had heard from the angel, and that this messenger from heaven always carried a number of dazzling flowers which at night could be seen shining in the sky and which men called stars.

One day Jesus gave John a bright and shining seed as a present. John rushed into his little garden where he planted the grain of seed and then in joyful glee he told his other playmates that he had planted a star in his garden. When autumn approached, lo ! wonderfully beautiful plants sprouted at the spot, carrying flowers resembling stars. The children, shouting with joy, called the flowers asters, star-shaped flowers, and by this name they are known till this day.[1]

THE MAN IN THE MOON

Many legends are told of the man in the moon. Thus a legend based on a passage in the Old Testament (Num. xv. 32–36) relates that the man in the moon is leaning on a fork on which he is carrying a bundle of sticks picked up on a Sunday. " This man with lantern, dog, and bush of thorns representeth moonshine " (Prologue in *Midsummer Night's Dream*). In other legends it is Cain who is the man in the

---

[1] Warnke, *l.c.* p. 200.

moon. In the legends clustering round the early childhood of Christ the story of the man in the moon is related in the following version :

One evening the Virgin sent the Holy Infant with a basket full of apples which he was asked to carry to his foster-father Joseph. On his way the basket became too heavy for the infant. Just at that moment he met a man whom he asked to help him carry the basket for a while. But the man being hard-hearted, replied :

" I carry your basket ? Carry it yourself."

" Then help me carry it," said the infant, but this, too, the man refused.

Jesus was embarrassed, and begged the Jew to keep guard over the basket and wait until he had run to fetch his mother.

" I keep guard over your basket ? " mocked the hard-hearted man. " I would sooner sit in the moon."

And ever since the uncharitable man has been sitting in the moon.[1]

The legend and superstition concerning the man in the moon is widespread. Some say that it is a man with a bundle of sticks on his back who has been exiled thither for many centuries and is beyond the reach of death.[2]

Dante in his *Inferno* calls him Cain, and Shakespeare [3] speaks of him as carrying a thorn load and being accompanied by a dog. He has in turn been accused of stealing or gathering sticks on the Sabbath,

---

[1] *Am Urquell*, iv. 68.
[2] See Baring-Gould, *Curious Myths of the Middle Ages*, p. 171.
[3] *Midsummer Night's Dream*, v. 1 ; *Tempest*, ii. 2.

and therefore condemned to reside for ever in the moon.

Douce, in his *Illustrations to Shakespeare*, narrates the following legend current in Ceylon :

Buddha, when he was a hermit on earth, once lost himself in a forest. While wandering about in great distress, he met a hare who thus addressed him :

" It is in my power to extricate thee from thy difficulty ; take the path to thy left and it will lead thee out of this forest."

" I am greatly obliged to thee," said Buddha, " but I am very poor and also very hungry, and I have nothing to offer thee as a reward for thy kindness."

" If thou art hungry," replied the kind hare, " then I am again at thy service. Make a fire, kill me, roast me, and eat me."

Buddha made a fire, and the hare jumped into it, and there it has remained ever since. And that is the reason why the natives of Ceylon have placed a hare instead of a man in the moon.[1]

In a classic tale the man in the moon is Endymion, while in Jewish legendary lore he is Joshua, the son of Nun. The nursery rhyme of the man in the moon who is supposed to have taken a fancy to pease-porridge and tried to devour it in such a great hurry that he scalded his mouth, is quoted by Halliwell (*Popular Rhymes*) :

> " The man in the moon
> Came tumbling down
> And asked his way to Norwich."

[1] See Douce's *Illustrations to Shakespeare*, p. 10.

There are numerous other superstitions connected with the moon.[1]

THE DEAD CHILD

It is quite natural that the mediæval Christian legends should ascribe to the child Christ the power of raising the dead. Had not Elijah and Elisha both worked such wonders? In Jewish legendary lore, by the way, we are informed that the key to resurrection is in the possession of God alone and that it had been taken away from Elijah. In the Messianic time this key would, however, be given to the just.[2]

More than one legend narrates how Jesus called the dead back to life out of pity and compassion. It was pity, love of humanity that induced him to make use of this divine power. Deeply moved by the poignant grief of a wailing mother, he called back to life a dead child. Another time it was a poor workman who had met with a fatal accident in his work. Pity again with the suffering family deprived of their bread-earner moved Jesus, as the legend tries to convey, to work miracles.

One day the child Jesus was walking in the neighbourhood where his parents dwelt, and he heard loud wailing and lamentations. When he inquired after the cause of the trouble he was informed that it was a poor mother weeping over her dead child. In haste Jesus hurried to the house where the dead child lay, and touching it on the breast, he said :

---

[1] See T. F. Thiselton Dyer in *Gentleman's Magazine*, July 1880.

[2] See *Sanhedrin*, 113a, and *Pesachim*, 68a.

" I say unto thee thou shalt not die, but live, and be with thy mother."

And lo ! the dead boy opened his eyes, looked up, and smiled. Thereupon Jesus said to the woman, the mother of the child : " Take thy child and give him some milk, and remember me."

And Jesus left the house and went to play with the other children.[1]

On another occasion Jesus was walking in a street where a new house was being built, when suddenly there was a great clamour and people were shouting, women lamenting, and children crying. Jesus, too, went nearer and beheld a man lying dead. He took him by the hand and said unto him : " Arise, and do thy work." And the man straightway arose.

THE DEAD PLAYMATE

One day Jesus was playing with other children on the top of a certain house. Now it happened that one of the children pushed another off the roof on to the ground, and he died. And although the parents of the deceased had not seen it, they cried out against Joseph and Mary, saying, " Your son hath thrust our son to the ground and he is dead." Jesus himself was silent and said nothing. And Joseph and Mary came in haste to Jesus and asked him, saying : " Tell us if thou didst thrust the boy to the ground."

Thereupon Jesus immediately came down from the roof to the ground, and called the boy by his

[1] *The Gospel of Thomas*, ch. xvii.

name, which was Zeno. And Jesus said : " Tell us, Zeno, did I thrust thee down from the roof to the ground ? Tell them the truth."

And the boy came to life again and answered : "No, thou didst not throw me down from the roof to the ground."

And the parents of the child who had been dead marvelled greatly and honoured Jesus for the miracle he had done.[1]

In the *Arabic Gospel of the Infancy* this legend is related in a different version :

When the unhappy child fell off the roof all the other boys who had been playing there fled at once, but Jesus alone remained. Thereupon the kindred of the dead boy came and accused Jesus, who had remained behind. " Thou hast pushed our son headlong from the housetop, and thou art his murderer." Jesus denied the accusation, but they would not believe him.

" Well, then," said Jesus, " let us ask the dead himself to tell us the truth, and let him bring the truth to light." He came down from the roof and, standing over the dead boy, he called in a loud voice : " Zeno, Zeno, I ask thee to tell us who has cast thee down from the house-top ? "

And the boy who was dead at once came to life again and answered : " Thou didst not cast me down, but such a one pushed me off." [2]

This legend is also found in the *Provençal Infancy of Jesus*, where the name of the dead boy is given as

---

[1] *Pseudo-Matthew*, ch. xxxii. ; *Gospel of Thomas*, ch. ix.
[2] *The Arabic Gospel of the Infancy*, ch. xliv.

Abramon, while his playmate who pushed him off (*un garso mal astrug*) was called Ferrier.[1]

This legend was evidently known to Moslem writers, and is told in a somewhat modified version :

One day, when Jesus was playing with his youthful companions, one of his playmates jumped on the back of another boy and rode him like a horse. He struck him with his foot and killed him. When the parents of the dead boy heard what had occurred, they dragged the boys and also Jesus before the judge. Mary also came, because she was anxious on account of Jesus. When the judge asked the boys who had killed their comrade, they all replied, " Jesus."

Thereupon the judge, turning to Jesus, asked him severely : " Why didst thou kill thy comrade ? "

But Jesus mildly replied : " O judge, thou shouldst have first asked me whether or not I have killed my playmate, and not why and wherefore." Thereupon he went up to the dead boy and said : " Rise up with the permission of God."

And the boy arose, and after pointing out his murderer he fell down dead.[2]

Dead men raised to life in order to indicate their respective murderers is a *motif* quite frequent in folktale and legend, and is related of numerous saints both Christian and Jewish.

Once upon a time, a Sicilian legend relates, two men had spent the night in an inn, where one murdered the other and hid his body under the straw, where it was found by other travellers. The inn-

---

[1] Bartsch, *Denkmäler der provenzalischen Literatur*, Stuttgart, 1856, pp. 270–305, 287–291.   [2] Hofmann, *l.c.* p. 227.

keeper was naturally accused of the crime, but unable to prove his innocence, he was condemned to death.

When the accused was already on the scaffold a beautiful youth suddenly came riding in hot haste, crying " Pardon ! " The youth thereupon led the people into the church before the coffin of the murdered man and cried aloud : " Rise, thou dead one, speak with the living and tell us who murdered you." Thereupon the dead man replied : " The innkeeper is innocent. It was my companion who killed me."

The youth thereupon accompanied the innkeeper home, revealed himself as St. Oniria, blessed him and his family, and disappeared.[1]

Similar legends, wherein people who had been assassinated are called to life for a short time in order to designate their murderers, are related not only of Christian but also of Jewish Saints.[2] The resuscitated, after indicating the name of their respective murderers, died again.

A Jewish mediæval legend relates that in Spain the Jews, having been accused of the murder of a boy, the famous Cabbalist, Don Salomo Halevi, placed a slip of paper with the Ineffable Name written on it under the tongue of the dead boy and thus brought him to life. The boy rose up and pointed out his murderer.[3]

Jesus helps Joseph to make a Throne

Now Joseph, who was a carpenter by trade, was constantly being sent for by the people on account of

---

[1] Crane, Th. F., *Italian Popular Tales*, p. 210.
[2] See Lucius, *l.c.* p. 388.   [3] See *Liber Shevet Jehuda*, p. 94.

his craft. He was asked to make doors and boxes and couches. And wherever Joseph went he took Jesus with him. Joseph himself was not very skilful at his work, but whenever Jesus stretched out his hand towards the work it was done immediately as Joseph wished it.

Now on a certain day the king of Jerusalem sent for Joseph and said unto him : " I wish thee to make me a throne of the exact measure as the place on which I have been used to sit."

Joseph immediately put his hand to the work and remained in the palace for two years, but when he had completed the throne and removed it to its place, he found, to his great distress, that the throne was two spans shorter than it should have been. The king was very angry when he saw this, and Joseph was greatly afraid. But Jesus said to him : " Fear not, nor lose heart ; but take one side of the throne and I will take the other, and together we will set it right." [1]

And so each pulled on his side, and the throne was made right and brought to the exact measure as it was needed. The wood, however, was of that kind which was celebrated in the time of Solomon ; it had figures and engravings on it and was very fragile.

Zacchæus teaches Jesus the Alphabet

There was at Jerusalem a certain man named Zacchæus, who was a teacher of boys. And one day he said unto Joseph : " Thou hast an intelligent child, and he hath great understanding, why dost

[1] Hofmann, *l.c.* pp. 235-237.

thou not bring him to me to learn letters ? Come, give him to me, that he may learn letters, and with his letters I will teach him all science, and how to address the elders, and to honour them and also to love those of his own age."

And Joseph gave his consent, and reported this to Mary. And so they took Jesus to the master, and as soon as he saw him he wrote the alphabet for him and told him all the letters from Aleph to Beth with much distinctiveness and clearly. And he then bade Jesus to say Aleph, and when he had said Aleph he ordered him to say Beth.

But Jesus said to him : " Tell me first the meaning of the letter Aleph and then I will say Beth."

And when the master went to flog him, Jesus only looked at Zacchæus and said : " Thou that knoweth not Aleph naturally, how dost thou teach Beth to others ? Thou art a hypocrite ; if thou knowest the nature of Aleph, first teach Aleph, and then we shall believe thee concerning Beth."

Then he began to puzzle the master about the first letter, and he could not answer him. And Jesus then explained to him the meaning of the letters Aleph and Beth, also which forms of the letters were straight and which crooked, which drawn spirally, which marked with points and which without them, and also why one letter came before another. And he began to tell and explain many other things which the master himself had never heard, nor had he read in any book.

And in the hearing of many, Jesus said to the master : " Hear, Zacchæus, the arrangement of the first letter Aleph, and notice here how it hath lines and a middle stroke which thou seest crossing those that are common, connected with top projecting and again contracting. They are triform of the same kind, chief and subordinate, but equal in length."

And when the master Zacchæus heard the boy speak and explain the allegories of the first letter he marvelled greatly and said : " I think this boy was born before Noah," and turning to those around him, he said : " I am at a loss, and I have brought shame upon myself when I took charge of this child who is wiser than myself. I entreat thee, brother Joseph, take him away, for I cannot bear the severity of his gaze. I cannot explain the matter at all. This child is not at all of earthly parents, for he is able to subdue even fire. Perhaps he was begotten even before the world was made. I know not what womb bore him and what lap nursed him, but I do know that he surpasseth me in knowledge, and never will I attain to his understanding. I desired to have a new pupil, but I find that I have a tutor. I am an old man, but I have been defeated by a child. I suffer affliction, for I cannot look into his face. What can I say or what can I tell of the lines of the first letter, which he has told me of? I know neither its beginning nor its end. I beseech thee, brother Joseph, take him away to thy house. Thou hast brought to me a boy who is wiser than all teachers."

And to Mary, Zacchæus said : " There is no need of instruction for this thy son." [1]

[1] *The Gospel of Thomas*, chs. vi. vii. viii ; *The Arabic Gospel of The Infancy*, ch. xlviii.

The Canonical Gospels never hint at the education which Jesus had received, and make no mention of his schooldays. Legend therefore preferred to represent the child Jesus as visiting the school like his youthful companions, but used the occasion to show his superiority and his supernatural intelligence.

Chapter VII

The Wanderings of Christ on Earth

" Forget not to show love unto strangers ; for thereby some have entertained angels unawares."—HEB. xiii. 2.

POPULAR IMAGINATION HAS INVENTED many legends which tell how Christ, accompanied by his Apostles and sometimes only by Peter, visited farmhouses and cottages and asked for food and shelter. Such legends are common all the world over. They may be traced either to Biblical passages where angels in disguise visited mortal men and partook of their hospitality, or to the old pagan faith and heathen reminiscences when the gods were walking on the earth dispensing justice among men.

In Jewish legendary lore it is generally the prophet Elijah who visits men, punishing the wicked and avaricious, and rewarding the just, generous, and charitable. Among the Slavonic peoples there are many legends which greatly resemble this cluster. German legends which deal with this subject and describe the earthly wanderings of Christ and St. Peter remind us rather of the wanderings and visits of Balder and Loki, or of Philemon and Baucis. In all cases the visitors either reward the just and the generous, and honour the kindly host who has offered them hospitality, or mete out punishment to those

who for some reason or other deserve it.   One *motif* of
these divine visitations is frequent in folk-lore.   When
a man, who is usually arrogant and proud, attempts
to imitate the wonder-worker, he always fails.   The
divine person, the saint, or the supernatural being,
then saves the imitator who is about to undergo the
penalty of his failure and reads him a moral lesson.
It is found, for instance, in Grimm's *Bruder Lustig* and
Das jung-geglühte Männchen, in the episode of the Medea
cauldron, and the same *motif* can be traced in many
of the legends told of the Saviour and St. Peter.

It must be remembered that in the days of
heathenism the Teutons worshipped Thor or Donar
and Woden, while among the Slavs the place was
assigned to the thunder-god Perun, the Lithuanian
Perkunos.   The worship of these divinities having
come to an end with the introduction of Christianity, numerous ideas and beliefs of the old faith
were merged in the new ; the attributes of the old
pagan gods were transferred to the sacred characters
of the new religion.   Thus in Russian and Teutonic
legendary lore the beliefs formerly associated with
Perun or with Odin and Thor were transferred to
Christian saints or to the prophet Elijah, and sometimes even to Christ himself.

PETER AND THE ROBBERS

Once, when Christ was journeying with the
Apostles, they found themselves at night out in the
fields, and took shelter in a cabin belonging to some
shepherds.   The latter received their guests rather
inhospitably, refusing to give them anything to eat.

Soon after a band of robbers came along, attacked the flock, and robbed the shepherds, who ran away. When the robbers came to the cabin and learned from the wanderers how badly they had been treated by the shepherds, they prepared some supper for themselves and for Christ and his Apostles.

" Blessed be the robbers," said Peter, " for they treat the poor better than do the rich."

" Amen," said the Apostles, " blessed be the robbers."

HOSPITALITY REWARDED

A German legend relating how Jesus rewarded hospitality but punished avarice runs as follows :

One day Christ, accompanied by Peter, came to a town on the Bodensee, and looked for quarters where they could pass the night.

But the well-to-do people in the town all refused to give them shelter, a night's lodging, or a meal. At last Christ and Peter knocked at the door of a miserable hut, the abode of a labourer and his wife. The poor couple gladly offered hospitality to the two wayfarers, put before them whatever food they had in the house, and spread some straw on the floor for them to rest. When Christ and Peter had partaken of their frugal meal they made themselves known to their hospitable and kind-hearted hosts.

" As a reward for your kindness of heart and your generosity," said the Saviour, " you may express a wish which will be granted." The modest couple did not lose much time to consider the matter, but asked for a small garden round their cottage.

" Your request is granted," said Christ.

Early in the morning, even before their hosts were awake, the two wanderers rose up and started on their wanderings. When the labourer and his wife got up in the morning and opened the door of their cottage, their surprise and joy knew no bounds. For in front of them they beheld not only a vast and beautiful garden with all kinds of fruit-bearing trees, but also flower-decked meadows and fields covered with heavy golden ears of corn. Just at that moment one of the wealthy citizens of the town was passing the cottage, and in the exuberance of their joy the happy couple told him all that had happened and of the luck which had fallen to their lot.

Greatly annoyed, the wealthy miser hurried back and related the matter to his friends.

They all regretted having driven away from their doors such wonder-working travellers, and decided to send out a deputation in search of them. The deputation soon overtook Christ and Peter, humbly apologized for their conduct last night, and begged them to return to the town. Christ having declined their invitation, the deputation asked him to grant them at least one wish.

" Mention it," said Christ, whereupon they asked for the growth of the vine in their country. In spite of their avarice and lack of hospitality, Jesus granted their request. But when Peter expressed his surprise at this, the Lord said unto him :

" They will only have what they deserve, for their wine will be sour." [1]

[1] See Merkens, *Was sich das Volk erzählt*, p. 76.

10

THE POOR WIDOW

A Russian legend runs as follows :

Long ago Christ and his Apostles were wandering about the world, and one evening they came to a village where they asked a rich peasant for shelter, but the peasant refused. "Go to the widow," he said, "who lives in yonder cottage, she receives beggars." The wanderers went to the widow, who was very poor and only had a crust of bread and a handful of flour in the house, but she was a good and charitable soul, and did all that she could for the wayfarers. She set before them all the food she had, and let them sleep beneath her roof.

The next morning Christ and his Apostles set out anew on their journey. On the road they were met by a wolf. The animal fell down before the Lord and begged for food.

"Go to the poor widow's cottage," said Christ, "slay her cow, and appease thy hunger ! "

The Apostles wondered, but refrained from making any remark. The wolf immediately set off, entered the cow-house of the poor widow, killed the cow, and devoured it. When the woman found out what had happened, she only said : "The Lord gave, the Lord has taken away. Holy is His will."

In the meantime, the wayfarers pursued their journey and suddenly saw a barrel full of money rolling on the road. Jesus addressed the barrel and said : "Roll on, O barrel, into the farmyard of the rich peasant."

Once more the Apostles wondered, but kept

silent. The barrel, obeying the divine command, rolled on until it reached the farmyard of the rich peasant, who found the money and stowed it away. He never offered any thanks to God who had sent him such unexpected wealth, but merely grumbled : " The Lord might as well have sent me a little more—and even twice as much while he was about it."

The sun had now risen higher, and the Apostles were thirsty. " Follow the road," said Christ, " and you will find a well where you may drink." The Apostles went along and soon found a well, but, alas, they could not drink thereat, for the water was impure and moreover was swarming with snakes and frogs. They returned to the spot where Christ awaited them and told him what had occurred. Thereupon they resumed their journey, and soon Jesus sent the Apostles out in search of another well. This time they found a well wherein the water was cool and pure. They slaked their thirst and had a short rest under the wondrous trees growing around the place.

When they returned to the Lord, he asked them : " Why did ye tarry so long ? "

" We did not tarry long," replied the Apostles, " but only slaked our thirst and rested for three minutes."

" Not three minutes but three years did ye spend there," said the Lord, " and now I will tell ye why I sent the wolf to slay the poor woman's cow, and commanded the barrel to roll on to the rich peasant's farmyard. The poor woman who gave all she possessed and never grumbled at the decrees of Providence will receive a greater reward in a future life, while the rich peasant's punishment is awaiting him in the next world. As it was in the first well which ye found, so will it be in the other world with the rich peasant ; but as it was in the second well, so will it be in that world with the poor widow.[1]

A Basque legend connected with Christ when he was wandering among men runs as follows :

CHRIST AND THE OLD SOLDIER

Jesus was walking with his disciples to Jerusalem. On the way he met an old man and asked alms of him.

" I am an old soldier," said the man, " and they have sent me away from the army with a couple of small coins. I have given away one on the road, and now I give to you the only one that I have left."

Then the Lord said unto the old soldier : " Which wouldst thou prefer, a sack of gold or Paradise ? "

Peter, who was standing near the old soldier, nudged him in the ribs : " Say Paradise," but the old man would not listen to Peter's kindly advice. " Afterwards," he replied, " we shall have Paradise as well, but in the meantime I prefer the sack of gold."

The Lord gave him a sack of gold and said : " When this sack is empty, thou wilt only have to say : ' Go into my sack,' and everything thou wishest for will immediately go into thy sack."

The man thanked the Lord and went on his road. After a while he passed before the door of an inn and saw a fine leg of mutton on the table. As he was

---

[1] See Ralston, *Russian Folk-tales*, pp. 332–334.

hungry, he opened his sack and said : " Fine leg of
mutton, come into my sack," and in a moment the
leg of mutton was in his sack. The old soldier was
very glad, and ever since he had everything he wished
for in the same way.

One day, however, the devil came to tempt him,
but once more the man opened his sack and said :
" Come into my sack," and the poor devil was in it
in an instant. Then the man who knew that he had
fooled the devil betook himself to a blacksmith,
borrowed a sledge-hammer, and for a long time
pounded and belaboured the devil.

But the day came when the old soldier died, and
without more ado he presented himself at the gates
of Paradise. Peter opened the gate and perceiving
the old soldier, angrily exclaimed : " Why art thou
standing here, and what dost thou ask ? "

" Paradise," boldly replied the old soldier.

" Paradise ! " shouted St. Peter, " Paradise !
Didst thou not prefer to have a sack of gold when the
Lord offered thee thy choice ? It is too late now,
be off, and here are the gates of hell ! "

Sadly our man went off and knocked at the gate
of hell, which a demon opened to him. But scarcely
had the devil perceived the new visitor when he
exclaimed :

" Shut the door ! Don't let him in. He will
cause us a great deal of trouble, for he is very
vicious ! "

And as the devil would not receive him, the poor
soldier once more betook himself to Paradise and
knocked at the door. But the Lord now had pity on

him, and in his mercy and loving kindness forgave the poor fool because he had proved such a foe to the tempter.[1]

THE STONE TURNED TO BREAD

A popular Italian legend runs as follows :

Once, while the Saviour was journeying with his Apostles, they came to a village where there was no bread to be had. Christ said : " Peter, let each one of you carry a stone." They each took up a stone, but Peter took only a little one. While the other Apostles were all loaded down by the heavy stones, Peter went along easily.

" Let us now go to another village," said Christ, " if there is bread we shall buy it, but if there is none, I will give you my blessing and the stones will become bread."

Thereupon they went to another village, put down the stones, and rested. As no bread was to be found in the village, the Master gave his disciples his blessing and the stones became bread. But while the other Apostles had plenty of bread, Peter, who had carried only a small stone, had hardly a mouthful. " Master," he said, " how am I going to still my hunger."

" Why didst thou carry such a tiny stone ? " said Christ. " Look, the others who loaded themselves down have bread enough."

Thereupon they went on, and Christ made them each carry another stone. This time Peter took a large one, while all the other Apostles who were not

[1] See W. Webster, *Basque Legends*, 1877.

hungry carried small ones. When they reached
another village the Apostles threw away their stones,
because there was plenty of bread to be had there.

THE LORD AND THE BOASTER

While Jesus was wandering about accompanied
by Peter and Andrew they met a wayfarer who said,
" Take me with thee, O Jesus, I will be one of thy
Apostles." Jesus knew full well that this man was a
great sinner, but he nevertheless granted the request,
and the new Apostle went with them.

They reached a town where they heard that the
king lay sick. And Jesus said to his followers : " The
king in this town is a very good and pious man, and
has always been a friend of the poor and the simple
folk ; let us walk up to his house and bring him back
to health."

When Jesus and his Apostles reached the castle
and asked admittance in order to cure the king and
make him well, they were told that they had come
too late. " Alas," the servants said, " our good king
is dead, and no mortal man can bring him back to
life."

But Jesus replied : " That is of no consequence,
and if you will let me in into the death chamber, I
will do what I can."

And when the queen saw the Saviour and heard
his words she granted his request and led him into
the chamber where her dead husband lay. Jesus
now asked for a bucket full of fresh water and for a
long knife, and locked himself in the chamber with
the dead body of the king, while the Apostles

waited outside. Tired after a long day's tramping, they soon fell asleep, but the newcomer, the stranger who had joined them on that day, was wide awake, for he was curious to know what the Master was doing behind that locked door.

He approached, peeped through a chink in the door, and saw how the Lord had cut the corpse of the king into four parts, washed them in the bucket and then put the parts together. He watched Jesus pray and make the sign of the cross, and saw the dead king came to life again. The king thereupon offered a great feast and invited Jesus and his Apostles. He also gave Jesus and his disciples some cakes to take on their journey, but Jesus distributed them among the Apostles.

The next day the wanderers came to a forest where they decided to pass the night, and the Apostles consumed their cakes for supper, while Jesus had none, as he was not hungry. A few cakes remained and were put aside. In the night the newcomer rose up and consumed them all, and when the others got up in the morning he said : " To-night, while you were all asleep, two wolves came out of the forest and devoured all the cakes, and only at the risk of my own life did I succeed in driving the beasts away."

But Jesus calmly replied : " The two wolves were thyself and thy greed. Hadst thou at least confessed the truth it would have been well, and I would have allowed thee to abide with us. But since thou hast spoken a lie thou canst no longer remain in our company. Get thee hence ! " And the liar went his own way.

He trudged along and soon came to a town where he heard that the Emperor's daughter had just died. " Now is my opportunity," he said in his heart, and presented himself before the Emperor. " I can bring thy daughter back to life," he said, " and I hope that thou will reward me for my service."

" It is well," replied the Emperor, " if thou canst perform this miracle, I will give thee my daughter for wife, but know, my friend, shouldst thou fail, then death will be thy reward."

The boaster now asked for a bucket full of fresh water and for a long knife, and locked himself up in the room where the dead princess lay. Here he proceeded to act as he had seen the Lord do. He cut the dead body of the princess into four parts, washed them in the water, and put them together. Then he blew over the body, but he had forgotten to make the sign of the cross, and blow as he might, the princess remained dead. Suddenly the door opened and Jesus entered the room.

" Thou art caught in the trap," he said to the boaster who had tried to imitate him ; " had I not come, thou wouldst have been lost. Thou didst boast to the Emperor that in such-and-such a place thou didst bring to life the king, and hast concealed the just action of God. For thy misdeeds and thy lies and for thy arrogance to do the work of God, thou wilt receive thy punishment."

Thereupon Jesus brought the dead princess to life again and turning to the boaster he said : "Go and stand in the middle of the world, and as thou didst blow upon the dead body, thou shalt blow until the

Day of Judgment." And ever since the man who had
tried to imitate the Lord has been blowing and raising
the wind over the world. And from whatever side
he blows from that side the wind comes, and so he will
continue until the Day of Judgment.[1]

THE LORD AND THE BLACKSMITH

Once upon a time there lived a blacksmith who
was so proud of his skill that his pride gave universal
dissatisfaction. One day the Lord, accompanied by
Peter, appeared at the blacksmith's shop.

" Master Blacksmith," said Jesus, " would you
kindly allow me to do a little work in your
forge ? "

" Why not? It is at your service," replied the
blacksmith, flattered at being called " master " and
addressed in such terms. " What is it you wish to
make ? "

" That you will soon see," replied the Lord.

Thereupon he took up a pair of tongs and seizing
Peter held him over the forge until he was red hot.
Thereupon he drew him out and hammered him on
all sides, until the old Apostle was forged anew into
a handsome youth.

Speechless with astonishment, the blacksmith had
looked on. When the Lord and Peter had left him
and he had recovered himself, he ran straight up to
his sick old father who lay in bed and cried aloud :
" Father, come quickly, I have just learned how to
make a young and strong man of you."

[1] See Dähnhardt, *Natursagen*, vol. ii. p. 86, quoted from a collection
of Ruthenian folk-tales.

" My son," said the old man, somewhat terrified, " have you lost your senses ? "

" No, no," cried the son, " you can believe me, for I have just seen it myself and know how it is done."

As the old man still protested, the blacksmith seized him forcibly and carried him to the shop. Here, in spite of the old man's protestations, entreaties, and shrieks, the blacksmith thrust his father into the forge, but, alas, he brought out nothing but a piece of charred leg, which fell to pieces as soon as he touched it with his hammer.

Seized with anguish and remorse, the blacksmith ran out and hurried in search of the two visitors whom he found in the market-place. " Sir," he cried, " you have misled me ; I wanted to imitate your skill, but, alas, I have only burned my father alive. For God's sake, come and help me if you can."

The Lord smiled graciously and said : " Go home and be comforted, for you will find your father alive and well, but an old man again." And great was the joy of the blacksmith when he returned home and found his father alive and well. From that time, however, his pride disappeared, and whenever people addressed him as " master " he replied : " What folly ! I am only a poor bungler and no master." [1]

THE MASTER-SMITH

A Norse version of this legend runs as follows :

Once upon a time, in those days when the Lord accompanied by Peter used to wander on earth, they

[1] See *Zahrbuch für romanische Literatur*, vii. 28 ; see also *La Tradition*, iii. 250.

came to a smith's house. The smith had made a bargain with the devil, according to which the latter was to have his soul after seven years, but during that time the smith was to be master of all masters in his trade. The smith, therefore, had written in great letters over the door of his forge the following inscription : " Here dwells the Master over all Masters."

When the Lord passed by and saw that, he decided to give the smith a lesson in humility. He went in and asked the proud smith : " Who are you ? "

" Who I am," proudly replied the latter, " you had better read what is written over my door ; but if you can't read writing, then better wait until some one comes along to help you."

Just at that moment a man came in and asked the smith to shoe his horse.

" Will you permit me to shoe the horse ? " said the Lord.

" You may try," replied the smith, " I shall always be able to make it right if you do it badly, for I am the Master over all the Masters in my trade."

Thereupon the Lord went out and, taking one leg off the horse, laid it in the furnace and made the shoe red hot, turned up the ends of the shoe, filed down the heads of the nails, and clenched the points. He then put back the leg on the horse again. When he was done with one leg, he took the other legs, one by one, and did the same. The smith all the while stood by and looked on.

" Well," he said, " you are not such a bad smith after all."

" Do you think so ? " said the Lord.

In the meantime the smith's mother, who was an old, ugly woman, came into the forge and called her son to come home for his dinner.

" Mark now what you are going to see," said the Lord to Peter. Thereupon he took the old woman, laid her in the furnace, and hammered her until a young and lovely woman arose.

" Well," said the smith, " I repeat again that you are not at all a bad smith ; although it stands over my door that here dwells the Master over all Masters, I nevertheless say that you, too, are not a bad smith, and that one learns as long as one lives." Saying this, the smith walked off to his house to eat his dinner.

When he returned to his smithy a man came riding up to have his horse shod.

" I will do it in the twinkling of an eye," said the proud smith, " for I have just learnt a new way how to shoe a horse ; it saves such a lot of time."

Thereupon he cut off the horse's four legs, laid them in the furnace, just as he had seen the Lord do, and threw on a heap of coal. But the legs were of course burnt to ashes, and the smith had to pay for the horse.

Just then an old beggar-woman came in, and the master-smith once more tried to imitate the Lord. Seizing the old woman, he laid her in the furnace, in spite of her shrieks and protestations, assuring her that he was going to turn her into a fair and lovely dame. " Shut up," he shouted, " you don't know what is good for you, in a few minutes you will be a young and lovely maiden, and I will not charge you a penny for it."

But, alas, the old woman was burnt to ashes.

The Lord called her to life and rebuked the smith for his arrogance and pride.[1]

The punishment for the sin of pride is a *motif* quite frequent in legendary lore. Thus an Irish legend of St. Eloi runs as follows :

St. Eloi was a goldsmith before he became religious, but often amused himself by shoeing horses. He often boasted that he had never found his master in anything. One day a stranger stopped at his forge and asked permission to shoe his horse. St. Eloi consented, but to his great surprise the stranger first broke off the horse's leg and carried it into the smithy to shoe it. When he had finished his work he again put on the horse's leg and, turning to St. Eloi, asked him whether he knew any one who was able to do such a good piece of work. St. Eloi tried it, but failed miserably. Thereupon the stranger, who was none other than St. Eloi's guardian angel, cured the horse, and reproved the smith for his pride, and disappeared.[2]

This legend of the smith forms the subject of an old English poem entitled *The Smyth and his Dame*, first printed by Halliwell in his *Contributions to Early English Literature* (1849) and included by W. Carew Hazlitt in his *Remains of the Early Popular Poetry of England*, 1866, vol. iii. pp. 201–220. The legend is another proof of the manner in which the miraculous

---

[1] See Dasent, *Norse Folk-tales*.   [2] See Crane, *l.c.* p. 361.

attributes of Jesus were adapted in the mediæval legends and tales to current superstitions.

" God that dyed on a tree,
 He glad them al with his gle,
 That wyll herken unto me,
  And here what I wyll say ;
 And ye shall here a maruel,
 Of a tale I shall you tell,
 How in Egypt it befell,
  And in that same countraye.

Tyll it befell upon a day,
 Our lorde came there away,
 And thought the smyth to assay,
  As ye shall after here.

Sayd our Lorde, go thy way,
 Now thou doest me pray,
 I shall helpe that I maye
  Her for to restore
 Anone as her se,
 He blessed her full fayrely,
 And bad her stande upon hy :
  Anone she rose up there ! "

DEATH AND TREASURE TROVE

One day Christ, accompanied by his disciples, was walking through a desert place, when suddenly those who were following the Master saw a quantity of gold pieces shining on the wayside.

Calling to Christ, and wondering why he did not stop, they said unto him : " Lord, let us take this gold, for it will compensate us for many labours."

But Christ turned and rebuked them : " Ye desire the things that rob our Kingdom of the greater part of souls, and what I tell ye is true, for on our return ye shall perceive an example thereof." Thus spoke Jesus and passed on.

Now it happened that later on two men found the gold and were very joyous about their discovery. But as the gold was too heavy for them to carry away, they agreed that one should proceed to the nearest village to get a mule, while the other remained on guard. But evil thoughts entered the minds of both men, and evil deeds followed.

When the man who had gone to the village for the mule returned, he thus spoke to his companion : " I have eaten at the village, but thou must be hungry and I have brought thee two loaves to still thy hunger ; eat, and then we shall load our mule."

" I am not hungry just now," said the man who had remained to guard the treasure, " and I think that we had better do our loading first."

Thereupon they set to work and loaded the mule, and when they had nearly finished the work the man who had returned from the village bent down to make the burden fast, when suddenly his companion fell upon him from behind and killed him with a sharp knife. Then, feeling hungry, he took up one of the loaves and ate it, giving the other to the mule. But the bread was poisoned, and both the man and the mule fell down dead, and the gold remained free.

Later on, the Lord, accompanied by his disciples, passed the same spot, and he pointed out to the Apostles the example of which he had spoken previously on that day.[1]

[1] See *Cento Novelle Antiche*, Nos. 72 or 73.

Another version of this legend is found in *Thousand-and-One Nights*, where the lust of gold caused the death of three men : " Thereupon Jesus, the son of Mary (on whom be peace), passed by, and seeing this besought God the Most High for tidings of the case. So He told him what had befallen the men, whereat great was Jesus' wonderment, and he related to his disciples what He had seen." [1]

There are several other versions of this well-known story, which may be familiar to English readers in Chaucer's *Pardoner's Tale*, but they are told of a hermit, and the name of Jesus is not connected with it. One version however, from an account of the Virgin Mary and Jesus according to Arabian writers, appeared in the *Orientalist*.

One day Jesus was going on a journey, and as he was proceeding, a Jew came up to him and went with him. Whilst they were walking, Jesus proposed to the Jew that they should put their loaves of bread together and thus make common property of the food they were carrying. To this proposal the Jew readily assented, but when Jesus opened his bag and brought out only one loaf of bread, while the Jew brought out two, the latter felt that he would be the loser by the bargain. Whilst the man's mind was thus occupied with the loss he was about to sustain by carrying out the proposal, Jesus retired for the purpose of performing his devotions. The Jew, taking advantage of his absence, thought that to eat one of his loaves was the best way out of the difficulty, and so the matter was settled. The Jew ate up one

[1] See John Payne, *Tales from the Arabic*, 1884, vol. i. p. 282.

II

of the three loaves. When Jesus returned and sat down to his meal with the Jew, he observed that there were only two loaves instead of three. He thereupon questioned the Jew how one loaf had disappeared, to which the Jew replied that there were only *two* loaves, and not *three*.

The two men resumed their journey, and encountered a blind man sitting by the roadside begging for alms. Jesus restored the man's sight, then turned to his companion, and said : " In the name of the power which enabled me to give sight to this man, I adjure thee to tell me who ate the missing loaf."

The Jew persisted in his statement that the number of the loaves was two.

On their journey the two then came upon a cripple to whom Jesus restored the use of his limbs by the touch of his hand, and once more he called upon the Jew in the name of Him who had given him the power to heal the cripple to say who it was that ate the loaf. But the Jew still adhered to his first answer.

They continued their journey and soon reached the bank of a river, but there was no boat in which they could cross the river. Jesus asked the Jew to follow him while holding him by his garment, and they both walked upon the water and reached the other side. Once more Jesus asked his companion to tell him who had eaten the third loaf, but once more he received the same answer.

Jesus and his companion ultimately came to a lonely place where Jesus made three heaps of earth and by the word of his mouth turned them into massive blocks of gold. Then addressing his travelling companion, he said : " One of these blocks is for me, one for you, and the third for the man who ate the loaf."

Thereupon the man exclaimed : " It was I that ate the loaf, and therefore I claim the two blocks of gold."

Jesus gently rebuked his companion for obstinately adhering to a falsehood, but made over to him the three blocks of gold.

Now the man endeavoured to take away the gold, but found the blocks too heavy, and while he was thus wasting his strength and trying to remove the blocks of gold, Jesus returned and said unto him :

" These blocks of gold will soon cause the death of three men ; have nothing to do with them, but leave them and follow me."

The man obeyed, and leaving the gold where it lay, he went away and followed Jesus. In the end the men who found the gold met their death.

It has been suggested that the entire legend can be traced to the *Kalila and Dimnah*, an Arabic translation of a Sanskrit work which contains the fables of the *Pantshatantra* and of the *Hitopadesa*, made towards the end of the eighth century. There is also a story in the *Katamantshari* which closely resembles Chaucer's tale, and runs as follows :

A Sanniyasi, who was free from all desire for wealth, as he was passing along a forest path came across some buried treasure. As if terror-stricken he took to his heels. Meeting two other Sanniyasis, accompanied by a servant, they asked him why he was in such hot haste. " I have seen the man-slayer over yonder," he replied, " and am running away out of fear."

Some time after it occurred to the two Sanniyasis that the man was a simpleton and that by man-slayer he meant " money." Proceeding to the spot, they took possession of the treasure and went on their way. Their servant, meanwhile, thinking to himself that he had only to kill them in order that the money might be his, mixed some poison with their rice when he cooked it for them. The two Sanniyasis, on their part, reflecting that possibly their servant would ask them for a share of the treasure, took the oppor-tunity when they were bathing in a tank of pressing him down under the water and so drowning him. After this they ate the rice cooked by him, and so themselves also lost their lives—an effectual proof of the saying that money is the " Man-slayer." [1]

MOSES AND THE DECEIVER

The same legend is also told of Moses. The latter, too, met a man who proved to be a liar, and in spite of the Prophet's insistence refused to admit the truth. The story goes on to relate how Moses performed miracles with the divine staff in his hand, and even revived a dead person. The man, how-ever, despite the miracles performed, persevered in his imposture. He, moreover, stole the staff, but in his hand it lost its miraculous power.

Moses thereupon put up three heaps of dust which he transformed into gold. The old man, having

---

[1] *The Orientalist,* 1884.

now admitted that he was an impostor, Moses left the whole treasure to him and departed from him for ever. Unable to carry the treasure himself, the old man solicited the aid of Bedouins on camels who were passing. The Bedouins dispatched the man to the nearest city to buy bread for them, and during his absence resolved to kill him, in order to appropriate the whole treasure. This they did, but they, too, paid with their lives for their crime, for the bread the old man had brought back was poisoned. Thus all the heroes of the legend meet with the fate they so fully deserved.[1]

The entire legend, connected both with Moses and with Christ and told by Chaucer, has been traced to an Indian source.[2] It is one of the *Jatakas* or Buddhist Birth-Stories, a translation of which appeared in the *Orientalist*, 1884, p. 165.[3]

THE BRAHMAN AND THE ROBBERS

In times gone by, when King Brahmadatta reigned in the city of Benares, there lived a Brahman who was versed in alchemy and knew a certain charm (*mantra*) called " Vedabha." When this charm was repeated at a lucky hour, with the eyes of the reciter turned up to the sky, it had the effect of bringing down showers of treasure from the heavens. This Brahman set out one day for the Cetiya country with Badhi-

[1] See S. Krauss in the *Hungarian Journal Ethnographia*, x. 277 ; see also *Jewish Quarterly Review*, New Series, vol. ii. pp. 339 ff.

[2] See *Contemporary Review*, April, 1881 ; *Academy*, 1882, and *Journal of Philology*, 1883.

[3] See also W. A. Clouston, *Popular Tales*, 1887, vol. ii. p. 401.

satva his pupil, and on their way they fell into the hands of a band of robbers, called Pesanakacora, from a practice they had of sending one of their captives for a ransom while they detained the rest as hostages till its arrival. Of father and son they were wont to detain the son; of mother and daughter, the daughter; of two brothers, the younger; of teacher and pupil, the teacher. In conformity with this practice they detained the Brahman and sent Badhisatva to fetch the ransom.

On taking leave of his tutor, Badhisatva entreated him not to avail himself of the charm, although there was to be a lucky hour that very day, at which the *mantra* might be repeated with effect; warning him at the same time that a disregard of this advice would result in the death both of himself and of the five hundred robbers. So saying, he went away, promising to return in a day or two with a ransom. The Brahman, however, unable on the one hand to bear his confinement, and on the other to resist the temptation which the approach of the lucky hour presented, gave way to his weakness and informed the robbers of his resolution.

Thereupon he performed the ablutions enjoined preparatory to the recital of the *mantra*, bedecked himself with flowers, and, at the advent of the lucky hour, muttered the *mantra*, when, to the amazement and gratification of the robbers, a shower of gems fell from the heavens. The robbers helped themselves to as much of the treasure as they could carry and, releasing the Brahman, set out thence.

Whilst they were on their march, another band

of robbers, more powerful than they, met them and made them captives. The captives informed their captors how they got the wealth, wherefore the captive robbers were released and the Brahman was laid hold of. On being told by the Brahman that they must wait for a lucky hour, the robbers were so incensed that they cut the Brahman into two, and throwing the two pieces on the way, pursued the five hundred robbers whom they had just released, killed them all, and took possession of the treasure.

After this, they divided themselves into two factions, not being able to agree in the division of the spoil. Each faction attacked the other, and all were killed except two. The two who were left helped themselves to the whole treasure and hid it in a place of safety near the village. One of them kept guard over it, while the other went into the village to procure some food. Both were tempted by covetousness and each planned the destruction of the other.

The robber who went to the village for food, bought some bread and poisoned it, but as soon as he returned and offered it to his companion, the latter rose up and killed him. The survivor then partook of the poisoned food, and died instantly on the spot.

In the meantime Badhisatva collected some treasure for the ransom of his tutor the Brahman, but when he entered the forest to offer it to the robbers, he found the body of his teacher cut in two. He at once knew that his teacher must have disregarded his advice and caused a shower of treasure to descend. Advancing farther, he saw the mangled corpses of the thousand-but-two robbers lying scattered on the ground, and he finally discovered the corpses of the two who were the last possessors of the ill-fated treasure. The Badhisatva then, after reflecting upon the consequences of covetousness, removed the treasure and spent it in charitable purposes.[1]

JESUS AND THE BEAR

While Jesus and Peter were wandering over the face of the earth they asked any animal they met whether it had any complaint. The bear alone complained against his lot. " I have to live in the forest where I cannot find any proper nourishment to still my hunger."

And the Lord Jesus said : " Eat raspberries and blackberries and other sweet plants and herbs, and above all, honey."

But the bear was too stupid to follow the advice, grumbled over his lot, and growled.

Thereupon the Saviour, who had compassion with the whole of creation, gently led the bear to a tree full of honey and advised the animal to taste the food. The bear refused, and Peter had to use force to make the animal do it. But when the bear started to eat the honey he would not stop.

" Go now and try the strawberries," commanded the Lord, but again the bear disobeyed and continued to eat the honey.

Thereupon the Lord commanded a swarm of bees to fall upon the bear so that he was obliged to run

---

[1] *The Orientalist*, Kandy, Ceylon, 1884, pp. 165, 166, translated by T. B. Panebokke.

away from the tree. And ever since the bear has been fond of honey, and the bees pursue him.[1]

THE DOVE AND THE HAWK

Another legend showing the gentleness of Jesus and his pity for the animals runs as follow :

One day, while Jesus was wandering in the desert, a dove came flying to him, imploring his protection. " A fierce enemy is pursuing me," cried the dove, " and I have come to thee to implore thy protection." Touched by this pitiful appeal, the Man of Sorrows offered a refuge to the homeless bird, taking it under his seamless garment.

Suddenly a pursuing hawk appeared, and thus spoke : " I am tormented by the gnawing pangs of hunger, and in vain am I searching for food. Hast thou any right to deprive me of my rightful prey and thus increase my torments ? Hand over unto me the dove thou has taken to thy bosom, and let me have my nourishment which God has promised to all creatures."

And Jesus replied : " Is it food in general, any food, thou seekest, or just the dove ? If it is food thou art after, then I will do my best to give thee satisfaction, but if it is this dove thou wishest to devour, then I will not let the bird go. It is under my protection, and under no condition will I betray its trust."

But the hawk replied : " No, it is only food I am seeking, no matter whether it be this dove or anything else that will appease my hunger."

[1] See *Rivista populara*, 1897.

Thereupon the Man of Sorrows cut from his limbs a piece of flesh, equivalent in weight to that of the dove, and gave it to the hawk saying : " Here is thy nourishment."

But suddenly the hawk disappeared, for it was Satan in disguise who had come to tempt Jesus.

The same legend, with a slight variation, is told of Moses in the *Tutti Nameh*.[1]

THE SHEEP AND THE OXEN

In former times the sheep were shy while the oxen were domestic and tame. One day the Lord in his wanderings stopped to observe a shepherd in his work. The poor fellow was just hopping about barefooted and with a broken leg, trying to gather his sheep and not let them disperse. And the Lord said to the shepherd : " My child, I am very thirsty, bring me a drop of water ; thou knowest where the well is to be found."

" I will bring thee some water," said the shepherd, " but my sheep are shy and ready to disperse, and I cannot leave the herd alone. As thou seest, I have no time even to cover my feet and must run after them barefooted."

" Go," said the Lord, " and bring me some water ; I will look after thy sheep."

The shepherd went and brought him some water, and the Lord blessed him : " Henceforth," he said, " thy sheep will no longer be shy and ready to dis-

[1] See *Tutti Nameh*, German translation by G. Rosen, vol. ii. pp. 32, 33 ; see also Rappoport, *Myth and Legend of Ancient Israel*, vol. ii. p. 262.

perse, so that thou will find time to sit down and put on thy shoes."

And ever since the sheep are no longer shy, and the shepherd has time to lie down when he is tired.

The Lord thereupon went to see a herdsman at his work. The oxen were lying down, and the herdsman, with bare feet, was preparing to lie down and have a rest. And the Lord said unto the herdsman : " My child, I am very thirsty and should like to have a drop of water. Go and bring me some from the well."

But the herdsman said : " Go and fetch it thyself. I cannot run to the well barefooted as I am."

And the Lord said : " Henceforth thou shalt constantly run after thy oxen and never have time to put on thy boots."

And immediately the oxen became shy and began to run hither and thither, and the herdsman had to run after them barefooted as he was. And ever since the sheep have been tame while the oxen are shy.[1]

The Marks on the Haddock

During his wanderings with Peter the Lord, in order to be able to pay the tribute, commanded Peter to catch a fish in the Sea of Galilee. Peter obeyed, and at his Master's command caught a fish and from its mouth extracted a piece of money for the tribute. Now the marks on the haddock are said to have been made by the Apostle's finger and thumb while holding the fish.

[1] See Strauss, *Die Bulgaren*, p. 67.

A Yorkshire legend, however, as well as legends in other countries, attribute an unholy origin to the dark marks on the shoulders of the haddock. According to this legend the Evil One was the builder of the well-known dangerous ridge of rocks known as Filey Brigg. As he was proceeding with this work, he dropped his hammer into the water. Diving in haste to recover it, The Evil One, by mistake, seized a haddock instead of the hammer.[1]

The Cottagers

Legends of towns submerged by water are quite common, and originally may have been based on the passage in the Old Testament which describes the destruction of the cities of the plain, and the formation of the Dead Sea. Several such legends are told in connection with Christ, who thus punished avarice.

There is a Yorkshire legend which, with the exception that it is told of an angel instead of the Saviour, accounts for the formation of Semerwater, in Wensleydale.

Once, so the legend runs, in the spot where now are the waters of Lake Semerwater in the mountains, there stood a town of considerable size. One day an angel came to the town disguised as a poor beggar, old, ragged, and hungry, begging from door to door for food and shelter. Alas, he visited every house in the town, but none of the inhabitants would give him any relief. At last, outside the town, he reached

[1] See Brand, *Popular Antiquities*, iii. 309 ; Parkinson, *Yorkshire Legends*, p. 121.

a humble cottage inhabited by an aged and poverty-stricken couple, to whom he repeated his tale of woe.

" Enter our humble dwelling," said the aged pair, " and partake of what we possess." And when the beggar had passed their threshold they brought forth bread and milk and cheese, the best they had. The guest ate and drank, appeased his hunger, and thanked and blessed his hosts. At their urgent request he passed the night under their roof. In the morning he departed, but before leaving the abode of the charitable pair, he looked back over the hard-hearted, uncharitable town, and lifting up his hands he repeated the following lines :

> " Semerwater rise ! Semerwater sink !
> And swallow the town, all save this house,
> Where they gave me meat and drink."

He had hardly spoken these words when the waters of the valley began to rise until they became a troubled sea which rushed over the town and flooded it, so that it disappeared beneath the waves. But as soon as the inrushing waters reached the lonely and hospitable cottage the proud waves were suddenly stayed as if by an invisible hand. And the cottage was all that was left of the once-flourishing town.[1]

LAUGHTER AND TEARS

One day, when the Lord was still walking on earth accompanied by his Apostles, he told one of them to look and see what the people were doing.

[1] See Parkinson, *Yorkshire Legends*, pp. 215, 216,

The Apostle looked and said : " It is strange, but I see people weeping."

And the Lord answered : " It is not the world yet ! "

The next day Jesus bade one of the Apostles look again and see what the people were doing. The Apostle looked and saw the people laughing. " It is curious," he said ; " I see the people laughing."

" It is not the world yet," replied the Lord.

The third day the Lord made the Apostle look again, and when he did so he saw that some people were weeping while some were laughing. " Master," he said, " I see some people laughing and some weeping."

And the Lord said : " Now it is the world, because in this world one is weeping, while the other is laughing."

Chapter VIII

The Passion

> " *And it was about the sixth hour, and there was*
> *a darkness over all the earth, until the ninth*
> *hour. And the sun was darkened, and the veil*
> *of the temple was rent in the midst.*"—LUKE
> xxiii. 44, 45.

IT WAS OVER. The final hour had come and gone.
The Saviour, the gentle prophet of Nazareth, had
finished his task, nailed to the cross and crucified.
He had drained the bitter cup to its dregs, and his
death-agony had lasted from noon to sunset. Refusing the traditional drink intended to deaden the
sufferings of the crucified, he suffered the agony of
death in fullest consciousness. And then " there
was darkness over all the earth." Just as nature had
rejoiced in the hour of the Nativity, so all creation
wept and mourned at the hour of his Crucifixion.

The religious mediæval mind, however, could not
feel satisfied with the meagre information contained
in the Canonical Gospels. What wonderful scope
was there for the flights of imagination, for poetry,
pious longings, and yearnings rising on the wings
of fancy. Legend has therefore taken hold of the
hours of trial and death, of the physical and moral
sufferings of the Man of Sorrows, and woven a garland
of pious legends round his last hours, from the walk
to Calvary to the moments of agony and suffering on
the cross, and every nation relates these legends in

its own way, according to its own particular conceptions and inclinations.

When the Saviour was suffering on the cross the whole creation groaned, heaven and earth, beasts and birds, were weeping and mourning. Nature was full of compassion, and her creatures were anxious to alleviate the suffering of their Lord. The splendour of the sun was veiled, the earth was rent, trees trembled, and birds were silent. John Mandeville, in his travels, mentions an oak at Hebron, a thirty-centuries-old and venerable oak, the tree under which the Patriarch Abraham was said to have sat and offered hospitality to weary travellers and angels. This tree, he says, had a circumference of 23 feet, and its branches were spread out over a distance of 90 feet. But at the Crucifixion of Christ this old oak, like all the trees in the world at that moment, suddenly dried up and has thus remained until to-day as an eternal reminder of the suffering of Christ.[1]

The Palm

When Christ entered Jerusalem the people came to meet him carrying palms. The palm has always played an important rôle both in pagan antiquity and among the Jews. The victorious hero was received and accompanied by his friends and admirers carrying palms. The tree has become a symbol of Christ, who is himself often referred to in Latin hymns as *palma bellatorum*. The cross, too, is called by Dante (*Paradiso*, ix. 41) the palm of victory

[1] See Mandeville, *Travels*, p. 68 ; cf. also Douhet, *Dictionnaire*, p. 54.

which must be gained with both hands, because *palma* also means the palm of the hand, and Christ was nailed on the cross with outstretched arms. The palm, however, not only points to Paradise, but, as legend relates, also comes from Paradise. According to Moslem legend, it was created by God on the sixth day of creation from the earth out of which Adam had been fashioned.

In another Moslem tradition the palm first appeared on the island of Ceylon, whither Adam came when he was exiled from Paradise, and it grew out of the tears shed by our first parent. In a previous chapter I have related how Christ commanded an angel to carry the branch of a palm into Paradise. This legend, by the way, may have been known to Raphael, who painted the Madonna under a palm tree.

" When Jesus and his disciples drew nigh unto Jerusalem, and were come to Bethphage, on the Mount of Olives, he sent two disciples, saying unto them, Go into the village over against you, and straightway ye shall find an ass tied, and a colt with her : loose them and bring them unto me. And if any man say ought unto you, ye shall say, the Lord hath need of them ; and straightway he will send them. All this was done that it might be fulfilled which was spoken by the prophet, saying, Tell ye the daughter of Sion, Behold, thy king cometh unto thee, meek, and sitting upon an ass, and a colt, the foal of an ass.

" And the disciples went, and did as Jesus commanded them, and brought the ass, and the colt,

12

and put on them their clothes, and they set him thereon.

"And a very great multitude spread their garments in the way ; others cut down branches from the trees, and strawed them in the way. And the multitudes that went before, and that followed, cried, saying, Hosanna to the Son of David : Blessed is he that cometh in the name of the Lord ; Hosanna in the highest. And when he was come into Jerusalem, all the city was moved, saying, Who is this? And the multitude said, This is Jesus the prophet of Nazareth of Galilee " (Matt. xxi. 1–11).

This passage in the Canonical Gospels,[1] describing the entry of Christ into Jerusalem, mounted upon an ass and the joy of the city, has given rise to many legends.

In memory of the entry into Jerusalem and as a reward for carrying the Lord, the ass has the sign of the cross on its back.

The Ass and the Sign of the Cross

Five days before the Passah Festival, Jesus, mounted upon an ass, held his solemn entry into Jerusalem. The ass, proud of the part it was acting, claimed a share in the honours bestowed upon Jesus.

"Lord Jesus," said the conceited ass, "I should like to receive a special favour and distinction which I might be able to bequeath to my descendants and to future generations."

"Stupid animal," replied Jesus, "do not ask for favours which will turn into a burden for thee.

---

[1] Cf. also Mark xi. 1–10 ; Luke xix. 29–38.

Hitherto thou hast only witnessed the triumph of the Son of God, but very soon thou wilt witness his suffering and pain. Soon thou wilt see how men will mock and beat him. Art thou so anxious to share also his humiliation and his suffering ? A distinctive mark will soon make thee conspicuous among all the other animals, and the result will be not honour and respect, but constant contempt and abuse for thee and the future generations issued from thee until the end of days."

Thus spake Jesus in his kindness and compassion, not wishing the poor animal to bear the burden and suffer in consequence of its consent to carry the Lord into Jerusalem. The ass, however, the ass which had already played an honourable part at the Nativity, remained obstinate and refused to listen to the wise words of the Saviour. It begged for a favour and a mark distinguishing it from all other animals. Its request was at last granted, and it received the sign of the cross on its back. Ever since, a long grey stripe, darker in colour than the hair of the ass, runs along the middle of its back and is crossed by another stripe in the region of the shoulders.[1]

KING SOLOMON AND THE HOOPOE

A somewhat similar legend of an animal (a bird in this instance) claiming by way of reward a distinctive mark is connected with the hoopoe and King Solomon. This legend, too, teaches a lesson, and shows how excessive pride and vanity are the undoing of man, beast, and bird.

[1] *Revue des Traditions populaires*, xii, 230,

A flock of hoopoes was flying just at the moment when King Solomon was on one of his many journeys. It was a hot day and the sun was scorching. Suffering greatly from the heat of the day, the king grew faint and longed for shelter which would protect him against the burning rays of the sun. When he saw the flock of hoopoes an idea occurred to him and he asked the birds to gather over his head and thus form a screen protecting him against the scorching heat of the sun. The king of the hoopoes granted the request, and like a cloud the flock of birds hovered above the head of Solomon.

Desirous of showing his gratitude to the birds for the service they had thus rendered him, Solomon promised to grant them whatever request they chose to make. " Consider well," he said to the king of the hoopoes, " what thou seekest, and I will grant thy request."

And the king of the hoopoes answered : " We have considered the matter, and this is the request which all my subjects and myself proffer. We desire to have crowns of pure gold on our heads."

" Thou art a foolish bird," said the king, " but my promise I will keep. Should ye, however, in days to come, realize and repent of your vanity and folly, come again to me, and you will always find me ready to help you." The king prayed, and lo ! all the hoopoes had crowns of pure gold on their heads.

The vain birds now grew excessively proud and haughty, and looked down with contempt upon all the other birds. They never lost an opportunity of

preening themselves, and when walking on the sea-
shore they constantly admired themselves in the
surface of the water, which reflected their images like
a looking-glass. The queen of the hoopoes was the
proudest and haughtiest of all the birds. Seated upon
the branch of a tree, she no longer deigned to speak
to her old friends and even to her own cousins or
kindred. "They are only common birds," she
thought, "while I am wearing a crown of pure gold
on my head."

But, alas, evil days soon came upon the vain
birds. For bird-catchers soon realized the profit
they could derive from the silly, brainless birds.
One bird-catcher set up a trap wherein he placed a
piece of broken mirror. Immediately a hoopoe came
to admire himself and his golden crown therein,
and was thus caught in the trap. The bird-catcher
at once slew the bird and brought the glittering
crown to a worker in metal. But the latter was
cunning, and although he well knew that the crown
was of pure gold, he said unto the bird-catcher :
" This is but a crown of brass, and worth sixty
farthings. I will buy it for this price, and take any
more such crowns which thou canst find. Say
nothing, however, concerning this matter to any
man."

The bird-catcher was well content. He took the
money, caught many more hoopoes, and sold their
crowns to the cunning worker in metal. One day,
however, the bird-catcher met a goldsmith who was
also an honest man, and he showed him the crowns
of two hoopoes he had just caught and slain. " These

are crowns of pure gold," said the goldsmith, " and I will give thee one talent of gold for them."

Overwhelmed with joy, the bird-catcher divulged the secret to his friends, and soon the knowledge of the value of the hoopoe crown spread far and wide. Men hastened to catch the priceless birds by means of traps and bird lime, slings, and arrows, in order to sell their golden crowns and thus grow rich. No sooner did a hoopoe appear than it was caught and slain.

Great was the distress of the haughty and proud birds whose lives were now being constantly threatened on account of their golden crowns. Many of them had already been caught and slain, and the few who were still alive bitterly bewailed their destiny. "Soon," said the birds, "we shall be wiped out from the face of the earth."

Then the king of the hoopoes remembered the warning of King Solomon and his promise to help the birds should evil days befall them. Straightway, therefore, the unhappy king of the hoopoes flew to the palace of King Solomon in Jerusalem. Standing before the steps of the golden throne, the king of hoopoes, groaning and weeping bitterly, related unto the king the tribulations of his subjects, and how the days of his race were numbered on account of the golden crowns.

King Solomon smiled kindly, and thus he spoke to the hoopoe : " I warned thee at the time when thou didst proffer thy request and told thee how foolish it was to choose golden crowns. You have now paid a heavy price for your pride and vanity, but, remembering the service you did me, I will help you. Henceforth your crowns of pure gold shall be changed into crowns of feathers, and men will no longer pursue you."

And so it happened, The hoopoes now wear crowns of feathers instead of gold, and bird-catchers are no longer eager to catch them.[1]

THE SEDGE LEAF

Another legend connected with the ass which Christ had mounted when he entered not Jerusalem but Bethlehem runs as follows :

Jesus, riding on an ass, proceeded to Bethlehem. The animal was hungry and, perceiving the sedge bordering the way they were coming along, it tried to tear off a leaf or two to satisfy its hunger. Christ, however, being in a hurry, the ass had to let the leaf go, but the trace of its bite on the leaf remained, and ever since the leaves of the sedge show the marks of three teeth.[2]

In another source the legend of the sedge leaf is connected with the night in the garden of Gethsemane. " Then cometh Jesus with them unto a place called Gethsemane, and saith unto the disciples, Sit ye here, while I go and pray yonder " (Matt. xxvi. 36). " When Jesus had spoken these words, he went forth with his disciples over the brook of Cedron, where was a garden, into which he entered, and his disciples " (John xviii. 1).

It is with these passages in the Gospels that the

[1] See J. D. Seymour, *Tales of King Solomon*, p. 98.
[2] See *Revue des Traditions populaires*, vii. 481.

legend is connected. " The leaves of the sedge show on their inner side two indentations side by side. They look as if some one had bitten into the leaf and left the mark of his teeth. When the Lord Jesus Christ in the night of the Passion crossed the brook of Cedron he bit, in his agony, into a bulrush leaf, and therefore the bulrush leaves bear the marks of his front teeth." [1]

I have related above the legend of the aspen which was condemned to tremble for ever. But another legend connected with the night in Gethsemane gives quite another version :

In the night in Gethsemane Christ sat down under a poplar, where he prayed to his Father in Heaven with great trepidation. And it is for this reason that the trees called the trembling poplars, remembering the agony of the Lord, tremble until this day. [2]

The Footsteps of Christ

Even to-day the traces of Christ's footsteps are shown on the Mount of Olives at the moment when he ascended to heaven. He also left the trace of his left foot in the house of Simon. In the abbey church at Fécamp the trace of Christ's foot is shown, on which, legend relates, the name of the Trinity had been written. [3]

Numerous other traces of the Redeemer's feet are shown in many churches on the Continent—at Rome,

---

[1] See Bartsch, *Sagen, Märchen und Gebräuche*, i. 522.
[2] See Bartsch, *l.c.* i. 522, 524.
[3] See Leroux de Lincy, *Essai sur l'abbaye de Fécamp*, p. 73.

St. Denis, and San-Sebastian ; at Rheims, Arles, and Poitiers, where a church was erected on the spot.

In the neighbourhood of Nazareth, on a rock rising above the brook of Cedron, the imprints of the Madonna's knees and of the feet and elbows of Christ are shown.[1]

On the night when Christ was betrayed, taken prisoner, and led away to Caiaphas (Matt. xxvi. 57), he prayed several times to his Heavenly Father in a cave at the foot of the Mount of Olives (Matt. xxvi. 37–44 ; Mark xiv. 35–41 ; Luke xxii. 41–46), kneeling upon a rock. In its compassion the rock became as soft as wax so that the impression made by the feet of the Saviour may still be seen.[2]

This legend reminds me of one told of the Patriarch Jacob. In the Book of Genesis, chapter xxviii. 11, we read : " And he took of the stones of that place, and put them for his pillows, and lay down in that place to sleep." Now legend relates that the stones began to quarrel among themselves, for each one said : " It is upon me that this pious man will lay his head." And the Lord said : " For many years Jacob did not sleep at nights, but studied the Law, and now he has set stones for his pillow, and they, too, quarrel." He therefore commanded the stones to merge into one stone and to be " as soft as a cushion." [3]

[1] See Geramb, *Pèlerinage en Terre Sainte*, quoted by Maury, *Croyances*, p. 301, note 2.

[2] See Sepp, *Symbolikzum Leben Christi*, 1843, p. 92.

[3] See *Pirke de Rabbi Eliezer*, ch. xxxv.

Similar traditions are current not only among Jews and Moslems but also among Buddhists and the followers of other religions.

In the neighbourhood of Medina the Moslems show the impression of the head of Mohammed when he is alleged to have ascended to heaven, while on Mount Carmel popular belief places the imprint of the foot of the prophet Elijah. Buddhists see on the summit of a mountain at Ceylon the impression of the foot of Buddha when, at the moment of ascending to heaven, he cast a look of love upon mankind. The Moslems of Ceylon, on the other hand, hold that it was the foot of Adam, who was standing there on one leg imploring divine forgiveness.[1]

THE SPRINGS OF JERUSALEM

In the meantime the Virgin Mary was following her Son, who had been dragged by his enemies before the tribunal of the High Priest. But she was not allowed to enter the council-chamber and stood at the door without. In her agony the mother was anxious to hear and learn what was being said inside, but, alas, the bubbling springs in Jerusalem made such a noise that it drowned the voices of the High Priest and the elders. In her impatience the agonized mother cursed the springs :

" Ye wicked springs," she cried, " be silent." And ever since the springs in Jerusalem have been silent and the city has no water.[2]

[1] See Rich. Andrée, *La Tradition* (ed. Carnoy), vol. iii. (1889).
[2] *La Tradition*, x. 11.

THE TEARS OF PETER

Peter had meanwhile betrayed his Master three times. " Verily I say unto thee, That this night, before the cock crow, thou shalt deny me thrice " (Matt. xxvi. 34). " Then began he to curse and to swear, saying, I know not the man. And immediately the cock crew. And Peter remembered the word of Jesus, which said unto him, Before the cock crow, thou shalt deny me thrice. And he went out, and wept bitterly " (*ibid.* xxvi. 74, 75).

These tears, legend relates, Jesus gathered up ; they will be counted in Peter's favour on the Day of Judgment. For Peter had immediately repented of his deed and shed bitter tears. Thereupon the Lord appeared to him in a dream and said : " Peter, I have forgiven thee." But the Apostle could not believe it, and asked for a sign. Silently Jesus pointed out to him a number of gooseberry bushes with berries on them which had suddenly grown up.

" Peter," he said, " these are the tears thou hast shed ; I have gathered them from the face of the earth and they will be counted unto thee on the Day of Judgment." [1]

THE TEARS OF ADAM

This legend, telling of the tears of Peter producing gooseberries, somewhat resembles a Moslem legend connected with Adam and Eve when they were driven out of Paradise :

After Adam had fallen he was excessively grieved

[1] See Dähnhardt, *l.c.* vol. ii. p. 199.

and penitent, and his tears flowed abundantly. Beasts and birds drank therefrom, and where the bitter streams sank into the earth gum-bearing trees and fragrant plants arose. Eve's tears, falling into the sea, were transformed into costly pearls, and into fragrant and beautiful flowers when they fell upon the earth.[1]

In another version the tears which came out of the eyes of our first parent formed two rivers, the tears out of the right eye the river of Euphrates and the tears of the left eye the river Tigris.[2]

THE RAVEN AND THE MAGPIE

Two French legends connected with the raven and the magpie run as follows :

Jesus, trying to escape from his pursuers, was wandering through a forest and sat down on the turf to rest for a while. Thereupon the magpies came and pricked the bare feet and head of the Saviour with thorns, but the compassionate swallow removed the thorns. Thereupon the Lord said : " The magpie shall build its nest on the summit of trees, and men will despise it ; but the friendly swallow shall bring up its offspring safe from all pursuit, and men will love it." [3]

THE SPARROW

A Russian legend relates that when his enemies and accusers were seeking for Christ in the garden, all the birds tried to draw away the attention of the

---

[1] See Weil, *Biblische Legenden der Muselmänner*, pp. 29–38.
[2] Weil, *l.c.*   [3] See Sébillot, *Folklore*, iii. 170.

pursuers from the hiding-place of the Saviour. The
sparrow alone attracted the attention of the pursuers
by its shrill chirruping. The Lord then cursed the
sparrow and forbade men to eat its flesh. The
sparrows, too, brought back the nails provided for the
executioners, which the swallows had carried off,
and when Christ was on the cross the swallows cried :
" He is dead " (in Russian, *Oumer*). The sparrows,
on the contrary, maliciously exclaimed : " He is
alive " (*Iif* in Russian), so as to urge on the tor-
mentors to fresh cruelties.[1]

The entry of a sparrow into a cottage is therefore
considered as a bad omen, while the swallow is
always a welcome guest among Russian peasants,
for it is supposed to bring luck to a house, and to kill
it is a great sin. " The legs of the sparrow," writes
Afanassyev, " having been fastened together by
invisible bonds, it is unable to run, and therefore
always hops."

THE WOOD OF THE CROSS

Numerous legends are connected with the species
of the tree which furnished the wood for the cross on
which Christ died, and many speculations have been
put forth as to its identity. The apple tree and the
fig tree, the mistletoe, the oak and the elder, the ash
and the aspen have in turn been mentioned as
having furnished it.

According to one tradition it was the fig tree,
because it was supposed to have been the fruit of
this tree which Adam and Eve tasted.[2]

---

[1] See Ralston, *l.c.* p. 331.   [2] See Rappoport, *Myth and Legend.*

Another tradition mentions the aspen as the fatal tree, because the leaves of this tree never cease from trembling.

That legend should have considered the oak as the tree which contributed the material for the cross of the Lord is quite natural. Has not the oak tree been sanctified by many mysteries and divine manifestations in Holy Writ ? It was under an oak tree, the oak tree of Mamre, where God made His Covenant with Abraham. Under an oak tree the Patriarch offered hospitality to the three angels who appeared to him as weary travellers. Deborah, the nurse of Rebecca, was buried under an oak tree, and under an oak tree Jacob buried the idols which Rachel had carried away from her father Laban. Under an oak tree, too, the angel appeared to Gideon.[1]

In some sources we read that the cross was made of three species of wood, namely, of cypress, pine, and cedar. This tradition may have been inspired by a passage in Isaiah : " The glory of Lebanon shall come unto thee, the fir tree, the pine tree, and the box together, to beautify the place of my sanctuary ; and I will make the place of my feet glorious " (lx. 13).

The *Vulgata* translates cypress, pine, and cedar. The three species of wood are, of course, a reference to the Trinity. In other traditions four varieties of wood are said to have been employed, for the number four has in the Scriptures a mystical meaning.

" The Holy Cross," writes the Venerable Bede (*Collectanea*), " was made of four species of wood,

---

[1] See Gretser, *De Croce*, iii. 13.

namely, cypress, cedar, pine, and box." Jacobus de Voragine, in his *Golden Legend*, declares that the cross was made of cedar, cypress, olive, and palm.

The apple tree is considered by some to have been the tree the fruit of which Adam had eaten. In the Talmud the Rabbis say that the apple was the tree of Knowledge, and that Seth brought from Paradise a cutting which ultimately provided the cross of Golgotha. Such tradition may have been derived from Canticles viii. 5 : " I raised thee up under the apple tree ; there thy mother brought thee forth ; there she brought thee forth that bore thee."

De Gubernatis relates the following legend :

THE EVERGREEN OAK

When Jesus was condemned to be crucified all the trees foregathered in the night, and decided not to allow their wood to be used for the cross on which the Saviour was to suffer and die. But there was a traitor among the trees. The common oak refused to submit to the decision of all the others.

The oak tree, therefore, was excommunicated for its treason and condemned to be excluded from the confraternity of plants. Now when the carpenter began to manufacture the cross he saw, to his amazement, that the wood could not be worked. Whatever wood he took up it broke, split, and crumbled in his hand. He tried first one tree and then another, but always with the same result. It seemed to the astonished carpenter as if the wood was be-

witched, for it would not lend itself to his work. But
he was persevering and went on trying until he
happened to take up a piece of wood from the oak
tree. This offered no resistance, so out of it the
carpenter made the cross. Therefore the evergreen
oak is a cursed tree, and woodcutters on the mountains avoid it, being anxious not to stain their axe or
soil the holy flame of the fire.[1]

THE ILEX AND MISTLETOE

Among the trees, legend observes, there was a
traitor, but the name varies in different countries.
Here is another version. When the trees heard that
it had been decided to crucify the Saviour they for-
gathered, held a council, and unanimously decided
not to allow their wood to be used for the instrument
of punishment. At the appointed time the executioners arrived with their axes to cut the wood for the
cross on which Jesus was to be crucified, but their
efforts were in vain. The trunks and branches of
every tree, except one, split themselves into a thousand
fragments, so that it was quite impossible for the
executioners to get a length of wood necessary for the
purpose of a cross. One tree alone, the ilex, gave
up its trunk without uttering any protest, and from
its wood the cross was made. It is said that, in
Greece, woodcutters even to-day have a horror of
it, and never bring their axes in contact with the
accursed tree.[2]

The mistletoe, too, is mentioned in some legends

---

[1] See Gubernatis, *Mythologie des plantes*, vol. ii. p. 85.
[2] See Folkard, *Plant Lore*, 1892, p. 385.

as the wood which was used for the cross, and as a
punishment it was reduced from its position as a fine
forest tree to the position of a parasite of the oak.
The custom of the mistletoe bough and the habit of
" kissing under the mistletoe " still prevails, and
would seem to discredit this legend.

THE PEAR TREE

The Roman soldiers, another legend relates, in
their hurry to make a cross for the Saviour, found a
broken wild pear tree, with the hard nature of whose
wood they were not acquainted. The broken tree
seemed suitable for their purpose because its branches
to the right and to the left were naturally in the shape
of a cross. So the pear tree was taken, but it was
with great difficulty that the soldiers managed to
drive the nails into the hard wood.

Then, the narrative goes on, as the blood of the
Saviour poured out over the trunk and penetrated
into its fissures, the curse which had rested on the
broken tree was blotted out. New life and sap rose
in its blighted branches, and again its roots were
quickened. When the time came for the cross to be
removed, the new roots held fast to the spot where
Christ had suffered, and remained on the skull-
shaped knoll. After the destruction of Jerusalem, when
all around the mount of Golgotha was reduced to a
waste field, lo ! from the fresh root there sprouted
forth a new tree. It was like the old wild pear tree
in shape and appearance, but its leaves showed fine
red veins and its fruit contained a blood-red juice.
The fruit was not only pleasant to look at, but

13

succulent and health-bringing to all those who
ate it.[1]

GOLGOTHA

Not only the early and mediæval Christians but
also the Church Fathers have woven a number of
legends round the place of the Crucifixion. Golgotha,
or the place of skulls, is connected with the skull of
Adam, our first parent, so that it has been declared
Christ was crucified in the very place where Adam
was buried. " The place was called Calvary because
it held the head of the whole human race," wrote
St. Augustine (*Civitate Dei*, chap. xxxii.), and St.
Chrysostom, too, alluded to this tradition.

Jewish legendary lore has many traditions concerning the spot where Solomon built the Temple,
and Christian legend has extended and applied them
to the place of crucifixion. It was there that Cain
and Abel brought their offerings, that Noah sacri-
ficed when he came out of the Ark, and that Abraham
offered Isaac.

> " We think that Paradise and Calvarie,
> Christ's Cross and Adam's tree stood in one place ;
> Look, Lord, and find both Adams meet in me ;
> As the first Adam's sweat surrounds my face,
> May the last Adam's blood my soul embrace." [2]

THE IMAGE OF CHRIST

There is an old, very curious but very beautiful,
legend connected with the true portrait of Christ,

---

[1] See Handtmann, *Neue Sagen*, p. 169.
[2] Donne, *Hymn to God, my God, in my sickness*.

and the likeness of his features. It is stated that when Christ was walking to Calvary, bearing the cross, drops of agony running down his face, a devout widow or maiden gave him her handkerchief with which to wipe his brow, and the cloth thus became miraculously impressed with the image of his countenance. This image became the *Vera Iconica*, or the true portrait of Christ's features. The handkerchief was afterwards sent to King Abgar and ultimately came to Rome, where it was kept for many centuries at St. Peter's Church. From the term *Vera Iconica* came the name of Veronica, who is revered as a female saint.

In an article published in the *Art Journal* (1861) a writer pointed out that the legendary portrait of Christ can be traced to the first century of our era. In the catacombs of Rome he found little glass vessels or sacramental cups on which pictures of Christ and his principal disciples, generally wrought in gold, could be traced. The portrait of Jesus is invariably represented as an oval head with parted hair. From careful examination the writer came to the conclusion that these portraits were dated from the days soon after the death of Christ, when the tradition of his personal appearance was still fresh in the memory of his followers. It is evident, he says, that the artist did not adopt a mere conventional type, but had availed himself of information which had reached him regarding the obvious and characteristic traits in the true likeness. Thus the Saviour is delineated with the hair parted in the middle and wearing a beard which was not at all the conventional type of a

Roman youth, and which the artist might have been expected to adopt.[1]

In some versions of this legend it is related that the handkerchief or veil was brought to Rome by Titus, who, thanks to the virtue of this holy relic, was cured from leprosy. There are numerous paintings of Saint Veronica representing her with the handkerchief with which she had wiped the face of Christ. One of these pictures is at Munich ; another, by Hemling, at Bruges ; and a third, by Allari, at Madrid.

The Venerable Bede (*opp*. iii. p. 365) gives another version of the legend. The holy relic, he declares, was stolen immediately after the Resurrection of Christ and kept as a precious heirloom. When the man who had stolen the relic died, he left to his sons the choice of taking either the handkerchief or all his other worldly possessions. The son who chose the estate soon became poor, whilst his brother who took the portrait of Christ grew very rich. A dispute subsequently arising about the inheritance of this precious handkerchief, the Caliph Moawiya decreed that the authenticity and virtues of the relic should be tested by fire. As soon, however, as the handkerchief was thrown into the flames, it flew up into the sky, whence it fell into the lap of a pious Christian, and was subsequently kept at Jerusalem with the highest veneration.

THE CROWN OF THORNS

Numerous traditions are connected with the Crown of Thorns set on the head of Christ. Sir John

---

[1] See Chambers, *Book of Days*, vol. i. pp. 100–102.

Maundeville informs us that he saw several relics of the Crucifixion at Constantinople, among them one half of the Crown of Thorns, the coat without seams, the sponge, and one of the nails of the Cross.

The Crown which the Roman soldiers plaited and placed on the head of Christ is the subject of many hallowed speculations, and the honour or ignominy of having contributed the material to this instrument of suffering has been conferred on various plants. Sir John Maundeville says that it was made of " jonkes of the See " —that is to say, of rushes of the sea which prick as sharply as thorns. According to this traveller the Saviour was crowned three times, first with white thorn, then with eglantine, and finally with rushes of the sea.

Not only the nature of the thorns but also the subsequent fate of the Crown is the subject of many legends. A branch of the holy Crown which is preserved at Piacenza is said to blossom on every Good Friday. The same virtue is attributed to the branches preserved at Malta, Mentone, and Donauwörth. At Brixen the thorn is said to sweat blood, while the white thorn is believed to sigh quite audibly on Good Friday.

There is a church at Pisa which bears the name of *della spina*, because a thorn from the Crown of Thorns is said to have been brought there. The Crown of Thorns, legend relates, came into the possession of Charlemagne, in whose hand it began to blossom. The tonsure of the monks is supposed to be in remembrance of this emblem of humiliation.[1]

[1] See Fleury, *Hist. Eccl.* xvii. 201.

Giacomo Bosio, in his curious work entitled *La trionfante et gloriosa croce* (Rome, 1610), which the author translated into Latin under the title of *Crux triumphans et gloriosa*, describes several wonders connected with the plants which are associated with the Passion of Christ. The author first describes a small pumpkin called " Zucca " which grew in the garden of the Church of Santa Pudenziana, wherein there was the sign of the cross so marvellously shaped that all the beholders contemplated it with astonishment and heartfelt joy. The aspect of the pumpkin was extremely gracious. In the white core of the pumpkin there was visible a green cross which filled all those who examined it with a feeling of intense devotion. A further wonder was also noticed. In each of the four corners of the cross in the bigger pumpkin there were exactly five small grains of seed representing the five principal wounds which Christ had received on Calvary.

In this work, which was written in 1609, the author makes a further reference to another plant-wonder, namely, the granadilla, a species of the Passiflora, a genus of the Passion flower of the New World. The Spaniards called it the wonderful and mystic Flower of the Five Wounds, and " the Creator of the world," writes Bosio, " had purposely selected it to illustrate the suffering and the Passion of his Divine Son so that in days to come it might serve to effect the conversion of the nations in the countries where it grows." " The flower," Bosio continues, " is a true representation of the cross on which Christ had suffered. In the middle of the flower there is the pillar on which the Redeemer was bound when he was crucified, and above it are the nails all of a light green colour. Above, is again the Crown of Thorns framed by a sort of veil consisting of seventy-two fringes, the number of thorns in the crown. In the middle of the flower, underneath the pillar, there are visible five blood-red spots clearly representing the five wounds which Christ received on the cross. The plant is rich in leaves shaped like the points of spears or lances, reminiscent of the spear with which one of the Roman soldiers had pierced the side of Christ. At night the flower shuts up, opening only in the day and then only partially, when it takes the shape of a bell."

This again the author considers to be a wonder of creation, indicating that the mysteries of the cross will be revealed to the pagans only after a certain time.[1]

THE LANCE OF LONGINUS

Legend relates that the lance with which the Roman soldier Longinus pierced the side of the Saviour was a relic particularly precious to the warlike German nation, and constituted one of the State jewels. Although carried by a pagan, the lance, having served the great work of Redemption, became a sacred instrument since it had touched the side of the Saviour. Longinus, the Roman centurion who recognized Christ at the cross, died as a martyr on March 15. His name Longinus may have been derived from the long lance, which is referred to in an old Latin hymn as *Dulcis hasta*.

[1] See Bosio, *La trionfante e gloriosa croce*, 1610.

There is a picture representing Christ with three
lances,[1] and legend relates that one day Christ
wanted to destroy the earth with those three lances
for the three great sins of pride, lewdness, and
avarice. But he was moved to clemency owing to
the intervention of his Virgin Mother. Mary pointed
out to Christ St. Dominicus and St. Francis, who
alone could free the earth of the three sins.

Another legend connected with miraculous lances
relates that when a number of heroic virgins in Spain
had revenged the death of Roland, they stuck their
lances into the ground, which immediately blossomed
and bore leaves and flowers.[2]

The Robin Redbreast

The beautiful legend of the robin redbreast is
known all over Europe, and is told in different
versions. Sometimes the central figure is Christ ;
sometimes it is the Virgin Mary, but the legend is
mostly connected with the story of the Passion.[3]

When Jesus was suffering on the cross, he beheld
not far away a tiny bird sitting on the edge of its
nest. Mournful and sad, the little bird looked on,
unable to help. Tears welled up in its eyes when it
beheld the Crown of Thorns pressed on the head
of the Saviour and saw how the prickly thorns were
lacerating his brow.

" No one," lamented the little bird, " no one
comes forward to alleviate his suffering. I must go

---

[1] See Kugler, *Berliner Museum*, p. 21.
[2] See Menzel, *Christliche Symbolik*, ii. p. 10.
[3] See Longfellow's poem.

and console him." So it flew to the cross and
succeeded in removing one thorn from the crown.
But a drop of the Saviour's blood fell on the breast
of the compassionate bird, which dyed its feathers red.

And Christ said : " Dear little bird, in remembrance of thy compassion all thy descendants shall
henceforth bear a red spot on their breasts, and man
shall call them robin redbreasts." [1]

Another version of this legend runs as follows :

Slowly, dragging his cross, Jesus is walking to
Calvary, for the hour of his Suffering has sounded.
Little birds surround him and utter cries of distress,
of pity, and pain. When the place of execution is
reached and the Roman soldiers are tearing off the
clothes of their victim, the little birds, fluttering
round the Saviour, try to drive away the executioners. But the latter, hurling stones at the birds,
disperse them.

The cross has at last been erected, and the little
birds, beholding it, utter a cry of lamentation. Suddenly a Roman soldier with his lance pierces the
side of Jesus, and his blood flows freely. The little
birds once more fly back to the cross and make a
supreme effort to staunch the flow of blood. But,
alas, once more the executioners hurl stones at them,
and, weary of the fight and tired out, the little birds
can only cry, " Jesus is dead." But the drops of the
Saviour's blood have left a red spot on the breasts
of the little birds. [2]

---

[1] See Sébillot, *Folk-lore*, iii. 157 ; Swainson, *Folk-lore of British Birds*,
p. 15 ; Gubernatis, *Mythologie des plantes*, i. 130.

[2] See Sébillot, *Légendes Chrétiennes*, 20.

Another version of this legend connects the robin redbreast with the Holy Virgin.

A tiny piece of a blade of straw once got into the eye of the Virgin. The robin redbreast, sitting on a bush nearby and noticing the tears of the Virgin, was moved to pity. What did it do ? It quickly flew to its friend the swallow, and fetching in its beak some fresh water from a neighbouring river returned to the Virgin accompanied by the swallow. The robin redbreast sat down on the Virgin's brow and while it was carefully letting fall drops of water into the eye of Mary, the swallow gently removed the particle of the blade of straw from her eye.[1]

" The robin redbreast," writes Henderson,[2] " is invested with a sacred character all over Christendom, though various reasons are assigned for it in different countries. In Brittany it is reverenced for an act of devotion to the Crucified Saviour, in extracting one thorn from his Crown, thus dyeing its own breast red ; in Wales for bearing in its bill drops of water to the place of torment. Boys always respect its nest ; they say in Cornwall :

> " ' Who hurts the robin or the wren
> Will never prosper on sea or land.' "

A boy in the neighbourhood of Dartmoor told the author that if he took a robin's nest all the " clomb " (crockery) in the house would break.

---

[1] See Swainson, *British Birds*.

[2] *Notes on the Folk-lore of the Northern Counties of England and the Borders*, 1866, p. 92.

The Robin Redbreast and the Magpie

Just as the evergreen oak tree proved a traitor among the plants, so the magpie among the birds was the only one not to be moved to pity by the suffering of Christ.

A French legend runs as follows :

When Jesus was suffering on the cross, two birds, one very beautiful, indeed in those days the most beautiful bird in creation, and the other small and ugly, came and perched themselves on the cross. They were the magpie and the robin redbreast. The former had a crown of feathers on its head and a tail which was as beautiful as that of the peacock. But the magpie was as wicked and cruel as it was handsome, and it dared to mock Christ whilst he was suffering on the cross. The other bird was rather small and insignificant with its simple dress of grey feathers. Modestly and timidly this little bird approached the Crucified Saviour and uttered a cry of lamentation, thus expressing its feeling of compassion. Gently it wiped away with its wings the tears falling from the eyes of the divine sufferer, and with its beak it removed the thorns lacerating the brow of Jesus. In doing so a drop of Christ's blood fell on the throat of the gentle bird, and for ever dyed its modest feathery breast.

" Be blessed," said Jesus, " because thou hast shown pity and compassion with my suffering. Henceforth, wherever thou wilt go, joy and happiness will accompany thee. Thy eggs will have the colour of the sky, and thou shalt be the bird of God, the bird of good omen, the harbinger of glad tidings."

"As for thee," said Christ, turning to the magpie, "henceforth thou wilt be a cursed bird. Thy crown of feathers and thy glowing and beautiful colours of which thou hast been so proud, but which thou didst not deserve, shall be taken from thee. Thy feathers shall henceforth have the colour of mourning and misfortune, and the rain of heaven will always drench thy nest."

In another version of this well-known legend the magpie is said to have been chattering all the time while the robin redbreast was making efforts to staunch the blood flowing from Christ's wounds. And the words of the Saviour have come true. The magpie is a cursed bird, and to meet it brings ill luck. Her once brilliant feathers are now dull and common. She is forbidden to build her nest in the foliage of trees and, exposed as she is to wind and weather, she is always drenched by the slightest rain.[1]

THE SWALLOWS

The swallows are usually considered to be kind birds and are favourites of men, because when Christ was suffering on the cross they consoled him, and tried to remove the thorns from his Crown of Thorns. When he was dead, they went into mourning and put on a black dress which they have never since laid aside.[2]

---

[1] See Rolland, *Faune populaire*, ii. 263 ; Sébillot, *Petites légendes Chrétiennes*, p. 20.

[2] See Swainson, *British Birds*.

In some legends, however, the swallows are said to have lost their gift of song as a punishment for their conduct in the hour of Christ's Passion. When Jesus was suffering the agony of death on Mount Calvary, the entire creation wept and wailed and mourned. The sun grew dark, the earth was rent asunder, the trees trembled, and the birds were silent. Suddenly Jesus heard a joyous warbling, and lifting up his eyes he beheld two swallows perched on a tree and singing lustily. The agony of Christ was so great and his pain so acute that he could not stand the joyous song of the callous and unfeeling birds. And that is the reason why the swallows have been deprived of the gift of song and can only twitter.[1]

THE MOURNING TREES

A beautiful legend describing the compassion of Nature at the moment of the Crucifixion runs as follows :

Jesus had exhaled his last sigh on the cross ; from his soul there fell a whisper : " It is finished." A shudder of dread came over the torturers, and the Roman soldiers who had mocked and reviled him and had driven the nails into his feet and hands with mighty hammer-blows, were struck by the tranquil countenance of the corpse. Nature wept and mourned. Dense dark clouds veiled the radiance of the sun, white flashes of lightning convulsed the air. Peals of thunder spread terror all round, and the earth opened in many places revealing abysmal

[1] See *Revue des Traditions populaires*, vol. x. 302.

depths. Terror-stricken men, beasts, and birds took refuge in distant corners, unable to utter a sound. The trees, bushes, and flowers alone conversed in subdued tones, wailing and uttering lamentations. The pine tree (fir) of Damascus said : " He is dead, and, as a sign of my deep mourning, I will henceforth offer no shade to men and live in distant climes."

The willow of Babylon whispered : " He is dead, and henceforth, as a sign of my mourning, my branches will bend down towards the waters of the Euphrates and shed bitter tears."

The vine of Sorrent lamented : " He is dead, and henceforth, as a sign of my mourning, my grapes shall be black, and the wine they yield shall be called lacrima Christi."

Sadly spoke the yew tree : " He is dead, and as a sign of my mourning I have grown darker, for henceforth I shall be the guardian of cemeteries ; no bee shall sit down on my poisonous blossoms, and no bird shall swing on my branches. Deadly shall be my breath."

The iris of Enze said : " He is dead, and as a sign of my mourning my golden cup will I veil with a shade of violet."

High up on the summit of Mount Caucasus the box tree suddenly felt a sad breath ; it was the sigh of the dying Christ wafted along from Golgotha and ascending to heaven. The sap of the tree chilled and froze in its branches, its leaves grew a shade darker, and the branches pressed one against the other. " He is dead," sadly wailed the box tree "and henceforth, in memory of his death, I will remain on stony, desolate, and uninhabited heights. My black branches shall cover graves and serve to sprinkle holy water upon the bier."

The bindweed, too, mourned and said : "He is dead, and henceforth, as a sign of my mourning, I will shut my blossom every evening and open it only in the morning."

The oak, as a sign of mourning, dropped its acorns, the fruit trees their fruit, and the plane tree lost its bark. From the proud cedars in the Lebanon down to the humble hyssop in the valley, woeful and plaintive sounds, laments, and dirges ascended to heaven.

The proud and haughty poplar alone remained unmoved and said : "He died for the sinners and the guilty, but I am innocent, and his suffering is no concern of mine."

An angel flying over the proud head of the poplar heard these words. He was carrying to heaven a golden cup filled with the precious blood which had dropped at the foot of the cross, and he let a few drops fall upon the roots of the poplar.

"That thou mayest take part in the general mourning, henceforth, on hot summer days, when no breath of wind will pass over all other trees, and plants and leaves will remain motionless, thy branches shall be agitated and thou shalt tremble all over."[1]

The *motif* of the legends describing the feeling of sadness and mourning which fell upon creation in the hours of supreme human tragedy is to be found

[1] Ledieu, A., *Nouvelles et légendes*, Paris, 1895, p. 154.

both in Jewish and Moslem legendary lore. Thus when Adam was exiled from Paradise all nature is said to have wept with him. The very beasts and birds, moved by his wailing and his tears, came to show him their pity. A rather beautiful Moslem legend relates that when Mohammed died all the trees gave up their foliage as a sign of mourning, but the turpentine tree alone retained all its leaves. The other trees reproached the turpentine tree for its lack of piety, but the tree showed them its gaping sides and the almost complete disappearance of its pith. " Real and genuine mourning," said the tree, " does not consist in external demonstration, but in the soul. See, I have lacerated my very inmost nature." [1]

THE SIGN OF THE CROSS

A few remarks on the sign of the Cross as alluded to in the legends connected with Christ will not be out of place here. The sign of the Cross, legend relates, is known in heaven, for when the penitent thief entered Paradise bearing a cross he was recognized by this sign.

While Enoch and Elijah the Tishbite were talking about the descent of Christ into Hades, there came a lowly man bearing a cross upon his shoulders.

" Who art thou ? " the Holy Fathers said unto him, " Thou hast the appearance of a robber, and what is that cross which thou bearest upon thy shoulders ? "

And the lowly man answered : " As ye say, I was

[1] See *Revue des Traditions populaires*, xvi. 310.

a thief and a robber in the world, and I was therefore seized and delivered to the death of the cross together with our Lord Jesus Christ. But when he was hanging upon the cross I, the thief and the robber, believed in him. I called upon him and said : ' Lord, when thou reignest, forget me not.' And he said unto me : ' Verily, verily, I say unto thee, to-day thou shalt be with me in Paradise.' Therefore, bearing my cross, I came to Paradise, and finding the archangel Michael, I said to him : ' Our Lord Jesus who was crucified hath sent me hither ; lead me unto the gate of Eden.' And seeing the sign of the Cross, the angel lowered the flaming sword, and I came in. Then the archangel said unto me : ' Wait a little, for Adam, the forefather of the human race, is coming with all the righteous that they also may enter into Paradise.' And now seeing you I am come to meet you." [1]

Planted in the garden of Eden, in the terrestial Paradise, the tree of the cross, as legend asserts, will appear in the Celestial Paradise borne by Christ on the day of the Last Judgment. [2]

[1] *The Gospel of Nicodemus, the Second Part ; or The Descent of Christ to the Underworld*, B. Harris Cowper, *The Apocryphal Gospels*, 1867, p. 310.
[2] Didron, *Christian Iconography*, i. 369.

14

Chapter IX

The Legend of the Holy Rood

*" Jesus, whom ye slew, hanging
him on a tree."*—ACTS v. 30.

THE HISTORY OF THE LEGENDS clustering round the
Holy Rood is interesting. As a rule the legend of
the cross and the wood it was made of is connected
with the legendary history of Adam and Eve, of
Paradise, the Garden of Eden, the Tree of Life, and
the Tree of Knowledge. Towards the end of the
Middle Ages the legend had spread over Europe and
was well known ; but in the sixteenth century, when
Catholicism had to stand the attacks and criticism of
Protestantism, this legend, among many others, was
abandoned as pure fiction. In the countries, however, where the blossoms of religious romanticism
survived the rough wind of the Reformation, the
legend has often been treated in prose and poetry
by those who, in spite of criticism, could not shake
off the charm of romance.

The legend relating the history of the cross, or,
better, the history of the tree or wood out of which
the cross was made, arose, in all probability, during
the twelfth century. In the course of two centuries
it gradually developed, and the love of the miraculous
was responsible for the addition of several new
elements. Thus we find references to the wood out
of which the cross on which Jesus died was made in
the famous *Historia Scholastica* of Petrus Comestor

(died 1178) ; [1] in the *Otia Imperialia* of Gervasius of Tilbury ; in the *Rationale divinorum officiorum* of Johannes Beleth (1170) ; and, of course, in the *Legenda Aurea* of Jacobus de Voragine. The legend, as related by this author, is based on the Gospel of Nicodemus and the works of Beleth and Comestor. The legend of the Holy Rood was also well known and popular in mediæval England, for it is found in the *Cursor Mundi* [2] and in a poetical text published by R. Morris in 1871. It is also related in the *Canticum de Creatione* [3] and in *Lyff of Adam and Eve*.[4]

In modern times Rückert and Simrock have written short poems on the subject, Mrs. Hemans a longer poem, while Calderon, the Spanish drama-tist, made the history of the Holy Rood the subject of two of his *autos sacramentales* : " Auto El Arbol del mejer fruto " and " La Sibila del Oriente y Gran Reeina de Saba." The legend is also related in a Cornish drama edited by N. Norris in 1859. In the following pages I will describe all the elements which constitute the legend of the Holy Rood in its final version, and how it was connected with Paradise, the Garden of Eden, the Tree of Knowledge, and the Tree of Life.

PARADISE LOST

Myth and legend have from times immemorial busied themselves with the subject of Paradise and

---

[1] *Historia evangelica*, cap. 81.

[2] See *Specimens of Early English*, ed. by R. Morris, 1867, pp, 140–145, verses 419–612.

[3] Edited by Horstmann, *Altenglische Legenden*, pp. 124–138.

[4] Edited by Horstmann, pp. 220–227.

the life of man in this blissful abode. With feelings of deep emotion and piety hun anity, in its cosmic and theogonic dreams, pagan, Jewish, or Christian, has always been dreaming of that distant and lost Eden described in the Book of Genesis in a brief but majestic style :

" And the Lord God planted a garden eastward in Eden ; and there he put the man whom he had formed. And out of the ground made the Lord to grow every tree that is pleasant to the sight, and good for food ; the Tree of Life also in the midst of the garden, and the Tree of Knowledge of good and evil. And a river went out of Eden to water the garden ; and from thence it was parted, and became into four heads. And the Lord God took the man, and put him into the garden of Eden to dress it and to keep it. And the Lord God commanded the man, saying, ' Of every tree of the garden thou mayest freely eat : but of the tree of the knowledge of good and evil, thou shalt not eat of it : for in the day that thou eatest thereof thou shalt surely die.' "

But Adam listened to the voice of his wife, who, in her turn, had listened to the serpent who "was more subtil than any beast of the field which the Lord God had made." And the Lord drove out the man and sent him forth from the garden of Eden.

Thus, our first parent having disobeyed the command of God and sinned, Paradise was lost, and humanity has never ceased to yearn for it. The brief account of the Book of Genesis has given rise to numerous myths and legends, and poets of all nations, in all climes and at all epochs, have been dreaming of Paradise lost, and pictured this abode of delight in glowing colours. The magic word of *pairadaeza*, or Paradise, has the power to touch the heart of man, to throw open the hidden gates of his fancy—which are not guarded by the angel with the flaming sword—and to set free the prisoner imagination. The literatures of India and Persia, of Jews and Greeks, contain poetical descriptions of an earthly Paradise, of a Garden of Eden for which man, the sinner, can only yearn, but where he is no longer allow'ed to dwell.

Descriptions of Paradise are found in the songs of the *Rig-Veda* and more particularly in the *Mahabharata*. In the *Ramajana*, the land of the highest delight is Uttara Kura, where grief and worry are for ever unknown.

The divine mountain *Meru* of the Indians is the *Alborsh* in the Persian *Bundehesh*. From this mountain issue the four rivers which water the world, and here also, at the source of the river *Arduisur*, grows the sacred white tree *Hom*, the tree of life and immortality.[1]

In Homer's *Iliad* we also read of an island of the blest in the distant ocean whither the favourites of the gods are transferred. Hesiod, in his *Works and Days*, tells us of an island of the blest where Kronos, the sovereign of the golden age, is ruling. A Paradisiac island we also find in Celtic myth and legend, a land of perpetual pleasure and feasting, variously described as the " Land of Promise," the " Plain of

[1] See F. Lenormant, *Les Origines de l'histoire d'après la Bible, et les raditions des peuples orientaux*, Paris, 1882, vol. ii. p. 65.

Happiness," the "Land of the Living." Celtic mythology tells of the beauties and wonders of this mystic and mysterious country, the tradition of which has never died out. It is unknowable except for favoured mortals, and reminds us of the British " island valley of Avilion " of which Tennyson sings :

> Where falls not hail, or rain, or any snow,
> Nor ever wind blows loudly ; but it lies
> Deep-meadow'd, happy, fair with orchard lawns
> And bowery hollows crown'd with summer sea.[1]

It is a realm of inexhaustible splendour and delight.[2]

Numerous legends describe the voyages of mortals who set out to find this island of the blest, the abode of peace and delight. Seth, the son of Adam, was allowed to look at it from the distance ; Alexander the Great knocked in vain at the locked gates. His pleading and insistence were of no avail, and he only received as a gift the fragment of a human skull.

In a novel dating from the thirteenth century it is related that when Alexander the Great had reached the Nile he decided to sail down the river until three-quarters of his provisions would have been consumed. When he was on the point of returning he espied in the distance a small house surrounded by a beautiful garden. An iron chain attached to the house and stretched across the river connected it with a marble pillar erected at the foot of a mountain towering into the clouds. The passage along the river was thus barred. The warriors rattled the chain, and

---

[1] Tennyson, *Idylls of the King.*
[2] See Ch. Squire, *Celtic Myth and Legend*, p. 133.

an old man with snow-white hair and a flourishing countenance looked out of the window.

" You are unwise," he said, " to try and penetrate the mysteries of the Lord of the Universe."

" Is there any other Lord of the Universe besides Alexander of Macedon?" asked the astonished warriors.

To which the old man replied : " Yes, there is another, and there is none equal unto him. He is younger than Alexander, but he was before him. He has placed me here as guardian, for yonder on the top of the mountain is a magnificent garden which no man is allowed to enter. A tree stands there, and whoever eats of its fruit will never die. For over three centuries have I been keeping watch here, and only two men have been allowed to pass in these three centuries ; one of them came before the Flood and the other afterwards. I will stay here until they return, but this will only happen when another king comes who will try to extend the frontiers of his Empire even farther than Alexander, for he will ascend even to the stars. Then *my* king will send out against him his two champions, and to let them pass I will take off the chain."

Thus spoke the old man with the snow-white beard, and he gave the warriors a stone in the shape of a human eye.

Alexander examined the stone sadly and meditatively, and then threw it into the Nile, but quicker than a deer or a greyhound it swam back to the Macedonian conqueror.[1]

[1] See *Recueil des Histoires des Croisades, Histoires Occidentaux*, ii. p. 586, cf. also *Myth and Legend of Ancient Israel*, vol. i. p. 126 ff.

THE TREE OF LIFE AND THE HOLY CROSS [1]

Legend and poetry have thus busied themselves with the wonderland of the earthly Paradise, and fantasy and imagination have painted it in glowing colours. On the wings of fancy the pious mind soared to the abode of a blissful and peaceful life. But the popular mediæval Christian legend was not satisfied with a lost Eden which was only a mere illusion, an empty dream. In order to give this dream a semblance of reality, legend connected the drama on Golgotha and the idea of salvation with the blissful abode lost to the human race through the sin of our first parents who had eaten of the forbidden fruit of Paradise. Heaven and Paradise, Adam and Christ, the Tree of Life, and the Holy Cross, were connected by magic threads woven by pious fancy.

It was only natural that the mysticism of the Cross should find a parallel in the Tree of Life, the only tree which, besides the Tree of Knowledge that had caused the fall of Adam, is mentioned in Holy Writ. The Tree of Life occupies an important and prominent place in the traditions of nations dealing with the primæval age of humanity, and pagan myths, both in the East and in the West, have invested it with a symbolical meaning. But it was Christianity which connected the Tree of Life with the idea of salvation and cast upon it the halo of mysticism.

In *The Book of Enoch* we read that " on the south-side of the earth there are seven hills of marvellous precious stones, and the hill in the middle is like a

---

[1] See F. Kampers, *Mittelalterliche Sagen vom Paradiese, l.c.* 1897.

throne surrounded by trees of a beautiful colour, bearing fruit, ripe and fragrant. In the midst of these trees stands the Tree of Life, the fragrance of which has no equal. Its leaves, blossoms, and wood never wither, and its fruits are wonderful to behold ; they are like the clusters of the palm tree." And the archangel Michael said : " On this hill the Lord of Splendour, the eternal King, will sit enthroned, and there His glory will rest when he comes to visit the earth. And no mortal will be allowed to touch this tree of delicious fragrance until the day of the Great Judgment. Of its life-giving fruit only the Elect will be permitted to partake." Some of the Church fathers, the mediæval commentators, and Dante in his *Purgatorio* (xxii. 131 ; xxiii. 67), have indulged in poetical descriptions of this sacred tree. It came to be considered as the symbol of Christ, who is the *lignum vitæ* in the midst of the Church, and gradually legend connected it with the Cross.

" Under a tree, under the oak of Mamre," wrote Justin Martyr, " the Lord manifested Himself unto Abraham, and with his staff, a portion of a tree, Moses, at the head of his people, crossed the Red Sea. With this staff he drew water from a stone, and with a piece of wood he changed the waters of Mara from bitter to sweet."

In the *Book of the Bee* it is related that, when Adam was driven out of Paradise, he cut a branch from the big tree which was the Tree of Knowledge, and this branch served him as staff all his life. He left the staff to his son, and it was transmitted from

generation to generation till it came into the possession of Abraham. It was with this staff that the
Patriarch smashed the idols of Terah. Jacob used
the staff when he tended the flocks of Laban. The
staff was subsequently concealed by an angel in the
cave of treasures, in the mountains of Moab. When
the pious Jethro was pasturing his flocks, he found
the staff and used it henceforth. When Jethro had
grown old, he asked Moses to go into the house and
fetch this staff. Scarcely had the prophet passed
the threshold of the house, when the staff moved
towards him. It was this staff which afterwards
swallowed up the rod of the Egyptian witch Posdi,
and it was on this staff that Moses hung up the
brazen serpent. The staff then came into the
possession of Phinehas, who buried it in the desert.
When Christ was born, the place where the staff
had been buried was revealed unto Joseph, who used
it all his life. He left it to his son James, who gave
it to Judas Iscariot, and it served afterwards as *one
of the planks in the cross on Golgotha*.[1]

The older legend, which is of Jewish origin,
connects the Cross of Golgotha not with the Tree of
Life, but with the Tree of Knowledge. The Cross,
which is considered to be the symbol of salvation, was
therefore made from the wood of the very tree which
had caused the fall of Adam. "The tree," wrote
St. Augustine, "which had brought about the fall
and the loss of Paradise, shall be the instrument of
redemption."[2]

---

[1] See *Book of the Bee* ; Grünbaum, *Neue Beiträge zur Semitischen Sagenkunde*,
1893, pp. 162 ff.   [2] Piper's *Evangel Jahrbuch*, 1863, pp. 17, 94.

The Various Versions of the Legend

The oldest version of the legend of the Holy
Rood is found in the so-called *Historia* in an MS. of
the twelfth century.[1]   Here we read that under the
reign of David a Jew found the wood of the cross
and brought it to the king.   The latter, in a pro-
phetic vision, immediately saw what purpose the
wood was destined to serve in the future, had it
covered with gold, and held it in high veneration all
his life.   King Solomon followed his father's example
until the Queen of Saba, during her visit to Jerusalem, informed the wise king of Israel that if he
knew what destiny was in store for this wood, he
would not pay it such homage.   Solomon offered
gifts to the queen, and persuaded her to reveal unto
him the meaning of her cryptic words.

The queen thereupon informed Solomon that
in days to come on this wood a man was destined to
be nailed through whom the Kingdom of the Jews
would be destroyed.   Greatly frightened, Solomon
divested the piece of wood of its golden covering and
had it thrown into a cistern.   At the time of Christ
the cistern dried up and the piece of wood was discovered.   Honorius Augustodunensis, the author of
the *Speculum Ecclesiæ* (*c.* 1125) repeated the legend
of the *Historia*, and Peter Comestor related it in his
Historia Scholastica and in his *Historia Evangelica*.

Gradually, however, the story of the Holy Rood
was connected not only with the Tree of Knowledge

---

[1] See W. Meyer in *Abhandlungen der K. Akad. der Wissenschaften*, i. Cl.
Band xvi. II. Abtheilung, 1881.

and the Tree of Life, but also with the life and death of Adam after he had been exiled from Paradise. Thus in an old English poem the legends of Adam's life and death and of the wood of the Holy Cross are amalgamated.[1]

In the *Latin Gospel of Nicodemus* we find the following description :

" And when father Adam, our first parent, heard that Jesus was baptized in the Jordan, he cried to his son Seth : ' Tell unto thy sons, unto the Patriarchs and the Prophets, all that thou didst hear from the Archangel Michael, when I sent thee to the gates of Paradise to pray God to send thee his angel to give thee the oil of the Tree of Mercy, to anoint my body when I was sick.' Then Seth, the son of Adam, drew nigh to the holy Patriarchs and Prophets and said : ' When I, Seth, was praying to the Lord at the gates of Paradise, behold, Michael, the angel of the Lord, appeared unto me, saying, I am sent to thee by the Lord ; I am appointed over the human body. I say unto thee, Seth, do not labour with tears by prayer and supplication for the oil of mercy to anoint thy father Adam, who is sick, for thou canst not receive it, not until 5500 years have been accomplished. Then shall come upon earth the beloved Son of God to raise the body of Adam and all the bodies of the dead, and at his coming he shall be baptized in the waters of the Jordan. But when he shall have gone forth from the waters of the Jordan, then with the oil of his mercy shall he

---

[1] See Horstmann, *Sammlung altenglischer Legenden*, Paderborn, 1878, pp. 124–147.

anoint all who believe in him, and that oil of mercy shall be for the generation of those who are to be born of water and the Holy Spirit unto life eternal. Then going down to the underworld, the beloved Son of God, Jesus Christ, shall lead our father Adam into Paradise to the tree of mercy.' " [1]

In the Christian *Book of Adam* another version appears. Here the fruit of the tree, instead of the oil, is spoken of. After the first pair had spent forty-three days in sorrow and distress, and in their hunger desired to eat of the fruits of the garden, God sent a cherub to them with two figs. And when they saw that these were from the trees among which they had hid themselves, and remembered that they had then perceived their nakedness, they refrained from the fruit, and prayed God : " O give to us of the fruit of the Tree of Life, that we may eat and live and may not again have to bear the sorrows of earth." Upon which the word of the Lord came to Adam, saying : "Adam, from the Tree of Life for which thou prayest, I cannot yet give thee the fruit, but after fifty-five hundred years have been fulfilled, I will give to thee to eat thereof, that thou mayest live for ever, thou, and Eve, and all the faithful of thy seed. Rest in patience till the covenant which I have made with thee shall be fulfilled."

The legend of Seth and the Tree of Life is repeated by Vincent of Beauvais and Jacobus Voragine.

In a Netherlandish poem of the thirteenth century it is the oil of mercy which was promised to Adam by God at the expulsion from Eden. When Adam asked

---

[1] *Latin Gospel of Nicodemus*, ch. xix.

Seth to go to Paradise for the oil of mercy he instructed him to follow the path eastward which would lead him to the Vale of Hebron, and here he would see the footmarks made by himself and Eve as in sorrow they took their way from Paradise. When Seth came to the cherub and stated the request of his father Adam, the cherub first asked Seth to take a view of Paradise, after which he would hear his request. Seth put his head through the gate, and casting his eyes around, he saw four rivers, and on the bank a high leafless tree upon which there was a serpent, while upon the top of the tree there was a child lying, newly born, and wrapped in clothes, whose weeping he could hear. Returning from his observation, Seth inquired concerning the child, and was told that the child that was weeping on the top of the tree was the Son of God.

> " And when the years have run their round,
> And reached the destined point of time, then joy
> Shall also visit Adam, not before.
> Forth from the child and from his sufferings th' oil
> Of mercy pressed, in richest streams shall flow
> To Adam, who shall then himself rejoice,
> His soul disburthened of the grief he brought
> To all the world." [1]

Seth thereupon hastened to Adam and related to him what the angel had said, namely, that the oil of mercy would come not from a tree but from the child he had seen in Paradise. This narrative has found wide currency in the works of poets of more modern times.

It was towards the end of the thirteenth century

[1] Berjeau, *The Legend of the Cross.*

that the legend of the Holy Rood, of the wood of the Holy Cross, was finally worked out in a consecutive narrative wherein the accounts of the trees of Paradise, of the life and death of Adam, and of the visit of the Queen of Saba are woven together. It runs as follows :

When Adam, our first parent, had reached a great age, he was weary of life and longed to die. He summoned his son Seth to his side and said unto him : " Go, my son, to the gates of the garden of Eden, the terrestrial Paradise, and there ask the angel Michael to send me some of the oil of mercy which God promised me when I was thrust out of Paradise. Thou wilt easily find the way to Paradise in following my own and thy mother's footsteps, because wherever we trod, the grass withered on account of our sin."

When Seth reached the gates of Paradise, the angel permitted him to cast a glance inside. Seth, dazzled by the splendours of Eden, saw the luminous source from which issued the four rivers, Pison, Gihon, Tigris, and Euphrates, and his eye contemplated a tree deprived of foliage and bark on account of the sins committed by his parents. He returned to the angel, who invited him to look again. And now Seth perceived a serpent winding itself upward along the tree. And when he looked for the third time he saw how the summit of the tree reached into heaven, while its roots penetrated down to hell, where he beheld the soul of his brother Abel. High above among the branches Seth saw an infant, and the angel said unto him : " This is the Son of God, who is lamenting and bewailing the sins of thy parents, but in the course of time, he will be the oil of mercy promised unto them."

The angel refused to give Seth the oil of mercy, which, he said, could not be bestowed on man before 5500 years had elapsed. In token of future pardon, however, he gave Seth three grains from the Tree of Life, and commanded him to put these grains under Adam's tongue when he was dead. " Your father," said the angel, " will die within three days, and out of these grains three branches will grow—one a cedar, the other a cypress, and the third a palm, the symbol of the Trinity." [1]

When Adam died, his weeping wife and children at first tried to restore him to life, when the angel Michael appeared and showed them what to do with the corpse. Adam was buried in the Vale of Hebron. The pippins which had been placed under the roof of Adam's tongue began to grow after a time, and three trees or wands grew up which stood in Adam's mouth.

When Moses had led the Israelites out of Egypt and they had reached the Vale of Hebron, the Prophet one evening came upon the place where the trees were growing. He greeted these signs of the Trinity and drew the wands out of the earth. A fragrant and noble smell issued, and the Israelites thought that they had reached the land of Promise. Thereupon Moses carried away the wands with him, and with their aid he healed the sick and performed many miracles.

When his end came near, Moses planted the wands

---

[1] See Seymour, *The History of the Cross*, pp. 83–85 ; Baring-Gould, *Curious Myths of the Middle Ages*, pp. 381–383.

beside a stream under Mount Tabor.   Here the trees
or wands remained for one thousand years until the
day when they were found by King David.   He
brought them home and planted them in a reserved
place.   In the morning he found the three trees
grown into one with three branches springing from
the top.   He built a strong wall around the tree and
under it he composed his Psalter.   David died, and
his son Solomon completed the building of the temple.
One day the carpenters required a large beam, and
King Solomon gave orders to cut down the tree which
his father David had planted.   But as the tree proved
either too long or too short, the king commanded the
carpenters to make a bridge of it over the brook
Cedron, or Kedron, and in this position the tree remained until the day when the queen of Sheba, or
Saba, came to visit King Solomon.   She discovered
the beam, and having paid great honour to it, advised
the king not to allow it to remain where it was.   So
the king caused the beam to be removed, buried, and
hidden from all men.   After a long time, however, a
deep well sprang up which was endowed with miraculous powers, for the visitors who bathed in the well
were all healed.   When Jesus came upon earth the
beam began to float.   It was this beam of which the
cross was made to nail the Saviour on it.

In this final version the legend of the Cross became very popular among all Western nations, and
known all over Europe, from " Iceland and Sweden
to Spain, and from Greece to Cornwall."

In a Cornish play, *The Beginning of the World*, it is
related that the beam was not used for a bridge, but

15

placed in the temple between two pillars. King Solomon then commanded his people to visit the holy tree once a year and honour it in the best manner. And one year, when the people came up to Jerusalem from far and near to pay homage to the holy tree, there was a woman among them by name of Maximilla who, in unbelief, sat upon the tree, when lo ! her clothes caught fire and burnt like tow.

Thereupon she began to prophesy, and called on Jesus to have mercy on her. She was accused of blasphemy and turned out of the town. The tree was therefore removed, but no one dared to burn it. It was cast into a dike, but the Lord sent his angels who moved the water in the dike so that the beam was not hidden by it, and all the sick who got into the ditch were immediately healed through virtue of the holy tree. Once more the beam was removed and used as a bridge over a brook, and there it lay until the queen of Sheba visited the king and went over it barefooted.

Now when the Emperor Constantine sent his mother Helena to Jerusalem to inquire about the Holy Rood, a Jew, named Judas, told her that his grandfather Zachæus had taken part in burying the rood on Mount Calvary. Thereupon the queen announced to the people assembled in her presence that if they failed to bring her the Holy Rood they would be burned. But the people cried out that Judas was really the only person to be dealt with. The queen then gave orders to seize Judas. He was kept in prison for seven days without meat or drink and was forced to give in. He thereupon proceeded to the spot at which his ancestor said the cross was buried. When they reached this place they took spade and shovel, and very soon found three crosses— that on which the Saviour was put to death and those of the two thieves.

On their way home they touched the dead body of a young man with the Holy Rood and he at once came to life, but the devil came yelling forth from the body. " I did overcome through a Judas," he yelled, " and by a Judas I am overcome."

Thereupon Judas went away, became a Christian, and took the name of Quiriac.

In an old Cornish poem entitled *Mount Calvary*, published by D. Gilbert, the legend is thus related. The cross was made from the wood of the tree whence the apple sprang that was the cause of Adam's fall.

After the death of the Saviour great virtues were attributed to the wood of the cross, and many legends and wonderful tales are connected with it. Fragments of the cross were eagerly sought after. Sandys, in his notes to the poem, relates a miracle which happened to a knight of Cornwall of the name of Sir Roger Wallysborow. The knight had visited the Holy Land and was anxious to take away with him secretly a piece of the true cross. He prayed to that effect, and a miracle happened. His thigh opened and received the piece of the cross. On his return journey he escaped shipwreck as the elements were appeased through the virtue of the cross. When he reached his native land of Cornwall, his thigh opened once more and he took out the fragment of the cross. The knight gave part of it to the parish church, which was thence called Cross Parish, and the remainder to St. Buryau.[1]

THE HOLY ROOD

The following version of the legend is also interesting :

King David was dead, and his son Solomon desired to build the temple at Jerusalem. As he required building material, stones, and wood, he ordered his workmen to cut out huge stones from the quarry. The workmen, however, were unable to do this, having broken their tools before they had cut even a single block. They told this to King Solomon, who prayed to God for guidance, and his prayer was answered. Thereupon King Solomon commanded his huntsmen to fetch him the young of a gigantic bird called Rokh, and when the huntsmen had carried out the royal command, a huge cauldron of copper was made. The bird was then placed in the cauldron, which was overturned in the courtyard of the palace so that the young Rokh was imprisoned, two of its wings only being visible. When the mother-bird returned to its nest somewhere on the summit of a high mountain and missed its young, it began to fly hither and thither in search for it, until it beheld it imprisoned under the copper cauldron in the palace courtyard at Jerusalem. Unable to release its offspring, the bird immediately flew away to the Garden of Eden, where it picked up a piece of wood from one of the trees in the garden and carried it back to Jerusalem. When it reached the spot where the young

[1] See W. Sandys, *Mount Calvary*, p. 184.

bird lay imprisoned under the copper cauldron, the Rokh dropped the piece of wood from the tree in the Garden of Eden on the cauldron which immediately split in two. The mother Rokh thereupon seized its offspring and flew away to its nest in the mountain.

Solomon then ordered his workmen to make use of the piece of wood in cutting the stones, and as soon as it was placed on a stone it split in two. The wood was ever since held in great esteem, and when the temple was finished it was preserved in the middle of the courtyard of the royal palace. Now when the queen of Sheba came to Jerusalem to hear the wisdom of Solomon, the king learnt that she had a goat's hoof and desired to see it. And what did he do ?

He caused his palace-yard to be flooded by water and had his throne set in the very middle. The piece of miraculous wood was thus covered by water. When the queen of Sheba arrived she dismounted from her horse, and before dipping her feet in the water raised her garments and thus displayed her goat's hoof. But while she was advancing through the water her foot struck against the miraculous piece of wood, and lo ! her goat's hoof was immediately changed into a human foot. The queen, greatly rejoiced, told Solomon what had happened to her.

" As I was coming through the water to approach thy throne," she told the king, " my goat's hoof struck against a hard object, and immediately it was transformed into a human foot." Thereupon King Solomon told the queen the history of the piece of wood which the bird Rokh had once fetched from the Garden of Eden. And when the queen had learnt of the miraculous power of the piece of wood she ordered a collar of silver to be made which she placed upon it.

King Solomon then commanded that the piece of wood should be placed on the altar in the temple, and he, too, had a silver collar made for it. And when later on the king's successors heard the history of the piece of wood, they, too, prostrated themselves before the altar and each of them brought an offering of a silver collar, so that when Christ arrived the wood was covered with thirty collars of silver. These thirty silver collars were given to Judas as his reward for betraying the Saviour, while the piece of wood from the Garden of Eden was given to the carpenter to fashion into a cross on which Christ was crucified.

It was thus on a cross made of a piece of wood from a tree in the Garden of Eden that Christ was crucified.[1]

The contents of Calderon's auto, *The Tree of the better Fruit*, are briefly as follows :

In the first scene, Solomon is being urged by two angels to proceed more energetically with the building of the temple. In the second scene, Solomon sends Hiram, king of Tyre, to the Lebanon to bring palm cedar, and cypress trees for the construction of the temple. Candaces, the king of Egypt, is commissioned to obtain from the queen of Sheba or Nicaula incense and perfumes.

The scene of action now shifts to Sheba or Saba. The dramatist describes the religious fervour and

[1] See Amélineau, *Contes et Romans de l'Egypte Chrétienne*, i. 144 ; cf. *Kebra Negast*, trans. by Budge.

agitation of the queen communing in solitude with her divinity. She breaks down in a swoon, scattering sheets of paper covered with writing and which, grouped in proper order, contained the prophecy of the heavenly tree destined to bring forth fruit at the right moment.

In the meantime Hiram, king of Tyre, arrives. The queen describes unto him the wealth of her country, while her royal visitor tells her about the great wisdom of Solomon. The queen decides to pay a visit to the wise king of Israel, anxious to ask him to solve the riddle of the first cause of existence.

The next scene leads us to the Lebanon. There is a tree, assure the hewers of wood, which had been planted by Jericho or Jonithus, a son of Noah. When the hewers approach the tree they are frightened away, but they nevertheless lay their axes on it. And lo ! drops of blood fall from the branches upon the men ; when the tree is felled, the earth trembles. And to their great amazement the men find that the trunk of the tree bears a triple foliage, that of a cedar, a cypress, and a palm. The tree is finally brought to Jerusalem, but found unsuitable for the structure of the temple, is employed as a prop for a wooden bridge over the brook of Kedron.

The scene changes again, and we witness the triumphal entry of the queen of Sheba into Jerusalem. Here the queen tests Solomon's wisdom with her famous riddles, and when Solomon mentions the cause of all things, the queen gladly seizes this opportunity to discuss with her host a subject which she has at heart. Solomon gladly instructs his royal visitor and informs her of the essence and nature of the infinite and all-powerful God of Israel. In solemn procession the queen of Sheba is now led to the brook of Kedron where she is suddenly seized with violent trembling. Once more the spirit of prophecy comes over the queen and, pointing to the piece of wood, she announces the future : the crucifixion and the salvation of the world. The queen once more, in her state of ecstasy, falls into a swoon, but idolatry mocks her. The piece of wood is then solemnly carried to the temple, where it is kept in veneration.[1]

The Nails of the Cross

A number of legends are also connected with the nails used at the Crucifixion. A Bulgarian legend gives the following version :

When Jesus Christ was about to be crucified, his enemies called a master to prepare the cross and also a gipsy to manufacture four nails. Neither of them made any objection, although they were aware that Christ was going to be crucified. The master made the cross as he had been commanded, while the Egyptian or gipsy manufactured five nails instead of the four which he had been asked to hammer.

"And why didst thou hammer five nails ? " he was asked ; " Wast thou not told to hammer four nails, two for the hands and two for the feet ? "

But the gipsy replied : " That may be so, but I have thought differently and hammered a fifth nail for the heart."

" Thou hast done well," they said, and were well

[1] See Kampers, *l.c.* pp. 113–117.

content.   But a poor shepherd who had overheard the conversation felt a great pity in his heart, and was sore grieved to know that a nail would also be driven into the heart of Christ.   He therefore stole the fifth nail and hid it in his garment.   When the messengers came to fetch the nails there were only four.

" One of the people lingering about here must have stolen the fifth nail," they said ; and they commanded the soldiers to search all the people and to drive the nail through the heart of the thief.   And when the kind shepherd heard this he was in a great agony of fear lest they found the nail on him.   But the Lord sent him advice in the last moment.   The shepherd swallowed the nail, which stuck in his throat.   And this is the reason why so many people have a prominence on the fore-part of their throats resembling a nail which is called " Adam's apple." They are all descendants of that shepherd who had stolen and swallowed the fifth nail manufactured for the heart of Christ.

The gipsy who had hammered the nails was cursed, and never gets anything to eat unless he begs for alms.   The master, too, who had made the cross was cursed, and none of his trade ever grow rich.[1]

Other legends give different versions.   Four nails had been hammered, and it was a gipsy who, thanks to the subtle art of sleight-of-hand, managed to remove one nail from the basket containing them.   And that is the reason why the skill in legerdemain is almost a monopoly of the gipsies.

[1] See Strauss, *Die Bulgaren*, p. 82.

Another legend runs as follows :

When the cross was made, the nails were still wanting, and a smith in the town was bidden to make three nails. When the man heard that the nails were required for Jesus who was a prophet, " true and good," he was greatly grieved. He determined not to make any nails for this purpose, and pretended that he had hurt his hand. He was asked to show his hand which he had laid in his bosom, and when he produced it, lo ! it really appeared as thought it were sore.

But now the smith's wife came out, who was a woman full of strife. She abused her husband for his pretence and offered to make the nails herself, and so she did.

Chapter X   The Legend of the
                              Wandering Jew

*" Verily I say unto you, There be some standing
here, which shall not taste of death, till they
see the Son of Man coming in His kingdom."—*
MATT. xvi. 28 ; MARK ix. 1.

IT WAS, NO DOUBT, on these words in the Gospel
that the legend of the Wandering Jew was based
and gradually developed during the Middle Ages.
No trace of this legend is found either in the
Apocrypha and the Oriental traditions of early
Christianity or in the numerous legends popular in
the Middle Ages, although there are older Jewish and
Moslem legends of persons doomed to wander all over
the world which may have given rise to the legend of
the Wandering Jew whom Christ condemned to live
until his return. As I have already pointed out in
the previous pages, the popular mediæval religious
mind of the Middle Ages could not content itself with
the meagre information contained in the Canonical
Gospels. People were anxious to know more about
the earthly life of Christ, and their imagination was
kindled by the actions of those who played a part in
the drama of the Passion, such as Judas, Pilate,
Longinus, the two thieves, Joseph of Arimathea,
and Veronica.

Another passage in the Gospel which may possibly

contain the germ out of which the legend of the Wandering Jew developed is found in John (xxi. 22), where Christ said to Peter : " If I will that he tarry till I come, what is that to thee ? Follow thou me."

Here, however, life eternal is a reward for John's piety, and no mention whatever is made of a curse or a punishment.

As for the *motif* of punishment, there is a passage in the Gospels which deserves consideration : " And when he had thus spoken, one of the officers which stood by struck Jesus with the palm of his hand " (John xviii. 22). This incident has been seized upon by popular imagination, and more than one legend current in the Middle Ages has been woven round it. An Italian version runs as follows :

Malchus was the leader of the Jews who killed the Lord. All the others were pardoned. Even the thief was forgiven. Never, however, did the Lord pardon Malchus, because it was he who had struck the Madonna. Confined in an underground room under a mountain, Malchus is now condemned to walk incessantly round a column as long as the world lasts. Every time when Malchus walks round the column he gives it a blow in memory of the blow which he once struck the Mother of Christ. The condemned man has now walked round the column for so long that he has sunk into the ground up to his neck. On the day when he will be below the surface, head and all, the world will come to an end, and God will send him to the place prepared for him. Whenever people come to see him, Malchus asks them whether children are still being born ; and when they answer " Yes," he sighs deeply and resumes his walk, saying : " The time is not yet ! For before the world comes to an end there will be no children born for seven years." [1]

Tradition has confounded this man with the High-priest's servant, Malchus, whom Christ and Peter met in the garden of Gethsemane (John xviii. 10). Chrysostom considers the two to be identical.

In the course of centuries, however, when the faith in Christianity began to waver, the Church found it necessary to strengthen the faith of the doubters by offering them a living example in the person of a witness of the coming of Christ. Thus the monk Johannes Moschos (beginning of the seventh century) of Cyprus says that Malchus was condemned to wander eternally.

It is only in the thirteenth century that the eternal wanderer, the immortal witness of the Passion, is for the first time designated as a Jew. In a Chronicle compiled by an unknown Cistercian monk we read the tale of Armenian pilgrims who came to Ferrara in Lower Italy in 1223. They declared that they had met in Armenia the very Jew who had seen Christ on his way to Calvary, who had driven him from his door, and called him the seducer of the people. For this action Christ had condemned him to perpetual life : " Ego vade, et tu expectabis me donec reverter." Every hundred years the wanderer becomes again young.

This legend, narrated in the Chronicle of the Cistercian monk, seems to have spread in ecclesiastical

[1] See Crane, *l.c.* p. 197.

circles, and we find the first lengthy account of it in England in the *Flores Historiarum* of Roger de Wendover (1236), a monk in the Abbey of St. Albans. After Roger's death Matthew Paris continued the chronicles of the Abbey under the title of *Chronica Majora*, and here we find the following account :

In 1228 an Archbishop of Armenia came to England on a pilgrimage and was received with great honour. During his stay at St. Albans the Armenian bishop conversed with the monks through an interpreter, and related unto them many wonders concerning his country and the East in general. The monks asked him whether he had ever seen or heard anything of Joseph, who is said to have been present at the Passion of the Lord and to have spoken to him. This Joseph was said to be still alive in evidence of the Christian faith. Thereupon a knight from Antioch, a member of the bishop's family who was also his interpreter, replied, speaking in French : " My Lord, the bishop, well knows this man, and shortly before going on this journey my Lord saw him, for he ate at the Archbishop's table." And when the knight was further asked what had actually passed between Christ and this Joseph, he replied as follows :

" At the time of the Passion and the judgment of Christ this man, then called Cartaphilas, was a porter of the hall in the service of Pilate. And as Jesus was passing the door of the chamber of judgment, he struck him impiously on the back with his hand, saying in mockery : ' Go quicker, Jesus, go quicker, why dost thou tarry ? ' Whereupon Jesus, looking

back on him with a severe countenance, said to him :
' I am going, and thou wilt wait until I return.' "

"Vade Jesu, citius vade, quia moraris ?   It Jesus severo
oculo et vulto respiciens in eum dixit :   Ego vado et expectabis
donec veniem !   Ac si juxta Evangelistam diceretur : Filius
quidam hominis vadit, sicut scriptum est, tu autem secundum
meum adventum expectabis." [1]

It is as if he had said in the language of the Gospel,
"The Son of Man is going, but thou wilt await his
Second Advent."   "And this Cartaphilas is indeed
still awaiting Christ's return.   At the time of the
Passion he was thirty years of age, and when he
attains the age of one hundred years he grows young
again and returns to the same age as he was when
our Lord suffered and was struck by him."

"He is seized by an apparently incurable malady
and falls into a state of ecstasy, whereupon he suddenly recovers and finds himself to be thirty years
old, just the age which he was at the moment of the
Passion.   Cartaphilas was subsequently baptized by
Ananias, who had also baptized the Apostle Paul,
and received the name of Joseph.   He passes his time
in the two Armenias, and in other Eastern countries,
amidst bishops and prelates of the Church.   A man
of a holy life and very religious, he is circumspect
in his behaviour, speaks but little, and only when
questioned by the bishop and the prelates.   Then
he tells them of olden times and relates the events
which had occurred at the time of the Passion of
Christ, when he was put to death and came to life

---

[1] See Matthæi Parisiensis, *Chronica Majora*, edit. H. R. Luard, London,
1876, vol. iii. pp. 161–164.

again. He also tells them of the witnesses of the Resurrection, of the creed and the symbol of the Apostles and of their separation and preaching. All this he relates without smiling or levity, but as one who in tears and fear of God is awaiting the coming of Christ who will judge the world.

" He is afraid lest at the Last Judgment he will find Christ in anger because on his way to the Crucifixion he had provoked him to just vengeance. From different parts of the world people come to him, and if they are reliable people and men of authority, he relates unto them all this and explains all doubts in answering their questions. Gifts offered to him he always refuses, for he lives very simply, content with moderate food and slight clothing. He places his hope on the fact that he had sinned through ignorance, and that the Lord himself had prayed for his enemies in these words : ' Father, forgive them, for they know not what they do.' "

A few years afterwards the brother of the Armenian bishop came to England in his turn, and the monks who accompanied him asserted that they were certain of the fact that Joseph, who had seen Christ on his way to Calvary, was still alive and awaiting the return of the Lord.

The story of Cartaphilas-Joseph is also related by Philip Mouskes, Bishop of Tournay, in his rhymed *Chronicle*, and based on the account of the same Armenian bishop who came to Tournay after visiting Cologne. The version given by Philip Mouskes somewhat differs from that of Matthew Paris :
" When the Jews were leading Christ to be crucified,"

Cartaphilas relates, " I said unto them : ' Wait a moment, I will go with you to see the false prophet crucified.' Whereupon the true God turned his gaze on me and said : ' They will not wait for thee, but know thou wilt await me.' "

> " Et cil om quant il faus Judeu
> Minèrent crucifier Deu,
> Lor dist : Atendès-moi, g'i vois
> S'iert mis il faus profète en crois
> Et li vrais Dieux se regarda
> Si li a dit que n'i tarda
> Icist ne t'atenderont pas,
> Mais saces, tu m'atenderas,
> Et encor atent cil ensi,
> K'il ne moru puis ne transi
> Al cief de laus le voit on
> Rajovenir en cel roïon,
> Et la, dient, teus gens i a
> Qu' Ananias le baptisa,
> Ki fu li uns des vrais profètes."

> (Baron de Reiffenberg, *Chronique rimée
> de Philippe Mouskes*, Bruxelles, 1838,
> vol. ii. p. 491.)

It will be noticed that in this account there seems to be little ground for the severe punishment inflicted by the Saviour on Cartaphilas. It has therefore been suggested that by Carta-philas (from the Greek κάρτα φίλος, the well-beloved) the beloved disciple of Christ, the Apostle John is really meant. John is referred to in several passages of the Gospel, all of which seem to indicate that he was destined not to taste death (John xxi. 22 ; Matt. xvi. 28 ; Luke ix. 27 ; Mark ix. 1). The religious mind of the Mediæval Ages, anxious to find some justification for

16

these passages, suggested that John might be still alive, and a belief soon arose that certain persons who had witnessed the Passion of Christ had miraculously escaped death and could testify to the truth. Their deathless life, however, was variously interpreted. Sometimes it was regarded as a mark of the highest favour, which is in accordance with the true character and teaching of Christ ; in other cases, under the influence of pagan and particularly Teutonic mythology, it was interpreted as a curse and a punishment.

In a narrative dating from the thirteenth century reference is made to a man who, when Christ was being dragged to Calvary, had driven away the Lord from his door. As a punishment for his action he was condemned to live and await the return of Christ.

Guido Bonatti of Forli, mentioned by Dante (*Inferno*, xx. 118), writes as follows in his astronomical work, *De Astrologia Tractatus* : " Some men have attained a very old age, and in my time I saw a certain Ricardus, who had lived at the court of Charlemagne and pretended to be four hundred years old. People also asserted at that time there was another man, whose name was John Buttadæus, who had lived in the days of the Saviour, and driven Jesus from his door when he was bearing his cross on the way to Calvary. To him Christ said : ' Thou shalt tarry until I return.' As for Ricardus, I saw him at Ravenna in 1223, while the afore-mentioned John passed through Forli on a holy pilgrimage in 1267." [1]

---

[1] See L. Neubaur, *Die Sage vom ewigen Juden*, 1884, p. 111.

The word Buttadæus is evidently derived from the Italian *buttare*, to beat, and Buttadæus would therefore mean " the man who beat God," though it has been explained differently.

The story of Cartaphilas, of the man who was begging for death but was condemned to live, seems to have been known to Chaucer, who connected the *motif* of treasure trove with that of deathlessness in the *Pardoner's Tale*.

In the thirteenth century a form of the legend was quite popular in Italy. It contained a certain amount of sympathy for the poor wanderer who, it was affirmed, had only advised Jesus to walk faster in order to escape the brutalities of the mob.[1]   Here his name was Buttadæus, and poets and authors made frequent allusion to him.   Neither a wanderer nor a Jew was he, but merely a " waiting sinner."

Gradually, however, popular fantasy commuted the punishment of waiting either in some subterranean vault or even in one place to that of globetrotting. In the fourteenth century the waiting sinner appears in the guise of a monk, of a wonderworker, of a scholar, a humanist, helpful and working for humanity, but always restless and suffering under the curse supposed to have been hurled against him by the gentle Christ.

Jan Aertz of Mecheln, who had joined a Portuguese expedition in 1484, gives the following report in his notes (published in the seventeenth century) : " In Jerusalem there was being kept in captivity a man who had been an eye-witness to the crucifixion

---

[1] See *Romania*, xii. 112.

of the Lord Jesus Christ. He was detained behind nine locked doors, and the key to the last door was in the possession of an official who, thanks to the gift of a few ducats, was induced to open it. There, under a gallery supported by four pillars, we found a man, Jan Roduyn by name, stark naked and of a gruesome appearance, who persevered in an obstinate silence. They told us that when Christ was being taken to Golgotha this man had thus addressed the Saviour : 'Forward, forward ! thou hast tarried too long on thy way.' Thereupon Christ replied : 'I will go, but thou wilt tarry till the end of the world and anxiously inquire after my return.' And, indeed, on every Good Friday the prisoner asks : 'Has the man with the cross not come yet ? ' " [1]

Thus the news of the wanderer, the undying witness of the Lord's Passion, had come to Europe, but it was only in the sixteenth century (1547) that the man himself was said to have made his appearance. The account is given in a letter signed Chrysostomus Dudulæus and dated August 1, 1613. In this letter, the wanderer, the wandering Jew, is for the first time named Ahasverus. The entire text of the letter was given by Grässe. [2]

Paul von Eitzen, doctor of the Holy Scriptures and Bishop of Slesvig, related for some years past that when he was young and studied at Wittenberg, he returned home to his parents in 1547. When he visited the church on the following Sunday he noticed during the sermon a tall man, his hair hanging over

---

[1] Quoted by L. Neubaur, *Die Sage vom ewigen Juden*, 1884, p. 12.
[2] See *Die Sage vom ewigen Juden*, 1844, pp. 13–20.

his shoulders, and standing barefoot facing the pulpit.
He was listening with the deepest attention to the
sermon, and whenever the preacher mentioned the
name of Jesus he bowed profoundly and humbly,
sighing and beating his breast. Although it was in
the midst of winter and bitter cold, the man had no
other clothing except a pair of hose torn about his
feet and a coat held fast with a girdle and reaching
to his feet. His age seemed to be about fifty years.
Several people present, some of title, now remembered
having seen the same man in various countries of
Europe, in England, France, Italy, Hungary, Persia,
Spain, Poland, Muscovy, Livonia, Sweden, Denmark, Scotland, and other places. All these people
wondered at the strange man.

Now when the sermon was over, Paul von Eitzen
made inquiries and having ascertained the whereabouts of the stranger, he sought him out and asked
him privately whence he came and how long he had
been in this place. Thereupon the stranger modestly
replied that he was a Jew by birth, and was born in
Jerusalem ; that he was a shoemaker by trade, and
that his name was Ahasverus.

" I was present," he added with a sigh, " at the
Crucifixion of Christ, and have lived ever since
travelling restlessly through various cities and countries." He thereupon related unto Paul von Eitzen
all the circumstances of the Passion of Christ, and
many other details which are not recorded either by
the evangelists or the historians. He also described
in detail the labours and deaths of the Apostles.

Dr. Paul von Eitzen, as may be imagined, was

greatly astonished on hearing this wonderful tale, questioned him further, and obtained even more accurate information. " I lived in Jerusalem," said Ahasverus, " at the time of the Crucifixion of Christ, whom I, like many others, had regarded as a deceiver of the people and a heretic. I had seen Christ with my own eyes, but, alas, I regarded him as a deceiver. When the sentence had been passed on Christ and he had been condemned by Pilate to be crucified, he was being dragged past my house. I ran home and called together my household to have a look at Christ. I myself had my little child on my arm and was standing in the doorway of my house to have a good look at the Lord Jesus Christ. When he appeared, bowed down under the heavy cross, he stood still for a moment trying to rest a little, but I, afraid of the others and anxious to obtain credit among my fellow-citizens, drove him forward, telling him to hasten on his way. Jesus obeyed, but looking at me, he said : ' I shall stand and rest, but thou shalt go till the last day.'

" At these words I was no longer able to remain where I was. I set down the child and followed Christ. I saw him crucified, I saw him suffer, and I saw him die. I could no longer return to Jerusalem nor see my wife or child, for I felt that I must go forth into foreign lands tramping and wandering like a sad pilgrim. Years afterwards I returned to my native town, but found it in ruins and full of desolation, not a stone having been left standing on another."

Thus spoke Ahasverus, and he added that he

believed that it was God's purpose to drive him about from land to land and to make him lead a miserable life. At the end of days God intended to present him to the unbelievers as a living token of the death of Christ so that they might repent. As for his own part, he would rejoice if God in his mercy were to release him from this vale of misery and tears, but, alas, he could not die, and death, which he had courted more than once, would not take him.

The wanderer was thereupon questioned by learned people, well read in history, and by a traveller who had seen the East, but Ahasverus was able to give them much information and to convince the inquirers of the truth of his story. As a rule this wandering Jew is reserved and only answers direct questions. He eats little and drinks in great modera- tion. He never remains long in one place, but con- stantly hurries on. Money was offered to him on several occasions, but he never accepted more than four pence and distributed the sum among the poor.

The wanderer never laughed and wherever he passed he spoke the language of the country like a native. People came from different places to see him, and all were convinced that the divine provi- dence exercised itself in the strange man in a remark- able manner. He always listened with great reverence to the Word of God or of Christ, and grew indignant whenever he heard some one curse or swear by God's death. " Hadst thou witnessed," he would exclaim, " as I have witnessed the suffering which the Lord hath endured for thee and for me thou wouldst sooner undergo great pain than take the name of the Lord in vain."

Christopher Krause and Master Jacob von Holstein, legates at the court of Spain, confirmed with solemn oaths the truth of the story of Ahasverus. They had come across him in Madrid and spoken to him. Another reliable person asserted that the wanderer had been seen at Vienna whence he had started for Poland. Many persons subsequently asserted that they had seen him in Moscow.

Thus it was in Germany, towards the end of the sixteenth century, that the wandering Jew appeared under the name of Ahasverus, and there the legend found a receptive and credulous public. The ground for this story was well prepared. In 1599 Europe was startled by the news that the Antichrist, the messenger of Satan, who was to unite under his banner all the powers of evil and darkness against Christianity, had made his appearance in Babylon. Antichrist was advancing, and the Jews, so the men of the Middle Ages believed, would acknowledge his power and pay him homage. The news came to Germany from Italy and soon spread over Spain, England, and all Western countries. Terror-stricken Europe was awaiting the arrival of Antichrist. Learned men, well versed in Holy Scripture and history, tried to pacify the terrorized public. The signs, they said, which will announce the birth of Antichrist had not yet been seen, and moreover, the Roman Empire had not yet crumbled down. Others, however, were convinced that it was true, and that Antichrist was coming to destroy Christianity.

In Paris the excitement of the populace was so great that King Henry IV., who had received a report from the Grand Master of Malta, gave orders not to speak about the subject.[1]

" Toutes ces fadèzes et faux bruits estoient creus de léger par la commune, qui est prompte a recueillir et ramasser toutes nouvelles, surtout les fascheuses tenant tous rapports pour véritables et asseurées choses " (vol. ix. p. 344).

At that time Europe was in a state of terror as the end of the world was expected either at the close of the sixteenth century or at the beginning of the seventeenth.

The German *Volksbuch*, which appeared in 1602 and gave the account of Ahasverus, was evidently composed by an ignorant man whose aim was to attack Catholicism and at the same time give vent to his inveterate anti-Semitism. His ignorance is proved by the fact that he gave his Jew the name of Ahasverus. Even if, as learned German authors maintain, the name of Ahasverus was not unknown in Germany of the seventeenth century,[2] there has never been a Jew with either the surname or the *Christian* name of Ahasverus. Jews may call themselves Kurt Cohen or Archibald Abrahams, Moses Meredith, or Christian Israelson, but never has a Jew answered to the name of Ahasverus, the old king of Persia, were it only for the sole reason that among Jews this merry monarch of pagan antiquity has become synonymous with " fool."

[1] See L'Estoile, *Mémoires-Journaux*, vols. vii., ix.
[2] See Soergel, *Ahasver-Dichtungen*, p. 13, note.

In the German *Volksbuch* the heathen sinner, the " eternal pagan," has thus become an " eternal Jew," wandering restlessly from place to place, bearing the cross of suffering, undying, although courting death. The whole legend, the germ of which is found in the Gospel and has been applied to John, who, like Enoch and Elijah, has never tasted death, gives an absolutely false impression of Christ.

In the case of the Apostle eternal life was a reward for his faith, so that he might preach the Gospel of Love in the spirit of the Master, but Ahasverus was said to have been condemned to wander eternally as a punishment for the crime he had once committed in striking Christ. In Christian legend the Apostle John is destined to fight against Antichrist, just like Enoch and the Prophet Elijah in Jewish legendary lore, but the wandering Ahasverus, who in some versions of the legend has been confounded with Malchus, is compelled against his will to suffer in order that he might bear witness to the historicity of the Crucifixion.

In the first centuries of the Christian era many legends were current among Jews and Christians of wicked and cruel men who were condemned to live for ever in order to testify to the existence of God and the truth of religion. Thus the tradition of the blood-stained shadow of Nero, the cruel persecutor, gave rise to a legend according to which he never died but was doomed to wait for the Last Judgment as a counterpart to the legends current about John, Enoch, and Elijah.

In Jewish legend the same *motif* is repeated.

Pharaoh, we read, was being tossed about in the waves of the sea, when he heard the children of Israel raise their voices to praise the Lord. " I believe in Thee, O God," cried Pharaoh, " I acknowledge that there is no God beside thee in all the world." But the angel Gabriel said unto him : " Thou art a sinner ! Yesterday only thou didst deny the Lord, but to-day, tossed about on the waves of the sea, thou art ready to repent." Thereupon the angel Gabriel carried Pharaoh to the city of Nineveh, where he became king. Pharaoh never died, for it had been decreed that he should live eternally. Stationed at the gates of hell, he receives the kings and rulers of the nations, whom he rebukes for their wickedness and the lack of knowledge of the Lord. " You ought to have learned wisdom from me," he tells them.[1]

Such legends were current in Europe for centuries. The undying wanderer, who lived through the ages as a punishment for his sin was first Cartaphilas, a pagan, but by the end of the sixteenth century he had become a Jew.

From Germany the legend of the Wandering Jew travelled to France, and in 1604 the man is said to have appeared in Paris. A Paris lawyer named Rudolph Botoreus, in his historical work describing the happenings from 1594 to 1609, makes the following remarks with regard to the year 1604 : [2]

" I am afraid that I shall be accused of giving credence to old wives' fables if I insert here a story

---

[1] See Jellineck, *Beth-Hamidrash*, vols. i. and ii. ; Gaster, *The Chronicles of Jerahmeel*, pp. 37, 128.

[2] *Commentarium de rebus toto paene orbe gestis*, liber xi. p. 385.

reported all over Europe of the Jew, a contemporary of the Saviour, and which is also mentioned in our popular histories, which have not scrupled to assert it. They say that this man who is restlessly wandering over the globe was one of those scamps who had insisted on setting free the murderer Barabbas instead of Christ. In addition to this, the wanderer we are referring to had also committed another crime, for when Christ wanted to rest for a moment in front of his house, the man, who was a shoemaker, drove him away. This man, who has appeared in Spain, Italy, and Germany not in one century only, was also seen in this year and recognized as the same individual seen in Hamburg in 1564. The common people know and relate more about him, but to this I only allude to."

A contemporary of Botoreus, the Jesuit Jules Cæsar Boulenger, who died in 1628, also mentions this story. He says that a Jew, a contemporary of the Saviour, was wandering about the world, having been an outcast and a vagabond for over a thousand years. This man, of the generation of criminals who had cried out and insisted on the crucifixion of Christ and the release of Barabbas, was condemned by God to rove over the earth for ever for this and another crime he had committed. When Christ, dragging the cross, and tired out under its burden, sought to rest in front of this man's house, he ordered him off. Thereupon Christ replied : " Because thou refusest me a moment of rest, I shall enter into my rest, but thou shalt wander restlessly." The man immediately fled through the whole earth and has been wandering ever since. It is said that he is the same man who was seen in Hamburg in 1564.

But Boulenger hastens to add that he himself had never seen the man nor heard anything concerning him when he was in Paris. " Credet Judaeus Apella," he adds cautiously.[1]

" The Discours véritable," which is a translation of the German *Volksbuch* and appeared in 1609, relates that two noblemen had met the eternal wanderer in Champagne, to whom he told his story, informing them that he had visited many Eastern countries and had now come from Spain and Germany on his way to England. And Ahasverus who, as has been pointed out above, everywhere spoke the language of the country like a native, added :

> " Quand l'univers je regarde et contemple
> Je croy que Dieu me fait servir d'exemple
> Pour temoigner sa Mort et Passion
> En attendant le Resurrection."

Towards the end of the seventeenth century a man calling himself the Wandering Jew also attracted attention in England. Despised by the educated, he was listened to by the ignorant. Men of the nobility took an interest in him as if he were a juggler, questioned him, half in curiosity and half in jest, and paid him. With slight variations he told the same story as reported by Matthew Paris, namely, that he had been an officer of the Sanhedrin and had struck Christ when the latter was leaving the judgment-hall of Pilate. He had known all the Apostles, and he described their appearance with all sorts of

[1] See *Historia sui temporis*, p. 357.

details. He had travelled all over the world and claimed the power of healing the sick. His familiarity with foreign languages was marvellous, and professors from Cambridge and Oxford came to converse with him and to question him. One nobleman conversed with the mysterious stranger in Arabic, and the wanderer told him that he had known the father of Mohammed, who was a man of intelligence. When the man once denied that Christ had been crucified, he declared that he was a living witness to the truth.

He further informed his listeners that he was in Rome when Nero set the city on fire, that he had known Saladin and Tamerlane, and could give details concerning the history of the Crusades.[1]

Since the days of Matthew Paris the legend of the Wandering Jew has thus wandered all over Europe and furnished a favourite subject to poets, dramatists, and novelists. Space will not permit me to give an exhaustive account of the literature which has arisen out of this legend, but a brief sketch of the place it occupies in English literature may prove interesting.

In Chaucer's *Canterbury Tales* (" The Pardoner's Tale ") the old man who is courting death in vain but cannot die is somewhat reminiscent of the undying Ahasverus. In vain he implores Mother Earth to receive him, but earth remains adamant, and God will not let him die.

> " I knokke with my staf, bothe erly and late,
> And seye : leve moder, leet me in."
>
> (Verses 729, 730.)

---

[1] See Dom Calmet, *Dictionary of the Bible.*

It is, however, doubtful whether Chaucer was really acquainted with the legend. After the publication of the German *Volksbuch* (in 1602), the legend of Ahasverus came to England, and in Percy's *Reliques* we find a ballad entitled "The Wandering Jew, or the Shoemaker of Jerusalem." [1]

In his novel *The Spiritual Quixote*, Richard Graves, a clergyman of the eighteenth century, made fun of and ridiculed the legend in which the common people believed and delighted to talk. Among these legends was also that of the Wandering Jew, the accursed shoemaker who thrust the Saviour out of the judgment-hall and was condemned to a vagabond life. [2]

Matthew Gregory Lewis, in his novel *The Monk*, brings in a person who is none other than Ahasverus, the eternal wanderer. The *motif* of wandering and roving and of a constant yearning for release was stressed by Wordsworth in his *Song of the Wandering Jew*. The Lake-poet Southey utilized the legend in his *Curse of Kahama*, where, however, the curse is hurled not by the Christian God but by a Hindu magician. Here, however, the accused, whom the *Volksbuch* contemptuously represents as a good, pious, and charitable Christian, becomes a mighty opponent and is finally victorious over Kahama. As the spirit of revolt, as an accuser and not a repentant sinner, Ahasverus appears to us in the poetical works of Shelley. Ahasverus is no longer the condemned sinner, waiting for forgiveness in meek repentance,

---

[1] It is also included in the *Roxburghe Ballads*, edited by Hales and Furnival, vol. vi.

[2] See Richard Graves, *The Spiritual Quixote*, p. 15.

but an accuser of God and Christ, a sort of Satan in Milton's *Paradise Lost*.[1] This new type of Wandering Jew was imported to England from Germany, inspired by Schubart's poem, a translation of which Shelley printed in his notes to *Queen Mab*, and which I reproduce at the end of the present chapter.

I must also briefly refer to Croly's novel *Salathiel the Immortal* (1827), to Sarah Norton's *The Undying One* (1830), to R. W. Buchanan's *The Wandering Jew : A Christmas Carol*, and to Temple Thurston's drama *The Wandering Jew*.

The interpretations of the legend of the Wandering Jew in European poetry, novel, drama, and art are numerous, but cannot be treated in a work dealing with the legends of Christ. Ahasverus has been represented as a propagandist for Christianity, as the personification of the entire Jewish race, as the living incarnation of radical political views and tendencies, " Die Freiheit ist der neue Ahasver " ; as the expression of world-weariness, of *Weltschmerz* (Wordsworth) ; or as the obstinate Titan, as " the victim of the Eternal Avenger," as a social reformer, as an apostle of Communism, and so on.

As far as the legendary life of Christ is concerned, the legend of Ahasverus represents the Saviour in an unchristian light, unlike the Christ with whom the readers of the Gospels are familiar. He is a Teutonic Christ, moulded after the Teutonic gods, Thor, Odin, and Loki.

Karl Blind [2] pointed out that the legend of the

---

[1] See Zirus, *Der ewige Jude*, 1928, p. 60.
[2] In an article in the *Gentleman's Magazine*, July 1880.

Wandering Jew was " moulded upon a figure of the
heathen Germanic creed."   The author of the article
tries to prove that the tale of the Wandering Jew
has been evolved, as regards the main component
parts of his individuality, in Germany from the figure
of the Wild Huntsman, who is regarded as a representation of the chief Teutonic deity Wodan, or
Odin, after he had been deposed by the spread of
Christianity.   Odin was always considered by the
old Teutons as a great wanderer, " the ever-
travelling," the " Indefatigable Wanderer."   The
link between Wodan and the Wandering Jew is the
tale of the Wild Huntsman, which is found in a
variety of forms.   It is upon the great wanderer
Wodan that the phantom figure of the Wandering
Jew has been grafted, and the link between the two
is the tale of the Wild Huntsman.   He is condemned
to wander over the seven mountain-towns every
seven years, because he would not allow Jesus Christ
to quench his thirst at a river, nor at a water-trough
for cattle, from both of which he drove Christ away,
telling him that he ought to drink from a horse-
pond.   For this reason the Wild Huntsman must
hunt for ever, wander about and feed on horse-flesh.

Thus the name of Christ has been pressed into a
legend which is typically Teutonic, nay, in several
places, on Swiss and German soil, the same phantom
form is alternately called the Eternal Hunter and the
Eternal Jew, as well as the Pilgrim from Rome or
the Wandering Pilate.

Now, without questioning the plausibility of
Blind's suggestion, I feel inclined to say that in any

17

case the Christ of the legend certainly resembles a Teutonic heathen deity rather than the Christ of the Gospel, who, while he was suffering on the Cross prayed : " Father, forgive them, for they know not what they do." He is *a Teutonic Christ* who, like Thor, hurls his curses rather than his blessings.

The Prophet Elijah and the Wandering Jew

In my opinion the legend of the Wandering Jew is to a certain extent connected with the traditions and legends clustering round the prophet Elijah. In Jewish legendary lore Elijah, the eternal wanderer, is active and benevolent. The messenger of peace, he encourages the irresolute, instructs those who are eager for knowledge, brings succour to the needy, but rebukes the impious and teaches lessons of humility to the boasters and the arrogant. One day he will be the harbinger of salvation to the whole race of Israel. He has never tasted death, is omniscient and ubiquitous.

Mohammed, who drew largely from Jewish sources, had heard of this legend of the eternal, immortal wanderer, and represented him as a sage travelling for thousands of years. He is watching the eternal geological changes of nature and the social changes of humanity, the deeds of the prophets and saviours of ancient times, and of the false prophets and selfish so-called saviours of modern times, and of the butchers of mankind in all times. He is smiling at human ignorance and watching the march of events from the Pisgah heights of his age. He is Khidr, the eternally young.

Now during the Middle Ages the legend came to the Christians, and naturally it underwent a certain change. On the one hand, there was the desire of the Church to find as many witnesses as possible for its existence, while, on the other, there was bitter feeling between Christians and Jews. Hatred of the Jew would not permit Christians to admit that the eternal and wise wanderer was like Elijah. He must be an evil Jew. The wanderer of the legend, therefore, was first Cartaphilas, an ignorant pagan hallporter, who eventually became Ahasverus, an insolent Jew. The changed character of the wanderer is very noticeable in the German form of the legend ; indeed, it might appear that it was the German spirit which developed it on these lines. Its changed character would appeal to the Teutons for two reasons, firstly because it was anti-Semitic, and secondly because it represented the gentle Saviour as a sort of revengeful Thor. Christ is made to appear as a typical figure of Teutonic fancy with the attributes and characteristics of the Teutonic mythology. Like many other legends of apparently Christian origin, that of the Wandering Jew was cast in this heathen Teutonic mould and grafted on to the New Testament.

AHASVERUS, BY SCHUBART

This poem was translated into English and published in the *German Museum* in 1801.[1] Shelley reproduced it in his notes to *Queen Mab* (vii. 67). " This fragment," he wrote, " is the translation of

[1] See Zirus, *Der ewige Jude*, 1928, p. 45.

part of some German work, whose title I have vainly endeavoured to discover. I picked it up, dirty and torn, some years ago, in Lincoln's Inn Fields.[1]

AHASVERUS, RISE !

Ahasverus the Jew crept forth from the dark cave of Mount Carmel. Near two thousand years have elapsed since he was first goaded by never-ending restlessness to rove the globe from pole to pole. When our Lord was wearied with the burden of his ponderous cross, and wanted to rest before the door of Ahasverus, the unfeeling wretch drove him away with brutality. The Saviour of mankind staggered, sinking under the heavy load, but uttered no complaint. An angel of death appeared before Ahasverus, and exclaimed indignantly, " Barbarian ! thou hast denied rest to the Son of man : be it denied thee also, until he comes to judge the world."

A black demon, let loose from hell upon Ahasverus, goads him now from country to country ; he is denied the consolation which death affords, and precluded from the rest of the peaceful grave.

Ahasverus crept forth from the dark cave of Mount Carmel—he shook the dust from his beard— and taking up one of the skulls heaped there, hurled it down the eminence ; it rebounded from the earth in shivered atoms. " This was my father ! " roared Ahasverus. Seven more skulls rolled down from rock to rock ; while the infuriate Jew, following them with ghastly looks, exclaimed : " And these

[1] See T. Hutchinson, *The Complete Poetical Works of Shelley*, 1904, pp. 912, 913.

were my wives." He still continued to hurl down skull after skull, roaring in dreadful accents : " And these, and these, and these were my children ! They could die ; but I ! reprobate wretch ! alas, I cannot die ! Dreadful beyond conception is the judgment that hangs over me. Jerusalem fell—I crushed the sucking babe, and precipitated myself into the destructive flames. I cursed the Romans— but, alas, alas ! the restless curse held me by the hair ;—and I could not die !

" Rome the giantess fell—I placed myself before the falling statue—she fell and did not crush me. Nations sprang up and disappeared before me ; but I remained and did not die. From cloud-encircled cliffs did I precipitate myself into the ocean ; but the foaming billows cast me upon the shore, and the burning arrows of existence pierced my cold heart again. I leaped into Etna's flaming abyss, and roared with the giants for ten long months, polluting with my groans the Mount's sulphurous mouth—ah ! ten long months. The volcano fermented, and in a fiery stream of lava cast me up. I lay torn by the torture snakes of hell amid the glowing cinders, and yet continued to exist. A forest was on fire : I darted on wings of fury and despair into the crackling wood. Fire dropped upon me from the trees, but the flames only singed my limbs ; alas ! it could not consume them. I now mixed with the butchers of mankind, and plunged into the tempest of raging battle. I roared defiance to the infuriated Gaul, defiance to the victorious German ; but arrows and spears rebounded in shivers from my body. The

Saracen's flaming sword broke upon my skull; balls in vain hissed upon me; the lightnings of battle glared harmless around my loins; in vain did the elephant trample on me, in vain the iron hoof of the wrathful steed! The mine, big with destructive power, burst upon me, and hurled high in the air I fell on heaps of smoking limbs, but was only singed. The giant's steel club rebounded from my body, the executioner's hand could not strangle me, the tiger's tooth could not pierce me, nor would the hungry lion in the circus devour me. I cohabited with poisonous snakes, and pinched the red crest of the dragon. The serpent stung, but could not destroy me. The dragon tormented, but dared not devour me. I now provoked the fury of tyrants; I said to Nero, 'Thou art a bloodhound!' I said to Christiern, 'Thou art a bloodhound!' I said to Muley Ismael, 'Thou art a bloodhound!' The tyrants invented cruel torments, but did not kill me. Ha! not to be able to die—not to be able to die— not to be permitted to rest after the toils of life—to be doomed to be imprisoned for ever in the clay-formed dungeon—to be for ever clogged with this worthless body, its load of diseases and infirmities— to be condemned to behold for millenniums that yawning monster Sameness, and Time, that hungry hyena, ever bearing children, and ever devouring again her offspring!—Ha! not to be permitted to die! Awful Avenger in Heaven, hast Thou in Thine armoury or wrath a punishment more dreadful? then let it thunder upon me, command a hurricane to sweep me down to the foot of Carmel, that I there may lie extended ; may pant, and writhe, and die ! ''

THE WANDERING JEW'S SOLILOQUY

Is it the Eternal Triune, is it He
Who dares arrest the wheels of destiny
And plunge me in the lowest Hell of Hells ?
Will not the lightning's blast destroy my frame ?
Will not steel drink the blood-life where it swells ?
No—let me hie where dark Destruction dwells.
To rouse her from her deeply caverned lair,
And, taunting her cursed sluggishness to ire,
Light long Oblivion's death-torch at its flame,
And calmly mount Annihilation's pyre.
Tyrant of Earth ! pale Misery's jackal Thou !
Are there no stores of vengeful violent fate
Within the magazines of Thy fierce hate ?
No poison in the clouds to bathe a brow
That lowers on Thee with desperate contempt ?
Where is the noonday Pestilence that slew
The myriad sons of Israel's favoured nation ?
Where the destroying Minister that flew
Pouring the fiery tide of desolation
Upon the leagued Assyrian's attempt ?
Where the dark Earthquake—dæmon who engaged
At the dread word Korah's unconscious crew ?
Or the Angel's two-edged sword of fire that urged
Our primal parents from their bower of bliss
(Reared by Thine hand) for errors not their own
By Thine omniscient mind foredoomed foreknown ?
Yes, I would court a ruin such as this,
Almighty Tyrant ! and give thanks to Thee—
Drink deeply—drain the cup of hate ;
Remit this—I may die.
(SHELLEY, published by Bertram Dobbell
in 1887.[1])

---

[1] See Th. Hutchinson, *The Complete Poetical Works of Shelley*, Oxford, 1904, p. 978.

Chapter XI

Christ in Mohammedan Tradition

The Birth and Life of Mary

Mary, the Holy Virgin, and Jesus are regarded with much reverence in the *Koran* and by Moslem writers. Many men, said Mohammed, have attained excellence and moral perfection, but only four women have arrived to that dignity and they were : Ashyah, the wife of Pharaoh, because she believed in Moses and from the very beginning respected him as a prophet ; Mary, the holy Virgin (Mariyam) ; Khadija, Mohammed's first wife, and Fatimah, his daughter. In the *Koran* Mary is often mentioned as a holy and devout woman always cheerfully obeying the commands of God. Her mother's name was Hannah and her father's Imran, while Thannan and Faukul were the names of her grandparents.

Now Hannah, the daughter of Thannan, who was a chieftain of his tribe, was advanced in years and had been childless all the days of her wedded life. One day, when Hannah was sitting by the door of her house, she observed a bird sitting on a date palm that grew beside her dwelling, tenderly feeding her young. The sight of the bird's solicitude for her little ones greatly agitated the childless woman who had all her life been yearning for maternity. Lifting up her eyes to heaven, Hannah cried out : " O God Almighty, if thou wouldst only gratify the desire of my heart and send me a son, I would dedicate him to the service of the temple. Freed from all desires and earthly pursuits, my child would then be wholly devoted to the service of the Sanctuary,"

Thus prayed Hannah, the daughter of Thannan, and her prayer was heard. Her vow was accepted by God and soon the woman who had been childless knew that her hopes would be realized. There was, however, a bitter drop in her cup of joy, and fear greatly troubled her mind. What if her child should prove to be a girl?

Hanna h's husband, Imran, died before the birth of the infant, and Hannah brought forth a female child. By this time her fears had gone. Undaunted by the birth of a girl, she resolved to fulfil her vow, and named the infant Mariyam, which signifies in Arabic " one devoted to worship." Mary, or Mariyam, was a child of extraordinary beauty, both lovely and amiable. Before the birth of her daughter Hannah prayed to God that the child might escape the touch of Satan. The cries of every child when it enters into this world betoken its sufferings under the malignant touch of Satan. To three persons only the Supreme Being vouchsafed an exception, and they consequently escaped the general penalty. They were Mohammed, the prophet of Allah, Mary, and her son Jesus. In these three instances it pleased God Almighty to place an impenetrable veil between Satan and the newborn child. Hannah was thus favoured. She had commended both herself and her child to God's protecting grace.

Thereupon Hannah, the mother of Mariyam or

Mary, swathed her child and carried it to the temple, where she dedicated her daughter to the service of God and commended her to the care of the priests in charge of the temple. The priests who were not only fascinated by the extraordinary beauty and loveliness of the child, but considered it also an honour to watch over the growth and upbringing of a daughter of their distinguished chief, rivalled with each other as to which of them should have the care and custody of the beautiful child. One of the priests, Zacharias by name, being the husband of the infant's aunt, claimed the honour for himself, but the other members of the sacerdotal confraternity contested his claim. Being the husband of the infant's aunt, they contended, was no valid ground of preference. It was therefore finally decided among the priests that the matter should be settled by the augury of a miracle.

The custodians of the temple, twenty-nine in number—according to others, twenty-seven—proceeded to the Jordan where each of them threw into the waters of the river a rod—some say a headless arrow—on which an extract of the Law had been inscribed. And lo ! the rod of Zacharias alone floated on the waters. Thus the custody of the child was committed to Zacharias by divine agency.

So Zacharias took the child under his care and built a separate apartment in the temple where Mariyam was placed in privacy and comfort. No access to this apartment could be gained except by means of a ladder. Seven doors led to this private apartment, the keys to which were in the keeping of

Zacharias. He alone opened and locked these doors. Every day he brought food and drink and oil unto Mariyam, and having placed before her these necessaries of life, he retired again, locking the seven doors and carefully guarding the keys. Great, then, was the astonishment of Zacharias when, on his returning visits, he found in the apartment an abundance of luscious and delightful fruit so rare and beautiful that it could only have come from the Garden of Eden.

Some unknown person, thought Zacharias, must be in the habit of invading the seclusion and privacy of Mariyam, and bring her such a supply of delicious fruit—summer fruits in winter and winter fruits in summer. He therefore questioned Mariyam concerning this provision of fruit and whence it came. But Mariyam answered that the provision of fruit came from the gardens in the heavens, and were gifts brought to her by the angels.

Mary, say other Mohammedan writers, was brought up on food sent from heaven, even as it happened in the case of Mohammed himself. One day, Moslem tradition relates, Fatimah, the prophet's daughter, brought a dish containing two loaves and a piece of meat, but Mohammed gave it back to Fatimah to be put by for a little while. Soon afterwards the prophet asked for the dish, and when Fatimah uncovered it, she found not only two loaves and a piece of meat, but a very ample supply of bread and meat. To Mohammed's inquiry as to whence this unexpected provision came, Fatimah quoted the words of the *Koran* : " This is from God, who provideth without measure for the wants of those who are found pleasing in His sight." Thereupon Mohammed gave thanks to God who had thus favoured his daughter Fatimah even as He had favoured Mary, the most excellent of the daughters of Israel.

When the Holy Virgin attained to years of maturity, she had, according to ceremonial law, to retire from the temple to the house of her aunt, the wife of Zacharias. On one of these occasions, we are informed in the *Koran*, God sent His angel Gabriel unto her in the form of a perfect man, and on seeing him Mary was alarmed and said to him : " I fly for refuge to the merciful God, that He may defend me. If thou fear Him, thou wilt not approach me."

And the angel answered : " Verily, I am the messenger of my Lord, and I am sent to give thee a holy Son."

" But how shall I have a son," said Mary, " seeing that I have known no man, and I am not a harlot ? "

But Gabriel replied : " Thus shall it come to pass : God hath purified thee and chosen thee, above all the women in the world." [1]

And the angel said unto Mary : " God sendeth thee good tidings, for thou shalt conceive and bring forth The Word. He shall be called Jesus, the Son of Mary, exalted in this world and in the world to come, for he shall be one of those who are privileged to come into the immediate presence of God. And as a child in his cradle he will speak to men, a perfect man, and he will be of the number of the just."

[1] See *Koran*, Sura XIX. v. 16–21.

And Mary said : " How could I have a son ? "

But the angel replied : " With God everything is possible, for He creates by the word of His mouth. And He will teach him the Book of Wisdom, the Pentateuch and the Gospel. Jesus will be His messenger to the children of Israel." [1]

Thereupon the angel Gabriel breathed into her bosom and the vitalizing breath was the cause of the conception. According to some authorities Mary was at that time thirteen years of age, but according to others she was sixteen.

Now Mary had a cousin named Yussufal who, too, had been dedicated to the service of the temple. Whenever Mary had an occasion to go to her aunt's house, Yussufal performed not only his own share of work in the temple, but also that of Mary. When Joseph discovered that Mary was with child, he began to suspect her chastity and bitterly reproached her for her misconduct.

" How," said Joseph, " can a plant grow without seed ? "

To which Mary replied : " Did not God at the beginning raise the corn, and cause the plant to grow without seed ? And how did God create Adam without a father ? "

THE NATIVITY

Mary's condition now attracted public attention and became the subject of public remarks. She was accused of secret crimes. At one time she had been greatly respected, but now people did not hesitate to

[1] See *Koran*, Sura III. v. 40–43.

talk openly of her guilt. Popular indignation rose so high that God, knowing that the safety of Mary would be imperilled, commanded her to leave her home, and to find shelter and security elsewhere. Thereupon, Joseph, placing her on an ass, took her away. While passing through a desolate and lonely spot on their journey, the thought entered Joseph's mind of taking away her life, and thus putting an end to all the calumny and shame which he felt sure he would have to endure.

Then the angel Gabriel came to Joseph and said : " Joseph, do not kill her, for her conception is of the Holy Spirit."

Joseph thereupon banished from his mind all murderous thoughts, and prosecuted his journey with Mary. They arrived at a place called Baital Laham (Bethlehem), where Mary felt the pains of labour strong upon her. In her agony she clasped the bare trunk of a withered date palm and exclaimed : " Would to God I had died before this, and had become a thing forgotten and lost in the obscurity of oblivion."

Then the infant in her womb spoke and thus he said : " Be not distressed ! God has provided for you a rivulet that, running past close to your feet, will refresh you. Shake the trunk of the withered palm, and in amplest profusion it will drop upon you ripe dates for your sustenance. Eat and drink and calm your troubled mind." [1]

And hardly had these words been spoken, when behold ! the dry trunk of the withered palm revived

---

[1] See *Koran*, Sura XIX. v. 22–25.

and blossomed ; its naked branches were suddenly covered with green leaves, while luscious clusters of ripe fruit hung all around. From the root of the fruitful palm tree a spring of water burst out and meandering grew into a stream. And Mary ate, and drank, and was refreshed.[1]

It was under this palm tree, rich in fruit and foliage, that Jesus was born. And at that very instant, in token of his supremacy, all the idols in every idolatrous shrine fell down broken and prostrate on the earth.

Thereupon the emissaries of Satan, who had hitherto infested these shrines, went up to their master and thus they spoke : " Hitherto we have been in the habit of creeping within the images of the idols and making them speak and thus deceive the sons of Adam who worship them, but to-day we find all these images prostrate on the ground. In our eagerness and anxiety to find out the cause of such an unprecedented event, we have travelled all over the world and searched the depths of the ocean, but neither on the earth nor in the sea have we discovered anything which could account for such a strange and singular event."

And Satan replied : " Stay here, my children. I will myself wander over the earth and soon ascertain the cause of this singular event."

Thus spoke Satan, greatly perturbed, and immediately he went forth and wandered to and fro all over the earth, until he came to the spot where Jesus was born. Here he found innumerable angels sur-

[1] See *supra*, p. 71.

rounding an infant. Great was the number of the celestials so that Satan was prevented from even approaching the object of admiration round whom the angels had gathered. Greatly dismayed, he flew back to his followers and myrmidons and thus addressed them : " Never until this day has any child, male or female, been born into the world without my knowledge, but this is the only child of whose advent into the world I have been kept in ignorance. He will certainly be a mighty power against us."

The legend of Mary and the palm tree, which I have related in the chapter dealing with the Flight to Egypt, is connected with the birth of Jesus in Mohammedan tradition, where Jesus is looked upon as the precursor of Mohammed. Not only the *Koran* but many Moslem authors refer to this legend.

When the hour of childbirth approached, writes Tabari, Mary, out of a sense of shame, betook herself to the outskirts of the city, and when the moment of travail arrived she saw in the distance a tree. It was a withered palm tree whose leaves had fallen off and whose branches were broken. Mary directed her steps to this tree as her pains did not permit her to go farther. She sat down under the tree, as it is written in the *Koran* : " Her labour-pains surprised her under a palm tree." And when she had given birth to Jesus, her pains and her sense of shame made her exclaim : " I wish to God I were dead and entirely forgotten."

When Jesus saw the light of day under the tree there was neither a spring nor a brook under the tree, but the Lord caused a spring to gush up and water flowed over the ground so that Mary could wash herself and the child. Thereupon a voice called out to her and said : " Shake the palm tree, Mary, and ripe dates will fall down for thee." And Mary shook the palm tree and immediately dates grew on it, became ripe, and fell down. She partook of the fruit, and her body gained strength. Ever since it has been the custom to give dates to women in childbirth.[1]

In another Arabic source we read :

And in a stormy night Mary saw in a solitary spot a withered palm tree. When she sat down at the foot of the tree near its root, the palm tree suddenly became green, covered with leaves and foliage, and by the will of God lowered its fruit to Mary. And from the soil beneath her God caused a bubbling spring to gush forth. And when the labour-pains overtook her she clasped the palm tree with her hand.[2]

A popular tradition explains the shape of the date, which resembles the letter *o*, as follows : " O, could I only have a palm," said Mary, and immediately the words which issued from her virginal lips impressed themselves upon the date, which ever since bears a round sign resembling the letter *o*.[3]

It will be noticed that in the various versions of this legend the tree and its fruit are always adapted to the soil of the country where the legend had found

[1] Tabari, *Chronique,* i. 541.
[2] See Rudolf Hofmann, *Das Leben Jesu nach den Apokryphen,*
[3] See *Revue des Traditions populaires,* iv. p. 409.

currency. In the *Apocryphal Gospels*, in the *Koran*, and in all the legends told in the East it is a palm tree, while in English Christmas carols and mystery plays [1] it is a cherry, and in the Provence it is an apple.[2]

After the birth of Jesus, Mary and Joseph removed into a cave, where they remained with the infant for forty days. After forty days Mary and Joseph re-traced their steps and returned home to their people. It was during their journey homewards that the infant Jesus thus addressed his Virgin Mother : " Blessed art thou, because thou art the mother of one who is the Servant sent by God." [3]

And thereupon Mary, carrying the infant, came to her own people, but they thus addressed her : " Mary," they said, " thou hast done something unheard of. O sister of Harun, thy father was not a wicked man nor was thy mother an unchaste woman."

But Mary pointed to the infant.

" How can we converse with an infant still in the cradle ? " her people asked in amazement.

But the infant spoke, and said : " Verily, I am the servant of Allah. He has taught me the Scriptures and appointed me to be a prophet. Wherever I shall be there His blessing will accompany me. He has commanded me to pray, to distribute alms all my life and to be respectful towards her who has given me birth, and He has not made me impudent or godless. Blessed am I on the day of my birth, blessed

---

[1] See Halliwell, *Coventry Mysteries*, p. 146.

[2] Arbaud, *Chants Populaires des la Provence*, i. 23 and ii. 237 ; *Cursor Mundi*, II. 668*b*, v. 11, 657 ; Horstmann, *Altenglische Legenden*, 1875, p. 6, 1878, p. 102, 112 ; see also *Notes and Queries*, 4th Series, xii. 461.

[3] The *Abdul Masiha*, see *Koran*, Sura XIX.

am I on the day of my death, and blessed shall I be when I rise again unto life." [1]

THE RETURN OF CHRIST

There are several legends in Moslem tradition referring to Jesus which may find a place here. The first shows the belief of the Moslem in the second advent of Christ :

Abu-hurairah said : " I swear by God, it is near, when Jesus, son of Mary, will descend from the heavens, on your religion, a just king ; and he will break the cross and will kill swine, and will take a poll-tax from Muahids ; and there will be great wealth in his time, so much that nobody will accept of it ; and at that time, one prostration in prayer will be better than the world and everything in it."

Abu-hurairah said : " If ye doubt about his coming to pass, then read this revelation, and there shall not be one of those who have received the scriptures who shall not believe in him (Jesus), after his coming down, in the latter part of the world.

" Camels will not be ridden in his time, because of the immensity of wealth ; in those days man will have all he wants ; and verily, enmity, hatred, and malice will go from man ; and verily, Jesus will offer money to people, and nobody will take it." [2]

Another tradition refers to Jesus as being near to Mohammed : " Verily, I am the nearest man to Jesus, in the beginning and end ; because there is no

---

[1] See C. F. Gerock, *Christologie des Korans*, 1839, p. 47.

[2] *Mishcat-ul-Massabih, Collection of Traditions*, Calcutta, 1810, vol. ii. pp. 558–581.

prophet between me and Jesus, and in the latter part of time he will be my vicegerent, and successor ; and the prophets are all brothers by one father, but their mothers are different ; and the root of all their religions is the same ; and there is no prophet betwixt me and Jesus." [1]

Moslem tradition further relates that on his nightly journey to heaven Mohammed saw Moses, Abraham, and Jesus : " Verily, the prophets have been shewn to me ; and behold, I saw Moses in a middling body, you might say of the tribe of Shanuah ; and I saw Jesus, the son of Mary, and the man who resembles him most is Urwah-Ibn-Masuud ; and I saw Abraham, and I resemble him more than anybody else. I saw Jesus a middling-sized man, his colour inclining to red and white ; with the hair of his head hanging down." [2]

The Miracles of Jesus

Many miracles performed by Jesus are related in Mohammedan tradition, but the majority of these legends are mostly different versions of those quoted above, as for instance, that of Jesus and the deceiver whose greediness and love of gold caused his death.

The more wonders Christ performed before the eyes of the people, the greater was their unbelief ; what they were not able to comprehend they attributed to be due to sorcery and delusion. Even the

---

[1] *Mishcat-ul-Massabih, Collection of Traditions*, Calcutta, 1810, vol. ii. p. 650.

[2] *Ibid.* p. 648.

twelve Apostles whom he had chosen to preach and propagate the Gospel, so legend declares, were not steadfast in their faith, and one day they asked their master to cause a table covered with viands to descend from heaven !

And a voice from heaven immediately said : " A table shall be given you, but whosoever shall thereafter continue in unbelief shall suffer punishment."

Thereupon two clouds descended carrying a golden table, on which there stood a covered dish of silver.

Many of the Israelites who were present exclaimed : " Behold the Sorcerer, what new delusion has he wrought ? " But instantly these scoffers were changed into swine.

Christ, however, on seeing it, prayed : " Oh Lord, let this table lead us to salvation, and not to ruin."

Then said he to the Apostles : " Let him who is the greatest among you rise and uncover the dish ! "

But Simon, the oldest Apostle, said : " Lord, thou art the most worthy to behold this heavenly food first."

Thereupon Christ washed his hands, removed the cover from the silver dish, and said, " In the name of Allah ! "

And behold ! A large baked fish became visible, with neither bones nor scales, diffusing a fragrance around like the fruits of Paradise. And round the fish there lay five small loaves, and on it salt, pepper, and other spices.

" Spirit of Allah," said Simon, " are these viands from this world or from the other ? "

But Christ replied : " Are not both worlds, and all that they contain, the work of the Lord ? Receive whatever He has given with grateful hearts, and ask not whence it comes. But if the appearance of this dish is not sufficiently miraculous to you, you shall behold a still greater sign."

Then, turning to the baked fish, he said : " Live, by the will of the Lord ! " Immediately the fish began to stir and to move, so that the Apostles fled with fear.

Christ, however, called them back and said : " Why do ye flee from that which ye have desired ? "

He then called to the fish : " Be again what thou wast before," and immediately the fish lay there as it had come down from heaven.

Thereupon the disciples prayed Christ that he might eat of it first, but Christ replied : " Have I lusted for it ? He that has lusted for it, let him eat of it now."

The disciples, however, refused to eat of it, because they now saw that their request had been sinful.

Then Christ called many aged men, many deaf, sick, blind, and lame, and invited them to eat of the fish ; thirteen hundred of them came. They all ate of the fish, and were satisfied. Whenever a piece was cut off from the fish, another grew again in its place ; so that it still lay there entire as if no one had touched it. As for the guests, they were not only satisfied with it, but were even healed of all their diseases. The aged became young, and the blind saw ; the deaf heard, and the dumb spoke, while the lame had their limbs restored.

And when the Apostles saw this they regretted that they had not eaten of the fish ; and all those who beheld the men who had been cured and invigorated regretted in like manner that they had not shared in the feast.

When, therefore, at the prayer of Christ, a similar table descended from heaven, the whole people, rich and poor, young and old, sick and whole, came to be refreshed by these heavenly viands. This lasted during forty days. At the dawn of day the table borne on the clouds descended in the face of the sons of Israel, and before sunset it gradually rose up again. But notwithstanding this, many still doubted whether it really came from heaven. So Christ prayed no longer for its return, and threatened the unbelievers with the punishment of the Lord. But from the hearts of the Apostles all doubt had disappeared, and they were now certain of Christ's mission. They now, therefore, travelled over Palestine, preaching faith in God and in his prophet Christ, and permitting unto the people certain food which had formerly been forbidden to the sons of Israel.

But when Christ asked his Apostles to travel into foreign lands and preach there the Gospel, his disciples excused themselves with their ignorance of foreign languages. Christ thereupon complained to the Lord of the disobedience and lack of faith of his disciples. And behold ! on the following day they had all forgotten their own native tongue and

each of them was able to converse in the language of
the country to which Christ was going to send them.

THE DEATH OF JESUS

When Christ had reached the age of thirty-three
years, his enemies plotted against him and wanted to
take away his life. But the Lord frustrated the evil
designs of Christ's enemies and took him into heaven,
while another man whom the Lord had made to look
exactly like Christ was executed in his place.

It is said that on the eve of the Passover feast
Christ and his Apostles were made prisoners and
condemned to be executed on the following morning.
But during the night the Lord manifested himself
unto Jesus and thus he spoke : " Thou shalt receive
death sent by me, but immediately after thou shalt
be borne up into heaven."

Christ thereupon expired and remained dead
for three hours. In the fourth hour the angel
Gabriel appeared, raised Christ up, and carried him
into heaven. But one of the unbelievers who had
stolen into the house in order to prevent Christ from
escaping was made to look so like Christ that even
the Apostles were deceived. And on the next day
the unbeliever who looked so much like Christ was
crucified in his place.

When Mariyam, the mother of Christ, was prostrate
with grief, her Son appeared unto her from heaven
and thus he spoke : " Mother, do not mourn or
grieve after me, for the Lord has raised me up into
heaven, and on the day of resurrection we shall be
reunited. Console my disciples and tell them to

persevere in their faith to be worthy of a place in heaven by my side. When the Day of Judgment is nigh I shall once more be sent down on earth, and then I shall kill the false prophet Dadjal and the wild swine who are causing equal mischief in the world. The world will then know a state of peace and friendship, and lambs and hyenas will live peacefully together. The Gospel which has been falsified by godless priests and the cross which some worship like an idol I will on that day burn, and the whole world shall accept the doctrine of the prophet Mohammed who will be sent in days to come."

After Christ had spoken thus to his mother Mariyam, he was again borne up to heaven on a cloud. But his mother Mariyam lived another six years after the death of her son, cherishing her faith in God, in her Son Christ, and in the prophet Mohammed whose coming had been announced by Moses in former days. The peace of God be with them all.[1]

THE LIVING WITNESS OF JESUS

When the Arabs had captured the city of Elvan, their leader Fadhilah, at the head of three hundred horsemen, pitched his tents, late in the evening, between two mountains in Syria. When Fadhilah began his evening prayer with a loud voice and spoke the words *Allah Akbar* (God is great), a mysterious voice immediately repeated not only these two

[1] G. Weil, *Biblische Legenden der Muselmänner*, Frankfurt-a/M., 1845, pp. 291–298.

words but each word of his prayer in a similar manner. Greatly astonished and not believing that the mysterious voice which had repeated his prayers so distinctly was a mere echo, Fadhilah cried out : " O thou ! who repeatest my words and answerest unto me, if thou art of the ranks of the angels, then the power of God be with thee, or if thou art of some order of other spirits, it is also well, but if thou art a man, let mine eyes light upon thee, that I may enjoy the benefit of thy presence and thy conversation."

Scarcely had Fadhilah spoken these words, when an aged man with bald head and holding a staff in his hand stood before him. He much resembled a dervish. Fadhilah saluted him courteously and asked him who he was.

" I am here," said the old man, " at the command of Lord Jesus, who has left me in this world, that I may live therein until he comes a second time to earth. I dwell behind yon mountains where I wait for this Lord who is the *Mamba al Saadat* " (the Fountain of all Happiness).

Thereupon Fadhilah asked him when the Lord Jesus would appear, and the old man replied that this would happen at the end of the world, at the Last Judgment.[1]

The Sayings of Jesus

In addition to legends and traditions found in Moslem literature connected with Christ, Mohammedan authors also mention speeches made and

[1] See Herbelot, *Bibl. Orientale*, vol. iii. p. 607 ; see also Grässe, *Die Sage vom ewigen Juden*, 1844, pp. 3, 4.

sentences uttered by Christ. Some of them are found in the *Koran*, while others are reported by the Commentators. Here are a few examples gathered from various sources.

Jesus the Son of Mary said : "He who is trying to acquire treasure is like unto a man who is drinking sea-water ; the more he drinks, the greater his thirst, and he drinks until he falls dead."

And Jesus the Son of Mary said to John, the son of Zacharias : "When a man speaketh the truth about thee, praise the Lord, but when he uttereth lies about thee, praise the Lord even more, for then thy treasure in the book of thy works will increase without any effort on thy part, because all the good the liar will have done will be credited to thee." [1]

One day the men who did not believe in the divine mission of Christ asked him to bring a dead man back to life again. They led him to the grave of Sem, the son of Noah, and asked him to perform the miracle.

The grave immediately opened and Isa asked : " Who art thou, and who am I ? "

" I am Sem," came the answer, " the son of Noah, and thou art the spirit of God."

" Why is thy beard grey ? " asked Jesus ; "it was black when thou didst die."

" Thou art right," said Sem ; " but, frightened at thy call and the voice of the angel of death, my hair must have turned grey."

[1] See Hofmann, *l.c.* pp. 327, 328.

And Isa replied : " Son of Noah, shall I pray to God to grant thee once more a long life ? "

But Sem replied : " No, I have lived long enough, and prefer to rest in the grave." [1]

[1] See Hofmann, *l.c.*

Chapter XII

The Legends of Joseph, Joseph
                of Arimathea, Judas, and
                Pilate

Joseph

THE CANONICAL GOSPELS say little about the life or
death of Joseph, the father of Christ in the flesh. We
know that he was of the tribe of Judah and a de-
scendant of David, the pious king of Israel. He was
a carpenter by trade and dwelt in the little city of
Nazareth, which was not even a city but a village in
Galilee. He had the reputation of being a just man,
pure-hearted, upright, kind, tender, and mild.
Nowhere in the Canonical Gospels is there any indica-
tion of, or reference to, the age of the husband of
Mary. Legend, however, has been busy with the
life and death of Joseph. He was a widower, and,
according to some versions, eighty-four years of age,
a feeble old man, while in other legends he is represented as a man of fifty, or even as a young man of
not more than thirty years. His conduct towards the
Holy Virgin was blameless, defending her and pro-
viding for herself and her son, for he loved and worshipped the child. I have related many legends in
which Joseph played a part, and will only add here
the legendary account of his death and of the respect
and love of Christ for his foster-father.

It is quite natural that Joseph should occupy a

prominent place in the legends clustering round the Saviour. Like the Virgin Mary he, as the father of the Son of God, *secundum carnem*, was revered by the faithful, and legend was anxious to attribute to him superior qualities. He became the " pater Christi," the husband of " Dei-paræ Virginis." Just as Mary is looked upon as the ideal of womanhood so Joseph is often presented in legend as the ideal of perfect manhood. And as all physical ills to which mortal flesh is heir to are the result of sinfulness, and as Joseph was free from sin, legend shows him even in an advanced age as suffering from no infirmity of body.

THE DEATH OF JOSEPH

The legend connected with the death of Joseph is fully narrated in the *Arabic History of Joseph the Carpenter*, where several incidents bear a close resemblance to the legends connected with the death of Adam.

Joseph, increasing in years, arrived at an advanced age, but he laboured under no infirmity of body. Never did his sight fail, nor did a tooth in his mouth decay. Like a youth he always displayed vigour in his affairs and he attained the age of one hundred and eleven years. When the departure of this pious man approached, an angel of the Lord made it known to him that the hour of his death was drawing near. Fear and great trouble of mind then came over Joseph. He arose and went to Jerusalem, where he entered the temple of the Lord and poured out his prayers, and thus he said :

" O God, who art the God of all mercy and the

author of all comfort and the Lord of the whole
human race, if my days are now finished and the
time is at hand when I must go out of this world,
send me, I pray, the angel Michael, prince of Thy
holy angels, that he may abide with me and not
allow my soul to depart from my miserable body with
terror and distress. All creatures which are under
heaven and into which a vital spirit hath been
breathed are seized with a great fear and terror on
the day of their death ; they are stricken with horror
when their souls depart from their bodies. Let
therefore, O my Lord and God, Thy holy angel
attend upon my soul and body until they are separated
from each other. Let not the angel appointed for
my keeping from the day when I was made, be
turned away from me. Let him be the companion
of my journey, until he hath brought me to Thee.
Suffer not that demons terrible in aspect should come
to me until I come happily to Thee. Nor let the
doorkeepers prevent my soul from entering Paradise.
O God ! Judge most just, who dost judge mortals
in equity and justice, let Thy mercy be with me, and
enlighten my way that I may attain to Thee."

When Joseph had thus prayed he returned to the
city of Nazareth and kept his bed. Now at day-
break on the twenty-sixth day of the month of Abib,
as he lay in his bed the soul of Joseph was restless, and
he cried aloud : " The same terrible hour which
overtook my father Jacob when his soul took flight
from his body is now upon me."

And at that moment Jesus went into Joseph and,
seeing his soul greatly troubled, he thus spoke :

" Hail, my father Joseph, thou just man, how are thou ? "

" Verily," replied the dying man, " verily, my beloved little son, the pain and fear of death surrounded me, but as soon as I heard thy voice, my soul found rest."

Thereupon the Virgin Mary rose, and coming up to Jesus, she said : " My beloved son, this pious old man Joseph is dying."

" My mother, most beloved," replied Jesus, " the necessity of dying lieth upon all creatures which are born in this world, for death hath dominion over the whole human race. Thou, too, my mother, must expect the same end of life with all other mortals. But thy death, as also the death of this pious man, is not death, but life for ever. It behoveth me too to die, as regards the body."

Thereupon Mary and Jesus entered the place where Joseph lay, and Mary sat at his feet looking at him while Christ held his hand. Now when the soul of Joseph was preparing to depart from his body, Jesus saw the angel of death approaching with his attendants. Joseph, too, saw him and groaned in a wonderful manner ; but Jesus repulsed the angel of death and thus he prayed to God : " O Father of all mercy, Eye which seest, and Ear which hearest,[1] hearken to my prayers and supplications for the old man Joseph. Send thy angels Michael, the prince of angels, and Gabriel, the herald of light, and let them take the soul of my father and bring it to Thee."

[1] See *Ethics of the Fathers*, ii. 2.

Thus prayed Jesus, and Michael and Gabriel came and received the soul of Joseph and brought it to the habitation of the pious.

And when Joseph's children knew that their father was dead, they began to wail and weep and lament, but Jesus said unto them : " Surely the death of your father is not death, but life eternal. He is delivered from the sorrows of this world, and hath passed away to rest, which is perpetual, and which will endure for ever."

Thereupon the inhabitants of the city of Nazareth and of all Galilee came and wept over Joseph from the third hour till the ninth. And at the ninth hour they took up the body and anointed it with excellent ointments. And two angels came, at the command of Christ, and spread out a bright white vestment and wrapped in it the body of Joseph.

Thereupon the chief men of the place came and bore away the body of Joseph to a place where there was a cave, and prepared to deposit it among the bodies of his fathers. At that moment Jesus remembered the day on which Joseph had delivered him from the wrath of Herod and endured great trouble on his account on the way to Egypt, and he bowed over the body, wept for Joseph's death a long time— and said :

" O death ! Who renderest all human knowledge vain, and callest forth so many tears and lamentations, it is certainly God who hath allowed thee this power. For through the transgression of Adam and his wife, Eve, men are doomed to perish, and death spareth not even one. Men, indeed, have existed

19

who have prolonged their life to as much as nine hundred years, but they, too, have died. Some of them may even have lived longer, but they ultimately succumbed to the same fate. And because Adam failed to do the will of God, my Father, but transgressed His commandment, God, my Father, hath caused death to enter the world. Had Adam kept the precept of my Father, death would never have befallen him. For the transgression of Adam, the violence of death descendeth upon the whole human race. Even Enoch and Elijah who have not tasted death must return into this world at the end of time and die, for they will be among the four witnesses whom Antichrist will slay ; he will shed their blood like water, for the reproach to which they will expose him and the ignominy wherewith they will brand him " (see Rev. xi. 3–12).

Having spoken thus, Christ once more embraced the body of Joseph, and wept over it. Thereupon the chief men opened the door of the sepulchre and laid the body of Joseph beside that of his father Jacob.[1]

This description of the death of Joseph, which includes the eschatological ideas current in such Jewish works as the *Shalsheleth ha-Kabbala* of Rabbi Gedalja ben Yahya, finds many parallels in the legends connected with the death of Adam and Moses.

Joseph of Arimathea. The Graal-Cup

When Joseph of Arimathea, the subordinate and friend of Pilate, heard of Christ's death, he obtained

---

[1] *The History of Joseph the Carpenter*, chaps. x.–xxxii.

from the latter the body of the Redeemer. The Jews objected to this, and Pilate ordered Nicodemus to support Joseph with his authority. He also gave Joseph a dish which had been brought to him from the house of Simon the leper, and which the Saviour had used for the Last Supper. (In another version it is Joseph himself who took the dish from the house of Simon.)

This vessel, legend narrates, was changed into one of emerald, with the intent of impressing Judas and saving him from perfidy. In other versions, however, it is said that the vessel really was of emerald. It was fashioned like a *catinus*, and out of this *catinus* Christ with his disciples ate the Last Supper, and thereof he said : " He that dippeth his hand with me into the *catinus*, he shall betray me."

Into this vessel, according to one tradition, Nicodemus, when he took down Christ's body from the cross, collected the sacred blood which was still moist, and which had been spilled about.[1] According to another tradition, however, it was Joseph who collected the blood from the sacred wounds while preparing the body of Christ for the tomb. This legend gave rise to the traditions of graal-cups current in the Middle Ages.[2]

The vessel containing some of the blood from Christ's wounds, together with a knife which had been used, was committed by Joseph of Arimathea to his nephew Isaac. By a miracle it was carried

[1] See J. de Voragine, *Chronicon Januense*, quoted by Dunlop, *History of Prose Fiction*, vol. i. pp. 44, 45.

[2] See *La Morte d'Arthur* and *The History of the Holy Grail*, published by the Early English Text Society.

over the sea to Normandy, where it was long preserved in the Monastery of Fécamp, where it was
said to have been in 1120.[1]

Another version says that Joseph, carrying with
him two silver vessels containing blood from Christ's
wounds, came to Glastonbury, where in deference
to his wish the two vessels were buried with his body.

JOSEPH OF ARIMATHEA AND TITUS

In another legend we read that an attempt was
made to kill Joseph and Nicodemus. The latter
escaped, but Joseph was imprisoned in a tower without light or food. Here the Saviour, in a great
brightness, appeared to him, and restored to him the
sacred vessel with instructions as to whom he was
to transmit it. He was also taught the secrets of
the great sacrament which is made on the Graal
—that is to say, on the chalice. And so the vessel
brought Joseph solace and provided him with
heavenly reflection during his captivity.

Now it happened that the Emperor Titus in
Rome, hearing of Christ's life and the cures wrought
by the Saviour, sent a commission to Judæa to inquire
into Pilate's conduct, and to bring back, if possible,
some article which had belonged to Christ. He had
been assured that such an article would have power
to heal his son Vespasian, who was afflicted with
leprosy. The commissioners brought back with
them to Rome an old woman, called Verrine, who
had preserved the towel with which she had wiped

[1] See Leroux de Lincy, *Essai Historique et littéraire sur l'abbaye de
Fécamp*, Rouen, 1840.

Christ's face. On looking upon the towel, the emperor's son was healed. Titus and his son thereupon proceeded to Judæa, and on their arrival Vespasian was conducted to Joseph's dungeon, descended into it, and was prophetically recognized by the captive.[1]

THE GLASTONBURY THORN

In an account of the miraculous Thorn of Glastonbury,[2] it is said that when Joseph of Arimathea came to England he landed not far from Glastonbury. Afterwards an oak was planted at the place to preserve the memory of his landing ; it was called " the Oak of Avalon." From this place Joseph and his companions marched to a hill on the south of the town, and being weary, they rested. The hill became known as Weary-ell-Hill. Here Joseph stuck his staff, a dry hawthorn stick, into the ground, and it subsequently grew and budded every Christmas Day. The thorn was afterwards grubbed up, but several trees raised from that thorn are said to have budded yearly upon Christmas Day.[3]

THE ROSE OF JERICHO

The Thorn of Glastonbury has been connected with the Rose of Jericho, a description of which is given by Brand in his *Popular Antiquities* (vol. iii. p. 357, 11) :

" The Rose of Jericho, that flourishes every year

[1] See *The Short Graal*, written by Robert de Borron ; Hucher, *Le Saint Graal*, vol. i. p. 368 ; Dunlop, *l.c.* vol. i. pp. 160, 166.

[2] See Hearnes, *History and Antiquities of Glastonbury*.

[3] See Chambers, *l.c.* vol. ii. p. 758.

just about Christmas Eve, is famous in Christian reports. Bellonius tells us it is only a monastical imposture. There is a peculiarity in this plant ; though it be dry, yet, on imbibing moisture, it dilates its leaves and explicates its flowers, contracted and seemingly dried up. . . . Suitable to this relation is the Thorn of Glastonbury, and perhaps the daughter thereof. Strange effects are naturally taken for miracles by weaker heads, and artificially improved to that apprehension by wiser. Certainly many precocious trees, and such as spring in the winter, may be found in England. Most trees sprout in the fall of the leaf or autumn, and if not kept back by cold and outward causes, would leaf about the solstice. Now if it happen that any be so strangely constituted as to make this good, against the power of winter, they may produce their leaves or blossoms at that season."

JUDAS AND THE THIRTY PIECES OF SILVER

The legend of the thirty pieces of silver of Judas runs as follows :

The coins which Judas received as a reward for his treason are said to have been struck by Abraham, and were used by the Patriarch to pay for the place of burial for himself and his family. The coins subsequently came into the hands of the sons of Jacob, who had received them from the slave merchants to whom they sold their brother Joseph. These self-same coins they afterwards took to Egypt to buy corn therewith. At the death of Jacob, the identical coins served to pay for the spices bought for the embalming of the body of the Patriarch. The coins thus came to the land of the queen of Sheba who sent them, among other gifts, to the temple of Jerusalem. From Jerusalem this money, *i.e.* the identical coins, were sent to Arabia, whence they were once more brought to Judæa by the three Magi among their gifts offered to the Holy Infant.

When the Holy Family fled to Egypt, the Virgin Mary took the coins with her, but lost them. They were found by a shepherd who kept the sum until the day when, stricken with leprosy, he travelled to Jerusalem to ask Christ to effect his cure. The shepherd expressed his gratitude by offering the thirty pieces of silver as a gift to the temple, and the priests afterwards gave them to Judas as the price of his betrayal. Judas, however, who repented his act of betrayal, returned the money to the priests, and they gave half of it to the Roman soldiers who guarded the Sepulchre of Christ and with the other half they bought a field to be used as a burial-ground for strangers.[1]

THE DEATH OF JUDAS

When Judas betrayed Christ he went out and hanged himself on a tamarind tree. The tamarind had formerly been a tall and beautiful tree, but after the death of Judas it became a shapeless, worthless shrub. Legend relates that the soul of Judas is condemned to wander through the air, and every time it beholds the shrub it pauses, imagining that it sees its body dangling from it.

[1] See A. Graf, *Roma nella memoria e nelle immaginazioni del medio evo,* Torino, 1883, vol. ii. pp. 462, 463 ; Delehaye, *l.c.* p. 43.

A popular legend about Judas who betrayed the Lord runs as follows :

When Judas betrayed the Lord, his Master said to him : " Repent, Judas, for I pardon thee." But Judas departed in despair with his bag of money, cursing heaven and earth. While he was going along thus desperate, he beheld a tamarind tree, and when he saw this tamarind tree, which was tall and beautiful, a wild thought entered his mind. He made a noose in a rope and there and then hanged himself. And hence it is that the tamarind tree dried up and became a short twisted and tangled bush ; its wood is good for nothing, neither to burn, nor to make anything out of, because Judas had hanged himself on it.

In other legends Judas is said to have hanged himself on an elder tree. Sir John Maundeville had evidently heard of this legend when he writes in his *Travels*, "By the pool of Siloam there still stands the elder tree on which Judas had hanged himself in despair when he sold and betrayed our Lord."

This legend seems to have been current in mediæval England, and both Ben Jonson and Shakespeare refer to it :

" He shall be your Judas, and you
    Shall be his elder tree to hang on."
    (BEN JONSON, *Every Man in His Humour*.)

Begin, Sir. You are my elder.
Well followed ; Judas was hanged on an elder."
    (SHAKESPEARE, *Love's Labour's Lost*.)

Shakespeare also refers to the elder tree as the symbol of grief when he writes :

" Let the stinking elder grief entwine
His perishing root with the increasing vine."

(*Cymbeline*, iv. 2.)

Possibly it was this legend which gave rise to the superstition which prevented religious people in England in the Middle Ages from using the wood of the elder tree as fuel.

Another legend relates that Judas hastened to hang himself as quickly as possible and to descend at once into Hades. He knew that Christ was to descend into Hades to liberate all the souls confined there and to conduct them to Paradise, and he hoped to precede the Saviour there and thus be saved. But his plan was frustrated. Satan came, and bending down the tree on which Judas was hanging so that his feet touched the ground, he kept it in that position until Christ had passed through Hades, and then let the branch go so that Judas would be hanged and go to the place he deserved.[1]

PILATE

The Roman governor, whose words, " What is truth," have become famous, is said to have become a Christian in later years, while according to another legend he is supposed to have committed suicide in his despair. Threatened by Emperor Caligula, so the legend runs, Pilate took his own life, and the Emperor had the body thrown into the Tiber. But

[1] See Seymour, *History of the Cross*, p. 95, note 1.

the evil spirits and demons who had possessed Pilate caused such storms and inundations that his body was dragged from the river and carried away to the Rhône near Vienne. As the evil spirits began again their hellish pranks, the corpse was once more dragged out of the water and thrown into a well somewhere in the Alps.

The legend of the evil spirits and demons accompanying the corpse of Pilate spread to Switzerland, and according to popular belief the well into which the body was thrown is said to have been the lake on Mount Pilatus, near Lucerne.

There is a popular belief that when something is thrown into that lake its waters grow troubled and bring on a storm. Traces of devils' claws are shown on the rocks all around, because every year on Good Friday demons drag out the body of Pilate with iron chains and place it on a throne while Pilate washes his hands.[1]

Another legend connected with Pilate runs as follows :

PILATE, THE SON OF A GERMAN KING

Pilate, the governor who condemned the Saviour to be crucified, was the illegitimate son of a German King *Atis*, and of *Pila*, the daughter of a miller living in the depths of a forest. When he grew up Pilate killed his brother, the legitimate son of his father, and was sent by the latter as a hostage to Rome. Once more he was found guilty of bloodshed, and sent to the Pontus, there to fight against the barbarians,

[1] See Berckenmeyer, *Antiquit.*, i. 317.

whence he received the name of Pontius. He distinguished himself by his courage and his cruelty, and was sent to the Holy Land to keep the Jews in order. Here he condemned Christ to be put to death, but afterwards regretted his deed and committed suicide. His corpse was thrown first into the Tiber, then into the Rhône, and ultimately into a well in the Alps.[1]

The legend may have arisen from the fact that many Germans were serving in the Legion stationed in the Holy Land, and hence the Westphalians are often subjected to cruel mockeries and accused of having crucified the Saviour.[2]

THE IMAGE OF CHRIST

A fuller and somewhat different version of the life and death of Pilate, collected from various sources, runs as follows :

He was the illegitimate son of a German King named *Tyrus* and the daughter of a miller named *Atus*, and hence his name Pilatus. The boy having killed his half-brother, his royal father sent him as a hostage to Rome. Here he killed a Gallic prince who was his prisoner, and the Romans, appreciating his cruelty, decided to send him against a rebellious tribe in the Pontus, whence his name Pontius Pilatus. Pilate thereupon made the acquaintance of Herod, to whom his cruelty, falsehood, and craftiness made a great appeal. The king of Judæa appointed the German as governor of the country, but Pilate played

[1] See Mone, *Anzeiger*, 1835 ; Hahn, *Passional*, 1845 ; Menzel, *Christliche Symbolk*, vol. ii. p. 235.

[2] See Menzel, *l.c.* p. 235.

his new benefactor false, and persuaded the Emperor Tiberius to make him the Roman ruler or Governor of Judæa independent of Herod.[1]

Now after the death of Christ, Tiberius Cæsar was suffering from a grievous sickness, and having heard that a certain physician, Jesus by name, was healing all diseases by his word alone, he bade Volusianus, one of his attendants, to fetch this physician. The Emperor, of course, was not aware of the fact that Jesus had already been put to death.

" Go quickly to Jerusalem," he said to Volusianus, " and tell my friend and servant Pilate to send me at once this physician, so that he may restore me to my original health." Volusianus departed immediately and went across the sea to Jerusalem, where he delivered the Emperor's message to Pilate.

" Tiberius Cæsar," he said, " emperor of the Romans, thy lord, having heard that in this city there is a certain physician who healeth all diseases by his word alone, commands thee to send him this physician that he may heal his disease."

When Pilate heard this, he was greatly frightened, knowing that he had already caused Jesus to be crucified. He therefore answered the emperor's messenger that the man was a malefactor who had drawn after himself all the people, and he had there-fore been crucified, according to Roman law.

As the messenger was returning to his lodgings, he met a certain woman named Veronica who had been acquainted with Jesus, and to whom he told all that he had heard from Pilate.

[1] See *Legenda Aurea*, ch. liii.

Thereupon Veronica began to weep, and said : " When Jesus, my Lord, went about preaching unto the people, I desired to have his picture painted for me, that while I was deprived of his presence, the figure of his likeness might at least give me consolation. Now one day when I was taking the canvas to the painter I met my Lord, who asked me whither I was going. And when I had made known to him the cause of my journey, he asked me for the canvas. He took it and gave it back to me painted with the likeness of his countenance. If my lord, the emperor, will therefore devoutly look upon this picture, he will assuredly be restored to health." Thus spake Veronica.

" Is a likeness of this kind to be procured with silver or gold ? " asked the emperor's messenger.

To which Veronica replied : " No, but with a pious sentiment of devotion. I will go with thee and carry the likeness to Cæsar to look upon, and will return."

And thus Volusianus came with Veronica to Rome, and informed the emperor that Jesus whom he desired to see had been fastened to the wood of the cross.

" But a certain matron, named Veronica," continued Volusianus, " hath come with me and brought the likeness of Jesus, the wonderful physician, and if thou wilt devoutly gaze upon it, thou wilt obtain the benefit to thy health."

So Cæsar caused the way to be spread with cloth of silk, and he ordered the portrait of Jesus to be brought to him. He looked upon it devoutly, and regained his original health.

PILATE AND THE SEAMLESS COAT OF JESUS

Thereupon Pilate, by command of Cæsar, was brought to Rome. And Cæsar, filled with wrath against him who had caused Jesus to be crucified, ordered him to appear before him. Now Pilate had brought with him the seamless coat of Jesus, and he wore it when he appeared before the emperor. As soon as Cæsar saw the coat, he laid aside all his wrath and could not speak harshly to Pilate. While in Pilate's absence he had been terrible and fierce, now, in Pilate's presence, he was quite gentle.

But as soon as he had dismissed Pilate, the emperor was once more inflamed against the governor of Judæa who had caused Jesus to be crucified, and had him at once recalled. And yet, as soon as Pilate, wearing the seamless coat of Jesus, appeared, Cæsar once more greeted him kindly and laid aside all the fury of his mind.

Great was the astonishment of the people who witnessed these changes of humour in the emperor, enraged against Pilate in his absence, and gentle in his presence. At length, however, by divine suggestion, the emperor had Pilate stripped of the seamless coat of Christ, and immediately the fury of his mind returned. Now while the emperor was greatly wondering about his curious changes of feeling towards Pilate, they told him that it had been the effect of the seamless coat of Jesus.

Thereupon Cæsar commanded that Pilate be kept

in prison till he had taken counsel with the wise men what he ought to do with him who had caused Jesus to be crucified. After a few days, sentence was pronounced against Pilate and he was condemned to an ignominious death. When he heard this sentence, Pilate with his own dagger put an end to his life. His body was thereupon fastened to a great block of stone and sunk in the river Tiber. But the wicked and unclean spirits, who had taken up their abode in his unclean body, moved about in the water and caused dreadful lightning and tempests, thunder and hail, so that all were seized with great fear. The Romans therefore dragged the body of Pilate out of the river Tiber and bore it away to Vienne, on the banks of the Rhône, where it was sunk in the river. Once more, however, the evil spirits did the same things as in Rome. And the men who were harassed by the wicked spirits and troubled by their vexations removed the body from the river Rhône and carried it to the territory of Lausanne. Here it was thrown into a pool surrounded by mountains, but where even now it cannot rest.[1]

[1] See *Legenda Aurea*, ch. lii.

BIBLIOGRAPHY

ALABASTER, H., *The Wheel of the Law*, 1871.
AMÉLINEAU, *Contes et Romans de l'Egypte Chrétienne*.
APOCRYPHA. See Cowper and Hennecke.
ARBAUD, *Chants Populaires de la Provence*.
ARNASON, I., *Icelandic Legends*, 1866.
BARBAZAN, *Fabliaux*, 1808.
BARING-GOULD, *Curious Myths of the Middle Ages*.
BARTSCH, C., *Denkmäler der provenzalischen Literatur*, 1856.
BEAL, S., *The Romantic Legend of Sakya Buddha*, 1875.
BENFEY, TH., *Pantshatantra*, 1859.
BERGEN, F. D., *Animal and Plant Lore*, 1899.
BERGH VAN DEN. See Eysinga.
BERGMANN, J., *Die Legenden der Juden*, 1919.
BERNHEIM, E., *Lehrbuch der historischen Methode u. der Geschichtsphilosophie*,
    1908.
BEZOLD, C., *The Cave of Treasures*, 1885.
BIGAUDET, P., *The Life or Legend of Gaudama*, 1880.
BIN GORION, *Der Born Judas*, 6 vols., 1914–1919.
BOSIO, *La trionfante e gloriosa croce*, 1610.
BRAND, *Observations on Popular Antiquities of Great Britain*, ed. by Hazlitt,
    1870.
Bundehash, The (Sacred Books of the East, vol. v.).
CABALLERO, *Cuentos, etc.*, 1877.
CALMET, DOM AUGUSTIN, *Dictionary of the Holy Bible*, 1830.
CHAMBERS, *The Book of Days*.
CHAUVET, H., *Folklore Catalan*, 1899.
CHILD, F. J., *The English and Scottish Ballads*.
CLOUSTON, W. A., *Popular Tales*, 1887.
COMESTOR, PETER, *Historia Scholastica* (Migne, *Patrologia*, vol. cxviii).
COSQUIN, E., *Contes populaires de Lorraine*, 1886.
COWPER, H., *The Apocryphal Gospels*, 1867.
CRANE, TH. F., *Italian Popular Tales*, 1889.
DÄHNHARDT, O., *Natursagen, Sagen zum Neuen Testament*, 1909.
DASENT, *Norse Folk-Tales*.
DEISSMANN, A., *Licht vom Osten*, 1908.
DELEHAYE, *Les Légendes hagiographiques*, 1905.
DIDRON, *Christian Iconography*.
DOBSCHÜTZ, E. v., *Christusbilder* (Gebhardt u. Harnack, *Texte und
    Untersuchungen*, N.F. 3 (1899)).
DOUHET, J., *Dictionnaire des légendes du Christianisme*, 1855.
DUNLOP, *History of Prose Fiction*, 2 vols.
DUTOIT, J., *Das Leben des Buddha*, 1906.
    20

DYER, F. THISELTON, *The Folklore of Plants*, 1889.
ETHÉ, H., KAZWINI's *Kosmography*, 1868.
EYSINGA, G. A. VAN DEN BERGH, *Indische Einflüsse auf evangelische Erzäh-
    lungen*, 1909.
FABRICIUS, *Codex Novi Testamenti*.
FOLKARD, *Plant-lore*, 1892.
GEROCK, C. F., *Die Christologie des Koran*.
Gesta Romanorum, ed. Oesterley, 1872.
GOMPERTZ, TH., *Griechische Denker*.
GRAESSE, J. T. G., *Die Sage vom ewigen Juden*, 1844.
GRAF, A., *Roma nella memoria e nelle imaginazione del medio evo*, 1883.
——— *Miti, leggende*, 1892.
GRETSER, *De Croce*.
GRÜNBAUM, M., *Neue Beiträge zur semitischen Sagenkunde*, 1893.
GUBERNATIS, ANGELO DE, *La Mythologie des Plantes*, 1882.
GUNTER, H., *Die christliche Legende des Abendlandes*, 1910.
HALLIWELL, *Popular Rhymes and Nursery Tales*, 1849.
HANDTMANN, E., *Was auf märkischer Heide spriesst*, 1890.
HARNACK, A., *Legenden als Geschichtsquellen : Reden und Aufsätze*, 1904.
HAZLITT, W. CAREW, *Remains of Early Popular Poetry of England*,
    1866.
HENDERSON, *Notes on the Folklore of the Northern Counties of England and
    the Borders*, 1866.
HENNECKE, E., *Neutestamentliche Apokryphen*, 1904.
HERBELOT, *Bibliothèque Orientale*, 6 vols., 1781–1783.
Histoire littéraire de la France, 1906.
HOFMANN, R., *Das Leben Jesu nach den Apokryphen*, 1852.
HORSTMANN, *Altenglische Legenden*, 1875.
——— *Sammlung altengl. Leg.*, 1878.
HUTCHINSON, T., *The Complete Poetical Works of Shelley*, 1904.
JAMESON, Mrs., *Legends of the Madonna as represented in the Fine Arts*.
JELLINECK, *Beth-Hamidrash*, 6 vols.
KAMPERS, F., *Mittelalterliche Sagen vom Paradiese und vom Holze des Kreuzes
    Christi*, 1897.
KAUTZSCH, *Die Pseudoepigraphen des alten Testaments*.
KAZWINI. See Ethe.
KEHRER, H., *Die heiligen drei Könige in Lit. u. Kunst*, 1908.
KELLY, W. K., *Curiosities of Indo-European Tradition and Folklore*, 1863.
KNOOP, O., *Volkstümliches aus der Tierwelt*, 1905.
KOEHLER, R., *Kleinere Schriften*, 3 vols., 1900.
KOENING, E., *Ahasver, der ewige Jude*, 1907.
Koran, The.
KRAUSS, F. S., *Sagen und Märchen der Südslaven*, 1883.
LANE, P. W., *Selections from the Koran*, 1843.
LEDIEU, A., *Nouvelles et légendes*, 1895.
LE GRAND, *Fabliaux*.
LENORMANT, F., *Les origines de l'Histoire d'après la Bible*, 1882.
LE ROUX DE LINCY, *Le Livre des Légendes*, 1836.
LIPSIUS, A., *Die apokryphen Apostelgeschichten u. Apostel legenden*, 1883.
LUARD, H. R., ed. *Chronica Majora*, by Matthew Paris, 1876.
LUCIUS, *Anfänge des Heiligenkults*, 1904.

Mahabharata, The (Roy's translation).
MALAN, S. C., *The Book of Adam and Eve*, 1882.
MALE, E., *L'Art religieux du XIII. Siècle en France*, 1893.
MAURY, A., *Croyances et légendes du moyen âge* (par A. Lognon et Bonet-Maury), 1896.
MENZEL, W., *Christliche Symbolik*, 2 vols., 1854.
MERKENS, *Was sich das Volk erzählt*, 1901.
MEYER, P., *Légendes hagiographiques en Français* (1906).
MEYER, W., *Die Geschichte des Kreuzesholzes vor Christus*, 1881.
MIGNE, *Dictionnaire des Apocryphes*, 2 vols.
MORGAN, *Mahomatism fully explained*, 1723-1725.
MORRIS, R., *Legends of the Holy Rood*, 1871.
NEUBAUR, L., *Die Sage vom ewigen Juden*, 1884.
NINO, A. DE, *Usi e Costumi Abruzzesi*, iv., *Sacre Leggende*, 1887.
NORRIS, *The Cornish Drama*, 2 vols.
OHSSON, D', *Tableau Général de l'Empire Ottoman*.
PARIS, GASTON, *La poésie epique de Moyen Age*, 1885.
PARKINSON, *Yorkshire Legends and Traditions*, 2 vols., 1888.
PAYNE, J., *Tales from the Arabic*, 1884.
PERGER, A., *Pflanzensagen*, 1864.
PETRUS ALPHONSIS, *Disciplina Clericalis*.
PITRÉ, G., *Usi e Costumi* (in *Biblioteca delle tradizione pop. Siciliane*, vol. xiv., 1889).
RALSTON, W. R. S., *Russian Folk-tales*, 1873.
Recueil des Historiens des Croisades, 1859.
REINSCH, R., *Die Pseudo-Evangelien von Jesu und Maria's Kindheit in der romanischen und Germanischen Literatur*, 1879.
RHYS DAVIDS, *Buddhist India*, 1903.
———— *Buddhist Birth Stories*, 1880.
ROBERTSON, J. M., *Christianity and Mythology*, 1900.
ROSEN, G., Translation of *Tutti Nameh*.
SALZBERGER, G., *Die Salomon Sage in der Semitischen Literatur*.
SANDYS, W., *Christmas Carols*, 1833.
SCHADE, *Narrationes*, 1870.
SCHROEDER, L. V., *Pythagoras u. die Inder*, 1884.
SCHULENBERG, *Wendische Volkssagen*, 1880.
SÉBILLOT, P., *Folklore de France*, 3 vols., 1905.
———— *Légendes Chrétiennes*.
SEPP, *Symbolik zum Leben Christi*, v., *Der mythische Christus*, 1846.
SEYMOUR, *The History of the Cross*.
———— J. D., *Tales of King Solomon*, 1924.
SHISHMANOFF, L., *Légendes religieuses Bulgares* (vol. xxi. of *Contes et chansons populaires*), 1896.
SOERGEL, *Ahasver-Dichtungen*.
SÖHNS, *Unsere Pflanzen*, 1897.
STRANTZ, *Die Blumen in Sage u. Geschichte*, 1875.
STRAUSS, A., *Die Bulgaren*, 1898.
SWAINSON, C., *Folklore of British Birds* (vol. xvii. of *Public. of the Folklore Society*, 1886).
TABARI, *Chronique*, 1867-1874.
THIERS, J. B., *Dissertation sur la Sainte larme*.

TISCHENDORF, C., *Evangelia Apocrypha*, 1876.
—— *Apocalypses Apocryphae*, 1866.
VORAGINE, J., *Legenda Aurea*.
WARNKE, FR., *Die Pflanzen in Sitte, Sage und Geschichte*, 1878.
WEBER, *Indische Skizzen*, 1857.
WEBSTER, W., *Basque Legends*, 1872.
WEIL, G., *Biblische Legenden der Muselmänner*, 1845.
WRIGHT, TH., *Latin Stories from MSS*, 1842.
WUNDT, W., *Völkerpsychologie*, 1909.
ZIRUS, *Der ewige Jude*, 1928.

PERIODICAL PUBLICATIONS

Academy, The, 1882.
Am Urquell.
Contemporary Review, The, 1881.
Early English Text Society, ed. by R. Morriss.
Folklore Record, The ; Folklore Journal, The.
Geiger's Zeitschrift, vol. ii.
Gentleman's Magazine, The, 1880.
Hungarian Journal of Ethnography, vol. x.
Jewish Quarterly Review, The, N.S., vol. ii.
Journal of Philology, 1883.
Journal of Sacred Literature, vol. vi.
Journal of the Royal Society, 1902.
Orientalist, The, 1884.
Revue des Études Juives.
Revue des Traditions Populaires.
Tradition, La (ed. Carnoy).
Zeitschrift der deutsch-morgenländischen Gesellschaft (ZDMG), vol. xlvii.
Zeitschrift für vergl. Literaturgeschichte, vol. xiv. (1901).

INDEX

A

Abraham, 97 ; birth of, 49 ; and Nimrod, 90.
Adam, expelled from Paradise, 212 ; and beasts of creation, 66 ; tears of, 187 ; " Adam's Apple," 233 ; *Adam and Eve,* Book of, 61.
Æsculapius, 49.
Afrodisius, 89.
Ahasverus, name of, 248, 249 ; *Ahasverus Rise,* by Schubart, 260.
Aleph, meaning of, 139.
Alexander the Great, at gate of Paradise, 214.
Anna, 31.
Annunciation, the, 31.
Apocrypha, authors of the, 22.
Apollonius, 68.
Art, and legend, 26.
Ashmodai, 95.
Asoka, King, 20.
Aspen, the, 72, 184, 190.
Ass, the legend of the, 51, 82.
Aster, the, 129.
Atis, King, 298.
Ave Maria, 36.

B

Balder, 142.
Balsam shrubs, 106.
Basil, the, 79.
Bat, the, origin of, 123.
Bear, and honey, 168.
Beasts, submission of, 64, 66.
Beetle, the, 84.
Ben-Temalion, demon, 94.

Birds, fashioned by Jesus, 118.
Blacksmith, the, and Jesus, 154.
Boulenger, 252.
Brahman, the, and the shrew, 95 ; and the robbers, 165.
Buddha, birth of, 48, 71 ; and the hare, 132.

C

Cannibal, the, 102.
Cartaphilas, 238, 259.
Cave, brilliant light in, 43.
Chaucer, 161.
Cherry tree, the, 57.
Christ, staff of, 11 ; severe judge, 12 ; childhood of, 107 ; power of raising dead, 133 ; and old soldier, 148 ; the footsteps of, 184 ; the image of, 194, 299 ; Teutonic conception of, 256, 258, 259 ; the advent of, 275.
Christianity, early converts, 21.
Christmas night, 50, 51.
— rose, 54.
Circumcision, 62.
Cleopas, 110.
Cross, the sign of the, 178, 189, 208 ; history of, 210, 216 ; mysticism of, 216 ; nails of, 175.
Crown of Thorns, the, 196.
Crucifixion, the hours of the, 175.

D

Daisy, the, 53, 115.
Dammachus, 100.
Date, shape of the, 273.

309